GOING TO SCHOOL IN SUB-SAHARAN AFRICA

GOING TO SCHOOL IN SUB-SAHARAN AFRICA

JIM NESIN OMATSEYE
AND BRIDGET OLIREJERE OMATSEYE

The Global School Room
Alan Sadovnik and Susan Semel, Series Editors

GREENWOOD PRESS
Westport, Connecticut • London

Library of Congress Cataloging-in-Publication Data

Omatseye, Jim Nesin E.
Going to school in Sub-Saharan Africa / Jim Nesin Omatseye and
Bridget Olirejere Omatseye.
     p. cm. — (The global school room, ISSN 1933–6101)
    Includes bibliographical references and index.
    ISBN 978–0–313–34071–0 (alk. paper)
  1. Education—Africa, Sub-Saharan—Cross-cultural studies. I. Omatseye,
Bridget Olirejere. II. Title.
    LA1501.O433 2008
    370.967—dc22   2007041055

British Library Cataloguing in Publication Data is available.

Library of Congress Catalog Card Number: 2007041055
ISBN: 978–0–313–34071–0
ISSN: 1933–6101

First published in 2008

Greenwood Press, 88 Post Road West, Westport, CT 06881
An imprint of Greenwood Publishing Group, Inc.
www.greenwood.com

Printed in the United States of America

The paper used in this book complies with the
Permanent Paper Standard issued by the National
Information Standards Organization (Z39.48–1984).

10 9 8 7 6 5 4 3 2 1

CONTENTS

PREFACE

Over the years, the slow pace of development in African countries has been traced to the challenges of education in the continent. For a long time, Africa's colonial legacy was the scapegoat on which the problem was blamed. After several decades of nationhood among these countries, it has become apparent that their leadership has failed to address the issue of education as an instrument of development. Endowed with tremendous national resources, the questions that have become pertinent are: Why has schooling failed to make much difference in the standard of living among Africans? What are the causes of this unfortunate development? Who is affected by lack of educational opportunity and why? How long has this been the case? How is the situation to be remedied?

Going to School in Sub-Saharan African has attempted to address these issues. The colonial legacy of the British, French, Portuguese, Dutch, Germans, and Spaniards in the ten countries picked for consideration constitutes the reality of the foundation of the challenges encountered. The seeming inability of successive African leaders to abrogate the social and political structures inherited was formidable and, as such, the problems have tended to persist. Such issues as funding, policy formulation and implementation, education reform, control of education, politicization of education, and a host of other factors have been identified as only a few of the challenges explored in the work.

The African child at the center of the problem is basically a victim of historical, political, and economic circumstances. From the very inception of colonialism, the colonial administrators were reluctant to educate African children for obvious reasons. Socioeconomic consideration could be blamed for the lackadaisical attitude of successive African leaders who could have done more to educate African children. The legacy of European culture entangled with African nationalistic tendencies created an anomie disposition which made some

African elite more French than the French or more British than the British. These factors have no doubt accounted for the ineffectiveness of curricula in many African schools—the outcome of which has been devastating to national systems.

Going to School in Sub-Saharan Africa has also considered the issues of education reform and access to schools in relation to the plight of children, especially in countries where civil wars have raged for decades. In countries with relative stability, who goes to the best schools or the worst schools in slums is determined by the parents' social class. Poor children end up in poorly funded government schools whereas children of the affluent parents find themselves in schools that can only be rivaled in Europe and the United States.

ACKNOWLEDGMENTS

We are grateful to Professor Alan Sadovnik and Debbie Adams for their editorial assistance. Our thanks also go to P. O. Ukwade, Margaret Odigie, and Maro Umukoro for their tremendous assistance with manuscript preparation. We dedicate this work to our children, Ete, Toju, and Val-Anire.

Chapter 1

SCHOOLING IN ANGOLA

INTRODUCTION

Although the annals of colonialism in Africa have hardly revealed the use of education as a means of self-determination, the situation in Angola clearly pointed to education as an instrument of subjugation. The Portuguese legacy in Angola can only be compared to the Dutch in Apartheid South Africa and the Belgians in the defunct Republic of Zaire (now Democratic Republic of Congo) where the Africans suffered humiliation in the hands of the colonial powers. If we accept knowledge, vision, and moral judgment as essential elements of education, it would be difficult to justify the actions of these countries as an expression of the civilization that education sustains.

After five centuries of exploitation and brutality in Angola, it is hard to imagine the Portuguese were still boasting in the 1950s that their rule would continue for five hundred more years. The attack of the Afro-Asian countries on them at the United Nations (UN) in the 1960s and the speed with which other European colonizers were granting independence to their colonies did not make any sense to the Portuguese. How visionless could any regime be! One could not agree more that "reality is not unitary but differs according to where one stands" (Marks 2000). Similarly, Cox argues that "there is no view from nowhere" in relating what reality is to theory (1981). Thus, it was an absurdity to think that the regime of oppression in Angola would continue in spite of all the warning signs the tiny-but-determined educated class were generating. The near absence of formal education in Angola itself speaks volumes about the state of education in the homeland itself. For one thing, nobody gives what he does not have.

The state of civil war and the anarchy that has engulfed the country since the flight of the Portuguese without handing power to another governing body is of historical significance. It was the first time a colonial power did not formally hand over power but abandoned it unceremoniously. It also showed how Portugal ruled and "educated" the African elite who have carried on their way of attrition that they started in Angola. According to a UN source, 30 million out of 170 million war deaths recorded worldwide in the twentieth century were victims of their own governments' killings. Of this figure, 7 million Angolans were "depopulated" by their own rulers for allegedly supporting the opposition (Thakur 1999). In the face of such brutality involving children, could anyone talk about schooling?

In spite of its past, Angola has continued to survive as a country trying to rebuild its shattered institutions and create a new image for itself.

ANGOLA'S PROFILE

Angola has a total land area of 1,246,700 square kilometers (481,400 square miles) and is about the size of Texas. Luanda, its capital with a population of 4 million, has been described as "the city of splendid squalor—a breathtakingly beautiful landscape tethered to a colonial artifact in the final stages of decay, where absolute vulnerability stands shoulder to shoulder with frontier prosperity, and existential uncertainty stands ready for abrupt recombination of mass and void" (Wilson 2005). Similarly, its diverse population of 13,000,000 (2004 estimate) has an ethnic composition of Ovimbundu (37 percent), Kimbundu (25 percent), Bankongo (13 percent), Molatos/mixed race (2 percent), and Europeans (1 percent). Other groups include Ambo, Chokwe, Ganguela, and Lunda. Portuguese is both the official and dominant language.

Angola is located between Namibia and the Republic of Congo on the South Atlantic. It is also bordered on the east by the Democratic Republic of Congo and Zambia. The country is well favored with a cool and pleasant climate: a hot and dry summer and a mild winter with intermittent rains from November through April. Angola is economically well endowed with abundant mineral resources including petroleum, gas, diamonds, iron ore, phosphates, bauxite, uranium, gold, granite, cooper, and feldspar. Its agricultural products include banana, sugar cane, coffee, sisal, corn, cotton, tobacco, and a variety of vegetables produced for export and local consumption.

Using purchasing power as an index, the gross domestic product (GDP) was US$45.9 billion in 2005 and a per capita of US$3,210. As impressive as these figures are in comparison with other African economies, Angola's inflation rate is about 24 percent. We must quickly add that millions of Angolans displaced by the civil war are not beneficiaries of the prosperity. The industrial sector is dominated by petroleum drilling and refinery, cement production, fish processing, brewing, and basic metal production. With petroleum and derivatives constituting 92 percent of exports, other shipments include diamonds, coffee, and timber to the United States, China, France, South Korea and very little to Portugal. Imports from these countries also sustain Angola's economy. But for the intermittent eruptions of the civil war causing the displacement of persons, the country would have done better in view of its resources.

Politically, Angola is governed by a president who is assisted by a prime minister and a cabinet of thirty ministers representing each of the eighteen provinces. Each province has a governor who is appointed by the president. The national assembly consists of 220 deputies: 130 are elected "at large" and five are elected to represent each of the eighteen provinces.

Angola's Supreme Court is the Appellate tribunal. The legal system is based on Portuguese and customary law and has been characterized as weak and fragmented by external jurists. The courts operate in each of the 164 municipalities of Angola (National Trade Data Bank 2007).

SOCIAL AND HISTORICAL CONTEXT

The history of modern Angola predates the arrival of the Portuguese in 1482 when they encountered the ancient African kingdom of Ndongo from which the country derives its name, Angola. As a result of several wars, negotiations, and treaties, the Portuguese acquired the territory in the sixteenth century. Shortly after, the Portuguese turned their attention to the slave trade, which fueled their sugar plantations in Sao-Tome, Principe, Brazil, and the Americas before it came to an end. However, they did not assume full control of Angola until the last millennium, when they turned to forced labor in place of slavery, especially in Mozambique and Angola. With British financing, the Portuguese used forced labor to construct the transcontinental Benguela railway linking the Port of Lobito with the cooper zone of the then Belgian Congo and present-day Zambia from which Dares Salaam in Tanzania is connected.

Even though the Roman Catholic and Protestant missions had contributed to education as part of their primary aim of spreading Christianity, many succumbed to pressure from the colonial government to victimize their African converts. For many, the task of "bringing the light to those living in darkness" had over the years been tainted by racial prejudice and an unhealthy sense of superiority. Emerson observed, "The standard French belief in the doctrine of assimilation as the proper aim of colonialism is often no more than a pale shadow of the persuasion of the Portuguese.... With pained and amused superiority they have watched the British and French abandon their African holdings" (cited in Okuma 1962).

Because Portugal was the poorest among European countries, holding on to their colonies in Africa was a matter of economic survival. This is in spite of the political humiliation suffered at the level of the international community. The attack on Portugal at the UN by the African and Asian countries for Lisbon's refusal to grant independence to its colonies was vehement enough that the USSR initially vetoed Portugal's application for membership. Also, the usual European tradition of democratic rule at home eluded the Portuguese. Indeed, Emerson asserted that it would be hard to find a lesser measure of self-government than in Portuguese colonies (cited in Okuma 1962).

In pursuit of its assimilationist policy, the Portuguese increased their population in Angola in the 1960s as a result of massive and forced migration of poverty-stricken Portuguese to the colonies. The move was intended to reinforce their claim that Angola was a province of Portugal in Africa. They thought the economic development of Angola would speed up in this manner. They also believed that the new immigrants would teach the Africans how to live a better life. Contrary to expectation, the half-baked and semiliterate Portuguese had nothing to offer by way of special skills. Instead, they scrambled for menial jobs with the poor Africans who themselves were struggling for survival (Okuma 1962).

Apart from the fairly favored Molatos and the assimilated Africans in the upper echelon of Angola society who had full and casual acceptance among the ruling Portuguese, the lower reaches of millions of Africans remained "natives" and were officially designated "uncivilized." They were subject to discriminatory administrative and judicial treatment. Those employed by whites were exposed to arbitrary punishment and discipline (Okuma 1962).

As a result of Portuguese determination to hold on to their colonies no matter what, schooling and other modernizing influences were kept to a minimum. Shielding future leaders from exposure to educational opportunities that might increase their levels of awareness and lead them to organize a rebellion became a matter of deep concern for the colonial administration. However, their efforts were quite unsuccessful. A handful forced their way to neighboring countries to acquire formal educations and economic power, endowing them with a new-found social status that also brought recognition and enabled them to start planning the revolt that the Portuguese dreaded very much.

While doing everything possible to shield young Africans from external influences, the colonial administration had plans to deal ruthlessly with any planned rebellion by isolating those involved.

Thus, in order to carry on the work of civilization that is Portugal's special mission it is necessary to guard the African against education and advancement and to view with suspicion all those who show any interest in the modern world or to succumb to that most dangerous of all diseases: thinking for themselves. Because those who think for themselves must come to the point of acting for themselves. (Emerson cited in Okuma 1962)

The abrupt departure of the Portuguese in 1975 and the civil war that has raged since then fulfilled the expectation that the best pupils in the colonial school would become the freedom fighters that would eventually liberate their land from the colonizers. In spite of the heavy toll on lives and resources, it was anticipated that social and economic reconstruction would bring about the emergence of an independent and democratic Angola. Even then, that would still be a tall order.

Meanwhile, the drive for freedom by the Angolan elite was facilitated by the cold war environment of the 1950s involving the USSR, China, the United States, and Europe. The freedom fighters drew their ideological inspirations from the cold war countries and African decolonizers, such as Nkrumah, Kenyetta, Azikiwe, and Mandela. Even as decolonization progressed everywhere in Africa, the shortsighted Salazar and Caetano dictatorships in Portugal failed to see the inevitable collapse of their empire in Africa.

After years of underground preparation, three groups of agitators for independence finally emerged:

1. MPLA: the Popular Movement for the Liberation of Angola led by Agostinho Neto, with links to the communist parties in Portugal, Cuba, and the Eastern Block;
2. FNLA: the National Front for the Liberation of Angola under the leadership of Holden Roberto, with links in the United States and to the Zairian dictator Mobutu Sese Seko; and
3. UNITA: the National Union for Total Independence of Angola led by Jonas Savimbi, with links to the People's Republic of China, United States, and Apartheid South Africa.

Fueled by ideological differences, the struggle for control of Angola led to armed conflict that began as the Portuguese fled the country they had vowed to keep for another five hundred years. With Luanda under Agostinho Neto's control, the MPLA's leader assumed the presidency of the country. FNLA and UNITA controlled the hinterland and declared war on Neto's government. Neto later died of cancer and was replaced by Jose Eduardo de Santos as Angola's president and MPLA's leader. As a result of several of FNLA's military failures and internal divisions within its ranks, the group was abandoned by its international backers before its final demise.

The internationalized civil war between UNITA and MPLA continued until 1989 when the United States attempted to broker a peace deal between the warring groups and later scheduled an election for 1992. The MPLA won the election with 49 percent of the vote; UNITA received 40 percent. UNITA rejected the outcome of the polls and returned to the bush to resume their guerrilla warfare. It was not until Jonas Savimbi's death in battle in February 2002 that UNITA agreed to a cease-fire a year later. Even as the war raged on, a low-level insurgence was taking place in the Cabinda Province where most of the petroleum resources came from. Cabinda has been pressing for independence from Angola. With such turmoil resulting in millions of displaced persons, formal education was the last concern in any Angolan community. Due to intermittent eruptions of fighting, a conducive environment for schools to function normally does not yet exist.

EVOLUTION OF EDUCATION

From its very onset, education in colonial Angola was viewed by the Portuguese as their way of introducing civilization to Africans. Against the background of indigenous education, Africans considered schooling a formality aimed at achieving higher social status in the oppressive colonial environment through knowledge acquisition and economic empowerment. In view of their educational agenda, the colonial authorities were bent on discouraging any opportunity that would enable Africans to rise above the level of "natives"—a pejorative term used to portray Africans as uncivilized. With such a mind-set, the stage was set in colonial Angola to educate blacks and whites in two separate school systems. The indigenous African education that has been the basis of family life and other activities was ignored by missionaries who were initially responsible for schooling in Angola. The colonial administration would later prohibit the use of African languages in schools and churches under Article 3 of Decree Number 77:

The use of native language in written form or any other language besides the Portuguese, by means of pamphlets, leaflets, or whatever kind of manuscripts, is forbidden in the religious teaching of the missions, in their schools or in whatever relations with natives. (1921)

Not unexpectedly, speaking Portuguese, especially among Angola's elite, has become a matter of prestige over the years. Encouraging Angolans to accept Portuguese as the lingua franca as was the case with English and French in their colonies was one thing, but enforcing the use of Portuguese by decree was an unusual authoritarian gesture that smacked of a human rights violation to Africans.

Similarly, a deliberate policy of using education to create a class society with members of one race as an underclass, as was the case in Angola, was also a violation of Africans' rights. Even though a handful of the so-called assimilated Africans were somehow tolerated in the European community after being separated from their kith and kin because of the "natural consequence of the[ir] degree of social and mental development," they soon realized that that distinction and supposed acceptance was superficial.

Critics of the dual system of education also faulted the scheme for entrusting the system to missionaries who neither had the resources nor the personnel to do a good job of providing quality education to Angolans. Even when some Protestant schools tried to improve on the rudimentary knowledge of reading, speaking, writing, and arithmetic of the young Africans, they did not receive any encouragement from the colonial administration that instead clamped down on them with all kinds of restrictions, including the infamous ban on the use of African languages in schools and churches. The colonial government insisted Africans did not need more education than that which would enable them to serve as court interpreters, clerics, and enlightened servants in white households. Instead, Article 24 of the Portuguese Constitution states:

Religious missionaries overseas being instruments of civilization and national influence, and establishments for the training of personnel for service in them and in Portuguese "Pradvoado," shall possess a juridical character and shall be protected and assisted by the State as institutions of learning. (Decree Number 18: 578 1930)

In the course of compelling Africans to accept Portuguese culture, there could not have been a better agent than the Roman Catholic mission, which transplanted the rigidly class-based and -oriented education system in Portugal to Angola. Their elitist educational orientation was beneficial to only a few assimilated Africans that constituted a diminutive class (about 30,000 in 1950). To join this group of *Assimilados*, the African was expected to be educated away from the norms of his community by disassociating himself from his "uncivilized family and his entire past." Even if and when he had done so, he was still socially considered inferior among the mestizos and whites (Marcum 1978).

The Portuguese determination to use education as a potent instrument for destroying their African roots led to the creation of a special school for the elite in the intensely Portuguese town of Sa da Bandeira. During the colonial era, this city was endowed with a salutary European cultural environment for the schooling of selected African students. The Bandeira secondary school taught advanced courses that were not available in similar centers of excellence as Nova Lisboa. It is quite informative, if not ironic, that Jonas Savimbi, one of the few privileged beneficiaries at the time, became the leader of UNITA, which has been part of the civil war that has bedeviled Angola during the last thirty years. Indeed, if Antonio Salazar, as leader of Portugal in 1963, had foreknowledge, he would not have said:

One hears it said, out, loud cries are raised claiming independence for Angola: Angola is Portuguese and does not exist without Portugal. The only national conscience rooted in the Province is not Angolans but its Portuguese of Angola. (1963)

The idea that Angola would never cease to be part of Portugal was so pervasive among the Portuguese that even Felgas, one of the most respected Portuguese historians in the twentieth century, stated:

The District, as for that matter all Angola, does not have racial problems. Blacks and Whites work side by side without conflict or hate…whether economically, politically, socially, the Portuguese Congo will give to this restless world an example of the effectiveness of Portuguese civilizing force in the lands of Africa. (1958)

Like President Salazar, the renowned historian could not seem to have learned from history that the human spirit would not tolerate injustice much longer than providence would allow and no matter how much effort is made to deprive any group of their freedom and access to education, soonest than later, the victim will usually find a way out. Hence in the 1950s, 95 percent of Angolan school-age children were in primary school—most of which were under the control of the Catholic mission because the Protestant schools were less favored. In spite of their disadvantage, they intensified their pursuit of quality education for the African population.

In pursuit of the Protestant agenda, the American Board and Canadian Congregation founded the Currie Institute for the training of African leaders for church and the business community. The Institute offered courses in carpentry, masonry, agriculture, tailoring, Bible study, and the 3Rs. While the Catholic mission focused on the training of priests in their seminaries, the Methodists started a trade school in Quessay in 1920.

Unlike forty years earlier, when education was available only to a few mestizos and assimilated Africans, the rapid growth of education as a result of the missions' activities, especially the Protestants, was not only phenomenal but also discomforting to the Portuguese authorities who thought that they were spreading education too fast among the blacks. This was one of the factors that prompted Portuguese authorities to slam the door with Decree 77, which banned using African languages in churches and schools.

With stricter government control of education, only teachers who were fluent in Portuguese would be hired to teach in all schools. All schools were also ordered to hire Portuguese and some assimilated Africans who were equally fluent in Portuguese as special teachers to be paid from a government subsidy. These special teachers were granted up to five hundred hectares of land and permission to cut free timbers, enabling them to build their homes near schools where they served (Henderson 1979).

This was the first step of the government's total control over education, which had primarily been controlled by the missions. In view of the Roman Catholic mission's tendency to support the colonial administration's policy, the government wished it had enforced an earlier 1940 agreement between Portugal and the Vatican that education in Angola would be a Roman Catholic affair. In doing so, it would have excluded Protestant missions—from other countries—from making their contribution to the educational development of the colonies. The growth of the Protestant school and church population, which went from 625 in 1910 to 983 in 1920 and up to 8,475 in 1930, became too alarming for the government to bear.

In the early 1950s, the Portuguese administration renewed its focus on primary education—now referred to as rudimentary education for Africans. However, this time around, the Catholic mission was specifically charged with the responsibility but without funding. It was not until 1954 when the state started to provide some financial support for the Catholic normal school at Cuima to train teachers to administer the Rudimentary Curriculum. The teacher education program had 153 students. Another normal school for women was later established.

The Politics of Angolan Education

When the Portuguese colonial administration remodeled primary education and christened it "Rudimentary Education," its main aim was "to contribute to the elevation of the native masses by means of the first level of instruction regarding the realities of the life of the people who are underdeveloped without alienating them from their class, their traditional hierarchy or from physical labor" (Henderson 1979). When the program was further renamed "Education for Adaptation," its proponents did not live up to expectation because nothing really changed. Critics even thought that it took a more negative turn from its original concept. The new curriculum posed more difficulties because many African children encountered more problems with Portuguese language, and teachers and parents were burdened with documentation and other bureaucratic bottlenecks in order to get children admitted into schools. To further reduce its effectiveness, the duration was reduced by one year. Many restrictions and requirements more or less crippled what would have brought education to the doorstep of the masses (Henderson 1979).

Because the government was not keen on secondary education, only the missions provided some service in that sector in their seminaries and institutes. Dating as far back as the seventeenth century, the Jesuits had attempted to train some African molatos in Portugal as priests. In 1906, a Catholic seminary located in Huila was later transferred to Luanda and located in the Bishop's courts. Classes did not start until a year later.

It was not until 1933 when the government built its first secondary school at Sa da Bandeira to educate very bright Angolans. As secondary education became available, the programs became very theoretical and classical. The need for a vocational and technical school arose to serve the practical and utilitarian aspirations of the less privileged members of the class society. In 1950, the vocational school offered classes in subjects such as commerce, electricity, mechanics, and home economics. Only 25 percent of 4,830,479 school-age children between ages five and fourteen attended school in 1960. When the age level was raised to ages between fifteen and nineteen, only 177,768 out of 1,561,877 children were registered in both primary and secondary schools in the same year. In all, only 7.5 percent of school-age children were in Angolan schools during the 1960–61 school year—a much lower percentage than in any British colony and surprisingly better than some in French colonies (Henderson 1979).

In terms of availability, tertiary schools were even less available than those at the secondary level. The political instability that had dogged Portugal and its colonies could not be unrelated to its reluctance to promote tertiary education. Even though most colonial powers in Africa were slow in initiating and promoting education at that level, it would appear that fear of opposition from the academic community, especially in Portugal, added to the reluctance of the Portuguese to act positively in this regard. Incidentally, some Africans in universities in Portugal were part of the Communist party and other radical groups opposed to the dictatorship of Salazar.

In spite of the near absence of opportunity in Angola, a few dozen Africans with good secondary education found their way to universities abroad, including Portugal. For example, Agostinho Neto went to Portugal in 1947, completed his degree in medicine in 1958, and was reported to have suffered arrests, interrogations, and imprisonment in Lisbon and Coimbra. He later returned to Angola to found MPLA and became the first president of independent Angola in 1975. That Angola can boast of only one university and a handful of other tertiary institutions today is certainly indicative of a long-standing neglect of tertiary education.

In spite of this inadequacy, Angola has a fairly good number of well-educated elite who, though engaged in the country's civil war, have also been involved in the economic development of their country.

Structure of Education

Until recently, basic education at its primary level consisted of eight years and was compulsory for all children between ages six and ten. Secondary education consisted of three years for general education and four years for vocational and technical education students. A two- to three-year preuniversity course is available to the few who are able to undergo and pass the difficult examinations to obtain admission into the university. As a result of an ongoing reform in education, six years has been proposed for the primary level and six to seven years for the secondary level with those in vocational and technical education spending a longer period in school.

The only state university, the Agostinho Neto University, was initially named University of Luanda in 1962 but was renamed University of Angola in 1976 before assuming its present name in 1985. The rector of the university is appointed by the President while the Minister of Education appoints other principal officers.

The baccalaureate degree is obtained in three years and followed by another two years to obtain the *Licenciatura*. However, the *licenciado* (a master's equivalent) is also obtained with a five-year course. A term of five to six years is expected for professional courses, such as medicine and engineering. The new reform calls for two cycles of *Bacharelato* after the first two years of general education. The language of study at all levels is Portuguese. The Angolan teacher education program runs at the secondary and tertiary levels in designated institutions in Angola.

In the last few years, the war situation has brought in nongovernmental organizations (NGOs) and some UN agencies to rehabilitate schools that have not been functional for many years. According to the United Nations Children's Fund (UNICEF), the projection for rehabilitation between 2005 and 2008 is for more than the 78,000 teachers currently in service in 38,000 locations in Angola. About 1,150 schools would be rehabilitated while 350 new schools would be needed to provide life skills. UNICEF, in collaboration with the Angolan government, would promote distance education to train at least 1,000 pedagogical supervisors for Angolan schools (UNICEF 2007).

Reflection on Angola and Educational Development

When we consider the level of underdevelopment in Angola in relation to the neglect of education, we must conclude that neither the Portuguese colonizers nor the African elite have demonstrated the true essence of education in relation to the lives of the masses. The recurring principle that any casual observer may pick up throughout the history of Angola is "might is right," a Hobbesian truth that world powers, past and present, have consistently resorted to international relations. What is the truth and who determines it in the case of the Angolan conflict and its effect on education? Could it be true that Africans, and indeed Angolans, do not care about who rules them and how? Is it true that Angolans were uncivilized and therefore needed to be educated for the land as their Portuguese colonizers claimed? One could not agree more with Foucault when he said:

Truth isn't outside power or lacking in power...truth isn't the reward of free spirits, the child of protracted solitude, nor the privilege of those who have succeeded in liberating themselves. Truth is a thing of this world: it is produced only by virtue of multiple forms of constraints (structured social processes). It induces regular effects of power. (cited in Marks 2000)

One of the powers that social institutions—governmental, educational, or economic—have is the ability to transform subjectivity into objective knowledge. Consequently, what is considered the truth tends to vary with the perception of the ones concerned. Because truth and power stand in dialectical relation, the production of truth is controlled by the structure of power. These power structures reproduce themselves by controlling access to truth to the exclusion of dissenting voices (Marks 2000).

However, the constructivists are quick to add that an institution can be reordered through the disruption of existing mechanisms for the production and reproduction of truth. Whatever truth or falsehood an institution has peddled over time collapses with it at the end of such regimes. When a regime attempts to sustain domination-power relations it tends to maintain existing structures and patterns of interactions that make the supposedly powerless dependent on the powerful who try to dominate them (Bull 1999).

In the light of the foregoing analysis of truth in relation to institutionalized power, the Portuguese powers in Angola concluded as true their notion that the Africans were without any form of education and, therefore, uncivilized. The existence of a pattern of governance under the rule of King Ndongo of Kongo and similar systems of government preceding their arrival did not alter their "truth." The fact that the peoples of Angola were militarily subdued gave the Portuguese the power also to subject them to slavery, forced labor, and loss of their freedom for centuries. Whatever was thought of them by their conquerors was true. During the colonial era, the Portuguese determined the prices that they would pay for the commodities exported to Portugal, and who would be educated, how, and to what level. Whatever decision was made by the Portuguese about the people of Angola was true. Somehow, the colonizers also believed that this situation would continue indefinitely because they were oblivious to the realities of the 1950s when other Europeans were disengaging from their colonies. From the Portuguese perspective, disengagement could not be a reality for them.

But the civil war engaged in by various political and ethnic groups could be nothing but an extension of the social structure established by the Portuguese and inherited by their African successors. When the African elite seized power in 1975, the principle of "might is right"" was retained as a dominant feature of the polity. Whatever peace accord was brokered by the various world powers, including the UN, had to be such that would bring about fairness, justice, and equity among all the ethnic groups and not just in favor of those with the most military might. In the absence of a just settlement of the conflict, every attempt by any mediators to do otherwise could only be a mirage.

However, it would be problematic to expect the war to end at all costs without regard to fairness to a majority of the people. For as Clauswitz (1976) once put it, war is politics because it has to do with a shift of power. Indeed, no one in a position of authority even within the law willingly relinquishes power without some element of persuasion or coercion. Inasmuch as war is heinous violence, it is also a historical process of reconfiguring power relations when other means of resolving deep conflicts nonviolently fail (Chingono nd).

As to whether Angolans really care who their rulers are, the abrupt end of Portuguese rule is enough evidence. For as the Nobel Laureate Wole Soyinka once said:

We are sometimes assailed by voices that have grown so insolently patronizing as to declare that Africans do not really care who governs them or how, as long as they are guaranteed freedom from diseases, shelter, and three square meals a day. I do not propose to give one more second to such racial slurs, least of all when they are given voice from our own kiths and kin in positions of, or slurping from one bloodied touch of power. (cited in Chabal 1997)

What is fundamental in the restoration of peace to Angola is that all parties be wary of the shortest route to nonviolence if interaction strategies must not reintegrate rather than transform hierarchical structures of wealth, privileges, incentives, and exclusion. In other words, if all freedom fighters (of external and internal aggression) in Angola must accept a settlement needed for peace to reign, the mediators, the UN agencies, and the NGOs working through the Peace Keeping Operations (PKO) ought to adopt the strategy of liberal peace.

The liberal peace initiative would usually reflect whatever consensus exists as a basis for conflict resolution. It must then be approached through a connected process of ameliorative, harmonizing, and transformative measures. Although this approach involves the provision of immediate relief and rehabilitation assistance, liberal peace "embodies a new political humanitarianism that lays emphasis on such things as conflict resolution and prevention, reconstructing social networks, strengthening civil and representative institution, promoting the rule of law and security sector reform" (Duffield 2001). This ought to take place within the context of a free market economy with a human face.

CONCLUSION

Having attained nationhood after three decades of bloody conflict, some critics may argue that Angolans ought to have settled down to the business of social and economic reconstruction using education as a potent instrument of transformation. Without justifying a prolongation of the civil war, it should be understood that the century-old colonial social structure on which the conflict is based cannot be dismantled overnight, especially in a country with a considerably low educational base. It should be expected that time is needed to reorder existing entrenched, institutional barriers through an interruptive mechanism whose outcomes are bound to be painful and of considerable duration.

If the pace of development must be accelerated in Angola, reform in the educational and political sectors ought to be given priority with a properly managed economy sustaining both. Within the context of a globalized economy, Angola is endowed with more than enough natural resources to pull itself out of its present predicament. However, it will take the commitment of the small class of educated Angolans who must shun corruption and enthrone transparency in order to install peace and raise the standard of living of the masses. The government's media blitz (CNN) on change must be positively translated into a real life-changing experience for a population that has been deprived of liberty for so long.

The international community through the UN, in proclaiming impartiality in its mediation of the crisis, has indicated that "impartiality for the UN operations must mean adherence to the principles of the charter in order to avoid complicity with evil" (United Nations 2000). With such an enabling environment, normalcy can be restored to Angola to enable education and to make a difference in its developmental aspiration and drive.

BIBLIOGRAPHY

Adibe, Clement. "Accepting External Authority in Peace-Maintenance." *Global Governance* 4, no. 1 (1998): 107–72.

Bull, Nancy. 1999. *Power, Alternative Theory of Encyclopedia of Violence, Peace and Conflict.* London: Academic Press.

Chabal, Patrick. 1997. *Apocalypse Now? A Post-Colonial Journey into Africa.* Inaugural lecture, King's College, London, March 12, 1997.

Chingono, Mark. "Reflections in War Time Social Research: Lessons from Mozambique Civil War." n.d.

Cox, Robert. "Social Forces, States, and World Orders: Beyond International Relations Theory." *Millennium: Journal of International Studies* 10, no. 2 (1981): 126–55.

Duffield, Mark. 2001. *Global Governance and the New Wars.* London: Zed Books.

Felgas, Helio Esteves. 1958. *História do Congo Português*. Uige, Angola: Carmona.

Foucault, Michel. 1997. *Ethics, Subjectivity and Truth*. Edited by Paul Rabinow. New York: New Press.

Henderson, Lawrence W. 1979. *Angola: Five Centuries of Conflict*. Ithaca, NY: Cornell University Press.

Marcum, John A. 1978. *The Angolan Revolution!* Vol. 2. Cambridge, MA: M.I.T. Press.

Marks, Susan. 2000. *The Riddle of All Constitutions*. New York: Oxford University Press.

Okuma, Thomas. 1962. *Angola in Ferment*. Foreword by Rupert Emerson. Boston: Beacon Press.

Salazar, Antonio de Oliveia. 1963. *Declaration on Overseas Policy*. Lisbon, Portugal: Secretariado Nacional da Informacito.

Sogge, David. "Angola: The Client Who Came in from the Cold." *Southern Africa Report* 15, no. 4 (2000): 4–6.

Thakur, Ramesh. 1999. "U.N. and Human Security." *Canadian Foreign Policy* 7, no. 1 (1999): 51–59.

United Nations. 2000. *Report of the Panel on U.N. Peace Operations* (A/55/305s/ 2000/809) New York.

United States Department of Commerce, National Trade Data Bank. Washington, D.C. 2007.

Wilson, J. Zoe. 2005. "Certainty, Subjectivity, and Truth: Reflections on the Ethics of War Time Research in Angola." In *Research Conflict in Africa: Insights and Experiences*. Edited by E. Porter, G. Robinson, M. Smyth, A. Schnabel, and E. Osagie. New York: U.N. University Press.

WEB SITE

Government of Angola, Permanent Mission to the United Nations Information Service: www.Angola.org.

Chapter 2

SCHOOLING IN CAMEROON

INTRODUCTION

Although the history of many African countries under colonial domination is characterized by diversity, none has the legacy that Cameroon has had to live with since its independence over four decades ago. The Republic of Cameroon is an African country with a very unique colonial experience. Unlike most, it has a legacy of at least four distinct European nationalities—the Portuguese, Germans, French, and English—in addition to over two hundred ethnolinguistic African groups in a small country with nearly 14 million occupying about 475,442 square kilometers. As will be seen later, it was the Portuguese who named the country *Cameroon*. As a result of its checkered colonial history, Cameroon has grappled with the challenges of national unity and has constantly struggled against the forces of disintegration due to clashing ethnic interests. On one side are the varying ideological orientations of the Germans, French, and the English in the major institutions inherited after nationhood, and on the other side is the variety of foreign and local influences and divisions that have created physical as well as cultural barriers.

As a result of these challenges, Cameroon has had to cope with at least two varying and competing education systems, the French and the British, out of which the country has attempted to forge one that all its citizens can call their own. This obviously has been a daunting task.

Without a doubt, the overriding issue of diversity has generally taken its toll on Cameroon's political, economic, and social cohesion because leaders are constantly engaged in a balancing act to ensure the country is kept together. As a result, education has experienced a considerable setback due to the same challenge—merging two foreign systems into a suitable one. Without question, these factors have been responsible for the inequalities and imbalance in educational opportunities in the country. The overall development of the country in terms of standards of living is not unaffected by these issues. Thus, Cameroon serves as a showcase of French, German, and English education systems juxtaposed within the context of an African milieu. The marrying of these systems with a view to evolve a suitable African system for the Cameroonians has been the daunting task confronting Cameroonian school authorities since independence.

The Republic of Cameroon as an independent state is located in West Africa. It borders Nigeria to the northwest, Chad Republic to the northeast, the Central African Republic to the east, and to the south. Cameroon also shares borders with Equatorial Guinea, Congo (Brazzaville), and Gabon. Cameroon also has her coastline lying on the Bight of Bonny in the Gulf of Guinea and the Atlantic Ocean. The topography of Cameroon is quite diverse. Cameroon has a natural geography of deserts, plateaus, mountains, rainforests, savannas, and beaches. Mount Cameroon (4,070 meters/13,354 feet) is the highest point of the country. The diverse nature of the country's topography has earned it the name, "Africa in Miniature." In 1986, the country suffered some major natural disasters. Lake Nyos located in northwest Cameroon released volumes of carbon dioxide, which left about 1,700 people dead. To this date, the suddenness of the gas eruption and subsequent disaster has puzzled scientists. Ways to eliminate further dangerous occurrences of this disaster have been worked on since then. Generally, one can describe the climate of Cameroon as tropical.

The total size and extent of Cameroon is approximately 475,442 square kilometers (or 183,568 square miles) of land surface and 1.3 percent water. Cameroon's population has grown tremendously. The first national census carried out in 1976 had an estimated population of 7,663,246 inhabitants. Between 1993 and 1997, it was estimated at 13 million and 14,100,000 million, respectively (United Nations Development Programme [UNDP] 1998). Of this figure, 56 percent of the population was twenty years of age and below (UNESCO 1995). However, the 2003 census reported a population of 15,746,179 million, with a density of eighty-eight people per square mile. An updated estimate in July 2005 revealed a population figure of 15,322,000 million. Cameroon is the fifty-third world's largest country, with a land size like Papua, New Guinea, but somewhat larger than the U.S. state of California.

Generally, Cameroon's population spread is evenly divided between the urban and rural areas, but with population density highest in the large urban centers rather than the western highlands of the northeastern plains. The population is sparse in the Adamawa plateau, southeast Benue depression, and most parts of the southern Cameroon plateau. The population is extremely heterogeneous with approximately two hundred ethnic and linguistic groups. The majority of the population comprises highlanders, constituting about 31 percent of the total population. Other groups include Equatorial Bantus, 19 percent; Kirdi, 11 percent; the Fulani people, 10 percent; northwestern Bantu, 8 percent; and Eastern Nigritic, 7 percent. Other African groups make up 13 percent of the total population, and non-Africans total less than 1 percent.

French and English are the official languages. However, there are twenty-four major African language groups and 270 indigenous dialects, most of which are of the Bantu and semi-Bantu groups. Bantu languages of varied dialects are spoken in southeast Cameroon by peoples such as the Douala and Fang. The Cameroon highlanders are Bantu and Sudanic. Languages like Hausa, Margi, and Kapsig are spoken by the Fulani immigrants. The Cameroonians in the east central region speak the eastern languages of Adamawa. Importantly too, Hausa, Fulani, pidgin English, and Douala are languages of trade or commerce in the region.

Since independence, the Republic of Cameroon has experienced problems with the choice of a national language. Maybe the government has paid lip service to it in view of its sensitive nature or for the sake of peaceful coexistence and national unity. Most educators and linguists are of the opinion that there is indeed a problem with the choice of a lingua franca that would reflect the wish of all Cameroonians. They have also suggested the need for a national language for the country (Ngijol 1964). Such a language, it is hoped, would enhance communication and promote literacy, and a national and cultural identity. For Bot Ba Njock (1966), even as Cameroon is a multilingual nation, it could have national languages. He suggested that the nation could be subdivided into linguistic zones, with each one having its own zonal language. Njock's idea may have prompted the promotion of six zonal languages since the 1960s. However, for Chumbow (1996), Cameroonians whose languages were not favored could revolt and result in a threat to national unity, which has always been the focus of political leaders in the country.

In December 1974, at the inaugural meeting of the National Council for Cultural Affairs held in Yaoundé, the government made an attempt to put an end to the national language issue by recommending that all Cameroonian vernacular languages be termed and considered as "national languages." However, Todd (1983) has argued that instead of the above generalization, the Cameroonian Pidgin English (CPE) that he believes is closer to all vernacular languages should be adopted as the national language. He further argued CPE was one language in Cameroon that is not associated with any particular tribe, region, religion, or a specific colonial government. CPE's neutral status makes it a strong unifying factor and clearly makes the language, a "no man's language."

On the usage of CPE educational purposes, Todd (1983) further states:

There would be a few linguistic or financial problems in the adoption of Cameroon Pidgin English as a language of education. It is widely understood, a shared lingua franca with Cameroon's African neighbours and while rarely, the only mother tongue of a child, is often one of the first languages he hears. It had long been used as a vehicle for Cameroon culture and has been found perfectly capable of expressing Christian teachings, parliamentary proceedings and financial negotiations.

Because Cameroon has about 247 indigenous languages, with English and French recognized as official languages, there is a quest for a national language. It would also be appropriate to know that CPE is its unofficial lingua franca.

Most Cameroonians are either Christians or Muslims. A good number are adherents of traditional African religions. Essentially, the ethnic groups in central and northern Cameroon, who are mostly cattle aisrers and semipastoral grain growers, practice the Muslim faith, while the majority of southern Cameroonians are Christians.

SOCIAL AND HISTORICAL EVOLUTION OF CAMEROON

From a historical perspective, not much is known of the early settlers in today's Cameroon. However, some historical findings suggest early settlers may have migrated from the northern arid savannah of West Africa. They were later followed by the Fulanis, who were basically cattle herders and had filtered in through northern Cameroon. The Cameroon region was discovered around 1472 by a Portuguese navigator, Fernado Po. On his arrival at the Bight of Biafra, he was said to have sailed up to River Wouri, which is situated in the coastal region. In his expedition, Po was quite surprised at the great number of shrimp that swamped the river. He named the river *Rio dos Camaroes* or the River of Shrimp. Thus, the country derived its name from this description of its river. When Cameroon became a German protectorate in 1884, the country was renamed *Kamerun*. It would later revert to its original name, Cameroon, when the British and French took over the administration of the colony after World War I.

In 1884, Cameroon was colonized by the Germans as a result of the signing of the German-Daouala Treaty in July of that same year. The treaty legitimized Cameroon as a German protectorate. In 1916 after the defeat of Germany in World War I, Cameroon became the trust territory of Britain and France. The territory was first administered under the League of Nation's mandate but later came under the UN's trusteeship. The latter arrangement involved sharing the administration of government: Southern Cameroon was administered by the British from Lagos in Nigeria, while the French got the larger share and declared it an independent territory on January 1, 1960, with Ahmadou Ahidjo as the first president. Thus, French Cameroon went on to full independence. Consequently, in a 1961 referendum, British Southern Cameroon was united with their French kith and kin. This unification was further consolidated on October 1, 1961. When Cameroon became a federal republic made up of the two, former West Cameroon and East Cameroon, it was renamed the United Republic of Cameroon in May 1972 and divided into seven provinces. In 1985 after the Bamenda Congress of the ruling Cameroon's People's Democratic Movement (CPDM), the country was again officially named a republic. In that same year, through a presidential decree, the number of provinces was increased to ten.

It is important to note that even though Cameroon enjoys the status of a republic, not much can be said of its education system. There are still traces of colonial legacy in the types of education systems in different parts of

Cameroon. In other words, two subeducation systems exist in the forms of the anglophone and francophone models. The Cameroonian government has noted with concern what threat could be posed to the survival of the union of the two systems—based on two cultures driven apart by language—in view of the unity and integration of the Republic of Cameroon. Consequently, since the 1960s the government has worked on such issues as harmonization, bilingualism, and ruralization, especially within the context of an emerging Cameroonian education system. To the present day, educational reforms have focused on ways to harmonize the British and French models toward the creation of a truly Cameroonian one. The main objective of these reforms is geared toward the uniformity of diverse cultural contexts.

Currently, the country is a one-party state ruled by Paul Biya and CPDM. Biya succeeded Ahidjo in 1982 and was reelected in 1984, 1988, and 1992 to date. Under Biya, Cameroon remained a de facto one-party state until 1990. In December 1995, a new constitution was adopted with the major aim of making way for regional representation yet retaining a strong central government. The outcome of this was the establishment of decentralized territorial communities. This political reform puts in place a senate with representatives of regions, traditional rulers, and special economic and social interests. Foremost, it created an opportunity for two additional seven-year terms for political incumbents, including President Biya. In May 1997, Biya won a majority in the legislative election and was reelected in October—opposition from the other parties notwithstanding.

Politics and Administration

At independence, and almost all throughout Ahidjo's presidency, his political party, the Cameroon National Union (CNU) was the majority political party. On Ahidjo's resignation in 1982, Biya joined CPDM's party platform. This remained the only legal political party until December 1990. By that time, other ethnic and regional parties had emerged. They included the National Union for Democracy and Progress under Maigari Bello Bouba, and the National Union for Democracy and Progress under Adamou Ndam Njoya. However, the main opposition to Biya's party is the Social Democratic Front (SDF). This is primarily an anglophone regional party headed by John Fru Ndi. Even with all of these oppositions, Biya's party has been in control of elections, especially that of the presidency and the national assembly. There is little wonder why Biya was reelected during the October 11, 2004, elections.

In terms of foreign policy, Cameroon still maintains links with France. This has also influenced some of the country's decisions. Generally, Cameroon is an African country that has enjoyed some relative calm in its political and social life. This stability has created the necessary atmosphere conducive for economic development and organized social life. However, in more recent times, the country has clashed with two African countries: its neighbor Nigeria over the possession of the Bakassi Peninsula, which was eventually granted to Cameroon; and Cameroon's president has had some encounters with President El Hadj Omar Bongo of Gabon. Cameroon is a member of the Commonwealth of Nations and La Francophone.

In terms of the country's administration, the president, who is elected by popular vote, is at the helm of affairs. As president, he has some broad powers that can be exercised without reference to the legislature. The president has the constitutional power to appoint officials at all levels of government from the prime minister to provincial governors, divisional officers, and urban councils. He can personally make these appointments especially in large cities, such as Douala, Yaounde, and Bafoussam, without reference to the legislature. In smaller municipalities, the citizens are free to elect their mayors and councillors by popular vote.

As specified by the 1996 constitution, Cameroon is divided into ten administrative regions: two English-speaking regions and eight French-speaking regions. The northwest and southwest are English-speaking provinces, while the French-speaking provinces are Adamawa (Adamaoua); North (Nord); Far North (Extrême Nord); West (Quest); Centre, Littoral, South (Sud); and East (Est). According to Delancey and Delancey (2000), the number, borders, and names of the regions may be changed by a presidential decree. Each of these regions is headed by a governor appointed by the president. These regions have some degree of autonomy, especially with regard to cultural programs, the economy, healthcare, sports, and social services. The governors are also given some measure of powers to make decisions concerning their provinces.

The provinces are divided into fifty-eight divisions (called departments in French). These divisions are headed by divisional officers or prefects who are presidential appointees. The major role of the divisional officer is to assist the governor. Divisions are further divided into subdivisions (*arrondissements).* These are headed by assistant divisional officers (*sons-préfets*). Finally, in the administrative cadre are the districts. These are the least of the administrative units, and according to Gwanfogbe et al. (1983), such units are only found in large subdivisions or in regions that are isolated or difficult to reach. The districts are administered by district heads (*chefs de district*).

Economic Trends

When Ahidjo became president, he tried to make the economy a priority. At that time, Cameroon could boast of an increase in its agricultural sector. The country's major agricultural exports include cocoa, coffee, rubber, cotton, and bananas. However, in the 1970s when petroleum was discovered in Cameroon, the country's attention shifted to the oil sector. Financial gains from this sector were judiciously used by Ahidjo's administration to assist other sectors of the nation. As noted by UNESCO (1995), economic growth in the Republic of Cameroon had been proceeding normally since the 1960s. The growth was reflected in all aspects of life in the country, particularly in the education sector. This was until the economic crises in the 1980s, which ushered in a significant slowdown in the economy and all that it sustained. For instance, the economic crisis of 1987 had a great effect on the education sector in terms of school enrollment, which dropped by 2.3 percent between 1990 and 1994, and the training of teachers, which also slowed down (UNESCO 1995). When the economy was still strong before the 1980s, Ahidjo was able to create a national cash reserve to assist farmers through small-scale loans and finance major development projects. Besides education, his administration also concentrated on health, communication, transportation, and the hydroelectric infrastructure.

Biya had hardly settled down as president when he had to grapple with the economic crisis, which actually erupted in the 1980s and continued until the late 1990s. The country suffered due to the falling world prices of petroleum. This affected the country and other leading oil-exporting nations. The result was a decline in the nation's actual per capita income from 1985 to 1995. Other causes of this decline included official corruption and mismanagement of public funds, and a steady increase in the population. The only option left for Biya to redirect the economy of the country was to turn to foreign aid. At the local and national levels, he tried to reduce funding in the health and education sectors as well as all other government institutions and parastatals. He also privatized industries. Beginning in 1997, economic programs as prescribed by the World Bank and the International Monetary Fund (IMF) to reduce poverty and increase economic growth were gradually introduced and enforced by the government. For instance, with the advent of the Structural Adjustment Program prescribed by the World Bank, teacher education institutions suffered a relapse as their closures were enforced. This led to a serious shortage of teachers in Cameroon during that period. In a World Bank study on teacher education, Leke and Tchombe (1998) have argued that the World Bank may have had a good case against such closure. In their view, the World Bank opined that the initial training of teachers was expensive and school-based teacher education would be more cost-effective. Their argument is that the World Bank may be justified from a purely economic perspective, but pedagogical and personal values in initial training and the education of teachers can in no way be provided in school-based training programs. In other words, economic consideration should not determine too rigidly educational matters.

Further economic effects from the 1980s to the late 1990s are indicated by an unemployment estimate of 30 percent in 2001, with about 48 percent of the population living below the poverty threshold in 2000. In more recent times, Cameroon's fortune has improved as its per capita gross domestic product (GDP) was estimated as US$2,421. For a developing African country, this was noted as quite high (World Economic and Financial Surveys 2006).

In terms of natural resources, the agricultural and forestry sector has served the country's economy better than the industrial sector. Available data indicate that in 2005 an estimated 70 percent of the population was engaged in farming; agriculture made up an estimated 44.8 percent of the nation's GDP in that same year (CIA 2006). Cameroon's agricultural cash crops include plantains, yams, cassava, millet, bananas, cocoa, palm oil, rubber, and tea. Other export crops include coffee, sugar, tobacco, cotton, groundnuts, and rice. The nation has a good record in agricultural exports. However, overreliance on agricultural exports has made the country vulnerable to shifts in their prices. Cameroon also subsists on livestock raised throughout the country by Fulani herders as a way of life. Seafood is a major agricultural engagement. According to Neba (1999), the fishing industry employs about 5,000 people and provides 20,000 tons of seafood yearly.

In terms of industry and infrastructure in Cameroon, and in contrast to agriculture and natural resources, factory-based industries accounted for only an estimated 17 percent of the country's GDP in the last few years. More than 75 percent of the industries are located in Douala and Bonaberi. Cameroon's industrial sectors include petroleum refining, food processing, and the smelting of imported aluminum. The economy also boasts of substantial mineral resources: cobalt, nickel, natural gas, bauxite, iron, ore, tin, and uranium. Although crude oil in Cameroon dropped since 1985, the importance of the oil sector has continued to play a dominant role in the nation's economy. In more recent times, tourism is fast becoming a thriving business in the country's economic growth.

EDUCATION IN CAMEROON

Traditional Education

Traditional education in Cameroon was typical of indigenous African education in precolonial Africa. Datta (1984) points out that there is no doubt traditional African societies possessed a kind of customary education and system that worked reasonably well, given the limits imposed by the society in which it had to operate. Datta highlighted the main aims of Africa's customary education as follows:

1. To preserve the cultural heritage of the extended family, clan, and tribe;
2. To adapt members of the new generation to their physical environment and teach them how to control and use it; and
3. To explain to them that their own future and that of their community depended on the understanding and perpetuation of institutions, laws, language, and values inherited from the past.

The traditional agencies of socialization in precolonial Cameroon included the family, the kin-group, social clubs, and age grades. Initiation and circumcision marked important stages of transition. Traditional values of obedience, loyalty to the group, respect for elders, and dignity of manual skill was upheld in typical traditional Cameroonian society where children were taught through stories, myths and legends, songs, proverbs, and dances. In the precolonial era, forms of education in the traditional context with their own structure existed, with a main goal of training and integrating its citizens into working groups. The educational process in traditional African societies in Cameroon was intended to bring cohesion and unity of purpose for the benefit of the community at large. The outcome was not only practical but also utilitarian in intent.

Precolonial Education

The arrival of the early Europeans in Cameroon around 1844 marked the advent of evangelism. Education was seen as a viable instrument for spreading the "Christian gospel." Thus, school buildings were used to facilitate evangelism. Somehow, the traditional values of Africans whose children would be attending these schools were undermined. Their social lives and economic aspirations were not taken into consideration as the foreign missions went about their work in the region. Even when the colonial government opened the first primary school in Bimbia the same insensitivity to native concerns existed. Attendance was not compulsory, but the natives who attended learned some new skills. Knowledge dissemination was generally geared toward changing attitudes, especially in response to positive Christian life and values. With time, this system of education gained ground and was accepted by the natives. In his study on the Cameroonian demand for primary education in this era, Amin (1997) revealed that mission schools were predominantly British oriented. This spread of mission schools was quite rapid by the time the Germans colonized and annexed Cameroon as its acquisition in 1884. There were already about fifteen primary schools with an enrollment of 368 pupils in existence. The schools were run by the London Baptist Missionary Society (Aloangamo 1978).

COLONIAL EDUCATION

Education in the German Era

Cameroon's colonial era can be said to have lasted from 1884 when Cameroon was annexed as a German colony until the early 1960s when the country attained independence. At the inception of the colonial era, it was expected that the Germans would do better at improving education than the missionaries did; however, they did not. Instead, the goal of education in the colonial era was to serve German interests, foster German culture, become part of German politics of colonialism, promote its economy in Europe, and cultivate its social life. In other words, the educational needs and aspirations of the natives were not considered.

Education in Cameroon actually began under the Germans who, initially, were not particularly interested in the growth and expansion of African education. However, some wealthy traders and merchants who arrived in the colony to trade found education as business to be a good investment. Thus, between 1887 and 1905, private schools sprang up in Douala, Victoria, Garoua, and

Yaoundé. In 1910, the School of Agriculture was opened in Limbe. The curriculum in the early years of primary school concentrated on the 3Rs, religious knowledge, and German language. This period also witnessed the enactment of an Education Law in April 1910. The Education Law addressed the following:

(i)   Prescribed the German Language as the only medium of instruction in schools. However, Douala Language could also be used, thereby restricting the use of Mother tongue in schools;

(ii) Primary education had a duration of five years of which stipulated minimum knowledge was to be acquired;

(iii) Primary education was made compulsory for all children of school age;

(iv) Subventions were given to mission schools on the condition that they encouraged and emphasized the use of the German Language and the expansion of the culture. They would also, promote the German colonial policy. To make this workable, Cameroonians were sent to Germany for further studies. (cited in Ngoh 1988)

Significantly in this period, some expansion in the establishment of schools was in progress. According to Amin (1997), at the dawn of World War I in 1914, there were 531 primary schools with an enrollment figure of 34,117 pupils. There were also few middle schools with the status of secondary school.

Education under the French Administration

Historically, Cameroon, a former German colony, became a League of Nations mandated territory after the defeat of Germany in World War I. In 1919, Cameroon was set between the French and the British. The French administration in Cameroon had one major goal in mind: to make their assimilation policy work. Their one major focus was to totally replace the African culture with that of the French. Also, they intended the language and the civilization of the natives would become French in every way.

In pursuance of their assimilation goals, they invested a lot of resources in the education sector. Schools established in French Cameroon were fully under the direct control and supervision of France. Every aspect of the education system—school structure, curriculum content, teaching method, language of instruction, examinations, and even certification were based on the French system. The French enforcement of their assimilation policy was such that in 1924 the French language was the only language of instruction, while other local languages were prohibited.

French Primary Education

The goals for primary education included basic education for all and education aimed at preparing children for secondary school.

There were two curriculum types to achieve the above goals: the metropolitan curriculum and another curriculum adapted to suit the Cameroonians. The overall goal of the curriculum was to impart French civilization in children.

Primary school entry age was six years old and school duration was for six years. In 1952, the directors of education in French-speaking Africa recommended a new school entry age of three or four years old. However, this recommendation was roundly rejected by the Cameroonians because it would affect the quality of their education.

Under French rule, primary education grew quite rapidly as a result—like the expansion of schools and increased enrollment. This area of success became a major focus of the second four-year development plan launched in 1953. Four years later, the Ministry of National Education was established to improve the quality of education and increase educational opportunities, especially for girls and those in northern Cameroon.

French Secondary Education

Just like the primary education, secondary education was patterned along the model in France. The curriculum was quite broad and is, to a large extent, what still exists today in French Cameroon. At the end of secondary school, students earn a baccalaureate obtained directly from France. Interestingly, by 1961, when the country had become independent, the number of secondary schools, similar to enrollment, had recorded great increases.

Education under the British Administration

Unlike what was obtained in French Cameroon during this period, the British did not opt for assimilation in their education. Their style of administration lacked the enthusiasm or zest exhibited by the French. The British policy of indirect rule did not encourage the paternalistic disposition found in the French and German styles of administration. The education policy under British rule in the colonial period was basically aimed at training civil servants for colonial exploitation (Ngoh 1988). Essentially, the British administration was quite decentralized, and education was dictated by British policy—the same used for Nigerians in that era. Although there was no deliberate attempt to impose British culture through their educational policy, it generally has been criticized for doing too little to educate the children of its colonies.

British Primary Education

Under British colonial rule, a partnership between the British missionaries and the native (indigenous) administration provided primary education. In other words, the British government per se did not quite take particular interest in education. According to Ngoh (1988), "Education was not vigorously pursued by the colonial administration in British Cameroon." Notwithstanding this, the following observation could be made about primary education in this era:

1. Primary education, which had a nine-year duration before 1932, was reduced to eight years;
2. The primary school curriculum was basically that of the British model;
3. Education was free at the infant level, that is, the early primary school stage;
4. Vernacular language was not allowed in public primary school; and
5. Primary schooling, which marked the end of primary education for some children, also prepared others for the standard six certificate examination, in anticipation of a secondary education.

British Secondary Education

Until about the late 1930s, citizens of British Cameroon had no opportunities to receive secondary education because there were no secondary schools. Many of the citizens had to go Nigeria for secondary educations. However, with great demand for secondary educations, the missionaries began establishing schools in British Cameroon between 1938 and 1939. Curriculum content followed the Cambridge School Certificate and the West African Certificate syllabi. Secondary school education lasted for five or, in some cases, six years.

Comparing French Cameroon and British Cameroon

The statistics in Tables 2.1–2.4 represent a comparative analysis between French Cameroon and British Cameroon for the number of available schools and enrollment figures in the colonial era. What can be deduced from tables 2.1 and 2.2 is that primary schools in both French Cameroon and British Cameroon maintained steady growth in enrollment as well as increased expansion of schools. However, at independence the increase in French Cameroon was quite significant.

In secondary education (see tables 2.3 and 2.4), following the trend in growth and expansion, especially at independence, French Cameroon had done well for its citizens. A total of twenty schools were in existence with an enrollment of about 4,742. The same cannot be said of British Cameroon with a

Table 2.1
Enrollment of Primary Schools in French Cameroon

Year	Number of Schools	Enrollment
1947	137	18,600
1951	203	28,594
1956	583	79,363
1961	977	151,635

Source: Ngoh (1988).

Table 2.2
Enrollment of Primary Schools in British Cameroon

Year	Number of Schools	Enrollment
1947	229	25,200
1951	266	28,960
1956	385	46,754
1961	499	86,257

Source: Ngoh (1988).

Table 2.3
Enrollment of Secondary Schools in French Cameroon

Year	Number of Schools	Enrollment
1947	3	704
1951	3	908
1956	5	1,479
1961	20	4,742

Source: Ngoh (1988).

Table 2.4
Enrollment of Secondary Schools in British Cameroon

Year	Number of Schools	Enrollment
1947	1	130
1951	2	322
1956	3	468
1961	6	903

Source: Ngoh (1988).

generally slow growth in school expansion and enrollment. By 1961, British Cameroon could boast of only six secondary schools and a total enrollment of 903. This low figure as previously highlighted prompted citizens to seek secondary education in neighboring Nigeria.

Education in Postcolonial Cameroon

As at independence and until 1976, two separate systems of education operated in Cameroon. East Cameroon's system was based on the French model, while West Cameroon's was based on the British model. During this period, Cameroonians as a people and an African nation had become more conscious of the kind of education they needed. They had also become aware of education as a stabilizing force—one to serve a political purpose as well as other roles in changing their people's socioeconomic circumstances. Cameroonians have also not lost sight of the colonial legacy inherent in their education. Judging from their historical past, Cameroonians have come to recognize that they are now a unified country but originally were characterized by geographical, linguistic differences and a multicultural heritage. They are also a people with different ideals borne out of multinational colonial policies. However, they are also certain the one binding force that can maintain and ensure stability and equity is education.

To further maintain this unification initiative that made the country a republic in 1961, there was a need for education system reform. In light of this, Nfor Gwei (1975) noted that the first civilian president, Ahmadou Ahidjo, began to seek an appropriate curriculum that would befit national development in light of suitable pedagogical practices. It would also meet the changes of an advancing technological world.

To achieve this goal, the federal government evolved a development plan for the period 1960–72. This plan emphasized the growth of a national system of education that also would be inclusive of higher education. There was also concern for quality education at all levels for the ultimate development of the nation's economy. In line with this, new educational policies were drawn and the structure of schooling at all levels was redefined.

Shortly after independence, Cameroon operated a federal government that allowed the different systems of education to continue in their initial colonial culture. Whereas, the French operated a highly centralized educational administration, the British opted for greater autonomy, allowing a decentralized system of education.

The harmonization of both systems became a major goal in the government's educational plan. The government was quick to note that in a situation with diverse cultures and backgrounds, harmonization was not without its structural and organizational problems. Thus, in June 1963, Federal Law Number 63/13 was enacted. It stipulated that curriculum content should focus on general education for the first three years of secondary education, while the last two years would concentrate on specific academic disciplines and professional studies. Notably, while the anglophone schools worked within the ambit of this law, the same could not be said of the francophone schools.

Because Cameroon operates a federal government system, it has tried to achieve unity in diversity in all spheres. In this case, the government took time to bridge the gap between the country's colonial and cultural histories, using a unified school system as an instrument. In effect, the federal government has always faced the issue of merging two education systems into supposedly one nation. The anglophone system of education was one of 7-5-2: seven years in primary school, five years of secondary education in cycle one, and two years of high school. The francophone system, on the other hand, was a 6-4-3 system: six years of primary education, four years of secondary school in cycle one, and another three years in cycle two of secondary school. However, in both systems, their technical education system was a 4-3 system: four years in cycle one, and another three years in cycle two. For both systems, besides the conventional secondary and technical schools, there is a third category of secondary education. The rural artisan and Home Economics Centers are profession-based secondary education schools.

In terms of certification, in both systems pupils are expected to take certificate examination. They are also specific to their systems of examination. For the primary level, anglophone schools take the first graduation certificate examination, while children in francophone schools took the equivalent known in French as the *Certificate Etude Primaires Elementaires* (CEPE). Secondary education in anglophone and francophone schools take cycle systems. For certification, in the anglophone system, the first and second cycles take the General Certificate of Education, Ordinary Level (GCE O/L) and the General Certificate of Education, Advanced Level (GCE A/L), respectively. In the francophone system, in the first cycle, the students take the *Brevet d' Etudes Premier Cycle* (BEPC), and for the second cycle, they take the Baccalaureate (BAC).

Certification for technical education in both the anglophone and francophone systems take the same certificate examinations known as the Certificate of Professional Aptitude (CAP). The francophone *Brevet de Technicien* (BAC) is taken at the second cycle in technical school. Anglophone schools can also take the London General Certificate of Education at both the ordinary and advanced levels. Other technical-based examinations that are offered in London include the Royal Society of Arts (RSA) and Chamber of Commerce and City and Guilds certificate examinations.

Having attained the status of a united republic under the leadership of President Paul Biya, the country continued its emphasis on education as a unifying force between the 1970s and mid 1980s. The government concentrated on the crucial issues that pertain to education, as well as its force to bond and sustain national unity. Such issues include ruralization, bilingualism, and harmonization. These were also reflected in the curriculum content at all levels. Indeed, the issue of ruralization of education became a government focus because of the rapid urban drift that resulted in high unemployment in the cities. Before the ruralization program, schools did not help matters as the prescribed subjects in the curriculum did not emphasize self-reliance skills to encourage living in villages. In effect, attention was not paid to such technical- or vocational-based subjects like agriculture, crafts, and arts. To bridge this educational gap, the government in 1967 introduced a rural-oriented primary teacher training institution. This was later redesigned as rurally applied education or a curriculum development center. Some of these centers were situated in Yaoundé, and later in 1974, another was established in Buea. Agricultural activities were gradually introduced as part of the curriculum. UNESCO and the United Nations Development Programme (UNDP) have commended Cameroon's ruralization of education program. For the Cameroonians, the ruralization of education had traits of colonial curriculum objectives.

The ruralization ideology conveyed a retrogressive view particularly when it was per-ceived that ruralization was almost synonymous with the adaptation of education to the actual conditions of Cameroon which is essentially agricultural and consequently oriented at the perpetuation of poverty and misery.... If the conception of ruralization was accompanied by other inputs intended to improve the quality of rural life (e.g. pota-ble water, good access roads, etc.) this would have been considered positive for national development. (Tchombe 1997)

To further standardize examinations, following the harmonization of the two systems besides the common entrance examinations organized by the Ministry of National Education, two other examination boards were created. They were the General Certificate of Education (GCE) board for anglophone examina-tions and the Baccalaureate board for francophone examinations.

In spite of the steps toward a successful harmonization, it is perceived in some quarters that there are still some basic problems. Tchombe (1997) argues that even when government tends to take the posture that both systems can operate independently, this can only be effective if both systems are accorded the same value and status. This idea of inequality may have stemmed from the British Cameroonians who saw themselves as the minority of both. They per-ceived the harmonization more or less as French assimilation rather than as a goal towards uniformity of an integrated system. Tchombe (1997) suggests that what Cameroonians actually need to function is adaptation and less inter-vention from the outside. Tchombe added, "It is about time we assume responsibility in directing our educational system. So far, the assertion is that there is uniformity in the anglophone system of education and the francophone system of education. In essence, for now, there is a partial harmonization, and may hardly be able to achieve a total one" (1997).

Higher Education in Cameroon

Higher education in Cameroon actually began with the creation of the National Institute for University studies in 1961. This institution came into being as a joint effort by the French government with the assistance of UNESCO. In 1962, under Decree Number 62-DF-289, the National Institute for University Studies became the Federal University of Cameroon. It provided degree courses in the pure sciences, arts, social science, and human science. Later, other professional programs were introduced in the Schools of Agricul-ture and Administration, respectively. The Military Academy and School of Education were created along with other professional schools and institutes for engineering, medicine, and international relations.

Entry qualification to those degree programs required the French Baccalau-reate or the English General Certificate of Education. Duration of programs or courses varied with courses of study. The Federal University of Cameroon is financed by France, so its programs are patterned along those of France and other higher institutions in francophone countries. Notwithstanding this, the university was created to cater to both French-speaking and English-speaking students. Instruction is either given in English or French depending on the disposition of the teacher. Because the university is run by French nationals, a majority of the population is French-speaking, as reflected in the number of teaching staff. Because this situation does not favor English-speaking students, there has been a heightened clamor for an English-speaking federal university.

So far, higher education has continued to expand in Cameroon since 1999, when about six state universities were established in Cameroon. Some of these universities may have high enrollment, but many may be lacking in the quality of teachers, teaching equipment, and resources. For instance, the following analysis discusses the quality of staff:

Because of the relatively low remuneration following the salary cuts and currency devaluation in 1994, (state) universities have not been able to employ qualified teaching staff and have gone back to recruiting holders of non-degrees as assistant lecturers. In some universities, assistant lecturers make up to 70% of the teaching staff. (Njeuma 2003)

It would seem that the main aim of Cameroon's state universities was to provide access to higher education to the populace, irrespective of the quality. Since 1990, the government has also made efforts to encourage private investors to establish tertiary institutions. Today, there are about sixteen private tertiary institutions, even through a good number of them have yet to meet government standards or obtain licenses. Most of the private universities have not met government standards in terms of infrastructure, equipment, and qualified teaching staff. Not surprisingly, they charge higher tuition than the state universities. Even at that, the attraction for potential students is still there. Their attraction may not be far-fetched based on the variety of courses offered and the duration of programs (usually, short-term courses).

Generally, education in Cameroon, in spite of its shortcomings, has been described lately as one of the best education systems in Africa. In the year 2000, the UN Human Development Indicator revealed in its statistics that about 70 percent of all Cameroonian children between six and twelve years old go to school. Also significant is the literacy rate, which is measured at 67.9 percent.

REFORMS IN EDUCATION

Bridging the Bilingual Gap in Education

Shortly after its independence, Cameroon like other African countries adopted different language policies. Cameroon is a subgroup of exoglottic countries that adopted two foreign languages, French and English. Before then, Cameroon had operated as two territories; that is, the UN Trust Territory of Southern Cameroon under the British administration and the rest under French administration. The latter adopted French as its official language, which meant it was also used in schools and an indigenous language acquired at home, while the former opted for English as its official language and the language used in school, in addition to a number of indigenous languages, and pidgin English as its unofficial lingua franca. Generally, those in the former English territory speak three languages, and in the former French territory, two languages.

When Cameroon attained independence and the unification of the two regions, the choice of a national language became even more difficult. In his submission, Kouega (2005) argues that Cameroon has over two hundred indigenous languages, four major regional languages (pidgin, Fulfuldo, Ewondo, and Duala), and two European languages (English and French) and should endeavor to preserve its national unity. He stated that the government's decision to shelve all language problems and settle for French and English as the joint official language of the country was a wise decision. The adoption of two official languages has made Cameroon quite a unique country. In the education sector, both languages are employed. This also means that bilingualism is encouraged and promoted in all schools.

Fonlon (1963) has advocated bilingualism begin early in the life of Cameroonian children. He suggests that as early as primary school, when children are psychologically and physiologically ready to learn new languages, English and French can be introduced simultaneously. To buttress this view, Cameroon's January 18, 1996, revised constitution, article 1, paragraph 3, made bilingualism an official government policy. It states:

The official languages of the Republic of Cameroon shall be English and French, both languages having the same status. The state shall guarantee the promotion of bilingualism throughout the country. It shall endeavor to protect and promote national languages.

By way of further promoting bilingualism, the government emphasized the use of two official languages in education, especially at the tertiary level. Echu explains: In four of the six state universities, English and French are used as languages of instruction in lecture halls wherein Anglophones and Francophones sit side by side in the same classrooms (2004). He also noted that teachers employ the official language they know better for their lectures. On their part, students take notes, take tests, and complete assignments in the language of their choice. This practice may not be without its own problems. Notable among these is the numerical advantage of the francophone teachers, which certainly affects the anglophone students who are in the minority, especially as most lectures delivered would be in French. To confirm this lopsidedness, Tambu (1973) and Njeck (1992) in their different studies on the language issue, arrived at the consensus that in the University of Yaoundé (their sample population), about 80 percent of lectures were delivered in French, and only about 20 percent were delivered in English.

On problems relating to bilingual education especially at the tertiary level, Echu (2004) has described evaluations in such a system as quite unreliable. He explains, "It is not uncommon for students to blame failure in examination to the fact that teachers concerned lack the linguistic competence to adequately understand students' examination scripts in the second official languages (LO2)." Another major problem is the adequacy and availability of teaching aids and facilities for better mastery by students of the second official language (LO2). According to Biloa (1999), in most cases, bilingual training classes are not well organized and lack the necessary infrastructural facilities, which could dampen the motivation of students. Ultimately, it makes bilingual educational efforts extremely difficult for both students and teachers.

Notwithstanding the loopholes experienced in bilingual education, a nation like Cameroon with its peculiarities needs bilingual education. As Echu (2004) put it, improvement especially in the area of teaching methods is quite pertinent. Teachers' proficiency in the second official language is also crucial. These factors will go a long way to reduce the students' suspicion of unfairness in matters of evaluation and other forms of assessment.

At the secondary school level, the language problem is still a delicate issue. For instance, in francophone schools, English is a core subject until the final school certificate examination level. The implication is that English is viewed as an important subject for all students and should be passed by all, however, this not the case with French in anglophone schools. French remains an optional subject even at the General Certificate Examination level. The resultant effect here is that secondary school graduates of francophone systems on entering tertiary schools are better equipped to confront problems arising from bilingual education. Those students have the advantage of both official languages, and there is a tendency that they can do better than their anglophone counterparts. Again, the dominating influence of the French in institutions would make up for such inadequacies. However, the French offer more opportunities in terms of subject offerings, and hence these subjects are compulsory. For instance, besides the emphasis on English as a core subject, the francophone student is also exposed to other foreign languages like Spanish and German. These are taught as subjects throughout the secondary school cycle.

As the country grapples with its bilingual challenges, most Cameroonian educators and linguists still believe there could be some silver lining if the issue is given more critical thought. It would seem in trying to protect unification, lip service is being paid to the language issue. As Ngijol (1964) argues, there is the need for a single national language in Cameroon, basically for community, education, literacy, and the promotion of a national cultural identity. Bot Ba Njok (1966), a Cameroonian, restates his agitation for zonal official languages for each of the linguistic zones into which the country has been divided.

CONCLUSION

The challenges posed by the unusually large number of regional and national influences on Cameroon's social, political, and economic landscape are not without their silver lining in terms of educational development. Even though French influence far exceeds that of the British in the current school system and the African component has yet to find its bearing, graduates of Cameroonian institutions are known to have done well within and outside their country in terms of cultural as well as economic adaptation to the emerging age of technology and international trade and sports. In addition to whatever African languages they may speak, the advantage of bilingualism in French and English is an asset that the Nigerian school system is currently striving to attain in pursuit of the country's free market economy. In spite of Cameroon's concern for possible political disintegration due to these factors of diversity, its economy has been growing steadily in relation to the level of education attained by the country's elite. Although corruption, which is generally the bane of many developing countries' development, is to some extent present in Cameroon, it may not be as problematic as in many of its larger neighbors.

If Cameroon ever overcomes its multifarious challenges of diversity, the deployment of education as a means of national integration remains the most viable option to adopt. The state must be courageous to allow at least two or three ethnic languages to be taught at all levels of education along with French and English, while pidgin English remains the unofficial lingua franca. However, several studies in Nigeria have revealed some damaging effects of pidgin English on the proper use of the English language in terms of writing and speaking. It is better to allow pidgin English to coexist with others at the informal level than promote its use as a national language. The idea of promoting one major language in each of the six zones into which Cameroon has been linguistically subdivided would also be a viable way of responding to the challenges of selecting a national language.

After several decades of juggling the difficulties of using education as a means of promoting national unity, at this point the effort must be intensified. One way to achieve this goal is to fund education adequately to enable the school system to produce better and highly educated Cameroonians who would rise above ethnic divisions and promote nationalism, instead of tribal loyalty or French or English orientations as opposed to Cameroonian aspirations. Cameroon is one African country to watch as a model among emerging African nations.

BIBLIOGRAPHY

Amin, Martin. 1997. *Report on the Demand for Primary Education in Cameroon, 1980–1995*. Washington, D.C.: World Bank.

Biloa, E. 1999. "Bilingual Education in the University of Yaounde I: The Teaching of French to English Speaking Students." In *Bilinguisme official et communication linguistique au Cameroun.* Edited by G. Echu and A. W. Grundstrom. New York: Peter Lang.

Bot Ba Njok, H. "Le probleme linguistic au Cameroon." *L'Afrique et l' Asie* 73 (1966).

Cameroon Tribune. April 17, 1998. Law No. 98/004 of April 14, 1998, Guidelines for Education in Cameroon.

CIA. 2006. *World Fact Book.* Washington, D.C.

Delancey, Mark W., and Mark Dike Delancey. 2000. *Historical Dictionary of the Republic of Cameroon.* Lanham, MD: The Scarecrow Press.

Echu, G. "The Language Question in Cameroon." *Linguistik Online* 18 (2004). http://www.linguistik-online.de/.

Fonlon, B. "A Case for Early Bilingualism." *ABBIA* 4 (1963): 56–94.

Gwanfogbe, M., A. Meligui, J. Moukam, and J. Nyuoghia. 1983. *Geography of Cameroon.* Hong Kong: Macmillan Education Ltd.

Kouega, J. "Promoting French-English Individual Bilingualism through Education in Cameroon." *Journal of Third World Studies* 22 (2005): 189–96.

Mbaku, J. M. 2005. *Culture and Customs of Cameroon.* Westport, CT: Greenwood Press.

Ministry of National Education. 1995. *National Forum Report on Education.*

Ministry of Plan and Regional Development. 1986. *Sixth Five-Year Economic Social and Cultural Development Plan, 1986–1991.*

Ngijol, P. "Necessite d' une langue nationale." *ABBIA* 7 (1964): 83–99.

Ngoh, V. J. 1988. *Cameroon 1884–1985: A Hundred Years of History.* Limbe, Cameroon: Navi-group Publications.

Njeck, Alice Forsab. "Official Bilingualism in the University of Yaounde: Some Educational and Social Issues." Mémoire de Maîtrise, Université de Yaoundé, 1992.

Njeuma, D. L. 2003. "Cameroon Higher Education Profile." In *African Higher Education: An International Reference Handbook.* Edited by D. Teferra and P. G. Altbach. Bloomington: Indiana University Press.

Tchombe, T. M. 1997. "Teacher Education and Deployment in Cameroon." In *Issues in Teacher-Education, Policy and Practice.* Edited by J. Bruce. Cameroon: Felicitas Academic Press.

Todd, L. 1983. "Language Options for Education in a Multilingual Society: Cameroon." In *Language Planning and Language Education.* Edited by C. Kennedy. London: Allen & Unwin.

UNESCO. 1995. *Report on the State of Education in Africa. Education Strategies for the 1990s: Orientations and Achievements.* Paris.

United Nations Development Programme. 1998. *Development and Human Report 1998.*

World Bank. 1995. *Priorities and Strategies for Education.* Washington, D.C.

World Economic Financial Surveys. Sept. 2006. *World Economic Outlook.* http://www.imf.org/external/pubs/ft/weo2006/02/data/index.aspx.

Chapter 3

SCHOOLING IN DEMOCRATIC REPUBLIC OF CONGO

INTRODUCTION

The Democratic Republic of Congo (DRC), formally Zaire, though similar in many ways to other colonized countries in Africa historically, is unique in several ways. In many respects, the country is sui generis among others because it has manifested some extreme forms of characteristics to the detriment of the social and economic development of its people in general and educational backwardness in particular. It was the only country in the annals of colonial Africa to become a personal possession of an individual at its inception as a country—King Leopold II of Belgium. After he acquired the territory as a fief in 1885 and named it the Congo Free State, he turned it over to Belgium's government in 1907 as one of its colonies.

In less than a decade after its independence in 1960, it was ruled for over three decades by one of Africa's most brutal dictators, President Mobutu Sese Seko. At every point in its history, the country has experienced patrimonial governance characterized by brutal imperial dominance of a people so impoverished, so uneducated, and so repressed. This trend has continued unabated because Mobutu's successors have so far been unrelenting in their authoritarian rule, in spite of recent intervention by the UN.

Consequently, education for the masses has always been viewed with suspicion by successive rulers of the country. Indeed, since the colonial era, they have paid little or no attention to education and, hence, with a current literacy rate of about 58 percent, the DRC may well be the lowest rate in Sub-Saharan Africa.

The current state of dilapidation in education may be traced to the colonial era when only the Belgian Catholic Mission had full responsibility for education with some support from foreign mining and agricultural companies in the

Congo. Though half hearted, their support to education was intended to produce a semiliterate workforce in the mines and large-scale farms. Their focus was on primary education as some of the schools were in fact located in the farms and mining camps.

After independence when the African-led government took over, they did not bother with the education of their people until a little over a decade later. Education, like other social welfare programs, was neglected because the political leaders were battling for control of the government. The emerging elite were more concerned about acquisition of wealth through control of the country's government.

At one time or another, there was a reenactment of a long-standing but tacit colonial policy of keeping the people of the Congo illiterate and obedient to their colonial masters and the emerging African elite in government. The apparent collaboration of the foreign business enterprises, some missionaries, and Congolese politicians indeed reduced education to a mere formality with no meaningful gain to the country's children. This is the case in the Democratic Republic of Congo with its unending civil war and instability.

With a vast land area of 2,345,000 square kilometers (905,630 square miles—about the size of the United States, east of the Mississippi) in Central Africa, the DRC is the largest country in Africa. Though sparsely populated with only 58 million, its capital is Kinshasa and ten provinces are spread around the famous Congo River basin. The country's annual population growth is 3 percent. With 30 percent of the population in urban centers, the rest live in rural areas engaged in subsistence agriculture. For the latter, education is a far cry because the few schools available are located in the cities except for a few found in agricultural settlements in rural areas.

The DRC has twelve main ethnolinguistic groups, in addition to 190 smaller ones of which 80 percent are Bantu-speaking, a few Sudanese in the North, some Nolitics in the northeast, and Pygmies and Hamites in the eastern region. The largest ethnic groups are the natives of Mongo, Baluba, Balunda, and the Kongo (or Bakongo). It is on record that a kingdom of Kongo existed in the fifteenth century and was visited by some Portuguese explorers and missionaries who converted the king of the Kongo to Christianity. The prince Alfonso, who later succeeded his father as king, had received some education in Portugal before his ascension to the throne, but when he tried to compel his subjects to accept Christianity, they rebelled against him. Nothing was heard about the old kingdom of Kongo when the Europeans returned in the nineteenth century.

In 1878, a British journalist, Henry Morton Stanley, in collaboration with King Leopold II of Belgium, conducted a survey of the territory and later acquired it as the personal fief of the king before it was later transferred to Belgium as its colony. For most of the colonial era, the country's affairs were in the hands of Belgian business firms in mining and agriculture.

The low priority accorded education in the 1950s was such that 98.2 percent of children in school were in primary, 1.7 percent in secondary, and 0.04

percent in tertiary (Hull 1973). Those who were in tertiary institutions abroad at that time were indeed in violation of a ban on Congolese from attending any university in Europe and elsewhere.

The DRC is a major producer of copper, cobalt, diamonds, cinchona, manganese, silver, uranium, tin, gold, zinc, and hydroelectric power. Congolese agricultural cash crops include coffee, tea, cocoa, rubber, cotton, cassava, and rice. European agricultural firms produce on a large scale for export while Africans are engaged in subsistence farming and mostly affected by the incessant droughts in East and Central Africa. The duality of the economy is such that large-scale farmers are able to export food and other products while poor African farmers can hardly raise enough food for themselves. Agriculture as the mainstay of the Congolese economy accounts for 56.3 percent of the GDP (2002), industry accounts for 18.8 percent, manufacturing accounts for 4 percent, and services account for 25 percent of the total GDP.

Within the last decade the annual income per capita has fallen from US$120 to US$98. Whereas the national budget was US$307.3 million in 1997, the total expenditure was US$601 million. Although this pattern of deficit budgeting is typical of successive DRC governments, it is significant to note that President Mobutu who had ruled the country since its independence was at this time being forced out of office.

Although French is the official language, other languages spoken include Lingala, Swahili, and Tshiluba. Due to the dominance of the Catholic Church, its share of religious groups is about 52 percent, Protestants make up 20 percent, Muslims make up 2 percent, and other sects make up 26 percent.

SOCIAL AND HISTORICAL CONTEXT

Although much has yet to be discovered about the origin of the DRC people, it is believed that the Pygmies were the first inhabitants but were later joined by some Bantu-speaking people who migrated from present-day Nigeria in the northwest. Records of early contact between the Bantu people and the Portuguese explorer, Diogo Cam, in the fifteenth century indicate a usual pattern of early Portuguese adventurism in Africa in the 1400s. It was reported that a group of Franciscan missionaries and craftsmen visited the Congo to promote Christianity. Although the contact indeed involved some promotion of educational activities, it was not sustained although Alfonso, the son of the king of Kongo, then was reported to be literate because of his sojourn and education in Portugal.

The same pattern of contact also took place in the old Warri Kingdom of the Niger Delta in Nigeria in about the same period in 1400. A prince named Don Domingo had an opportunity to study in Portugal after his father and the Itsekiri accepted Christianity. The prince would later return to Nigeria to reign as King (Olu) Atuwase I among his Itsekiri people of Warri in West Africa. Whereas the Kingdom of Kongo in the DRC disappeared before the return of the Europeans in the nineteenth century, others like the Benin and Warri King-doms in West Africa have survived. Our reference to these ancient African king-doms is pertinent in view of the level of subjugation that seems to have occurred in the Congo River area of Central Africa. The patrimony that has dogged the Congolese until this date may not be unrelated to the level of resistance to colonial repression in the post-Portuguese era in the Congo.

At every point in DRC history, starting from the colonial era to date, the treatment of the natives has been anything but subjugation. Like in South Africa, the discovery of strategic minerals attracted to the Congo many Euro-pean business interests to invest in the extraction and refining of copper, gold, diamonds, and other mineral resources, especially in the Katanga province where their succession bid in the early 1960s was reportedly attributed to the intrigues of foreign investors.

Because the mining companies dominated every phase of life in colonial Congo, the following statement was found in a school notice board in a mining settlement: "The good pupil should be pious, polite, obedient, hard working in order to please God, his parents and masters" (Glinne 1976). Such was the mind-set of people who were part of the network of paternalistic organizations shaping the lives of ordinary Congolese from cradle to funeral and on to para-dise. According to Glinne, the promoters of such social policy would also see these natives "as people who would forever remain children" (1976).

After nearly two hundred years of foreign and African domination of the masses in the DRC, during which education received little attention, it is to be expected that the cumulative effect of this legacy would take its toll on the overall development of the country. During independence in 1960, only a tiny group of African politicians with less than tertiary educations took over the reins of government. The struggle for control of the state since then has con-tinued with several invasions, succession bids, and an ongoing civil war.

The Congolese political aristocracy has manifested a weak sense of public purpose and collective societal good. By its actions, it has demonstrated a notably feeble commitment to increase the standard of living of the citizens over whom they rule. This is amply demonstrated by the analysis of the poli-cies governing their allocation of resources and commitment to their imple-mentation. The venality of the political aristocracy over whom President Mobutu presided exemplifies this point. "Development" programs usually got only what is left after the political aristocracy had achieved its interests (Call-aghy 1984).

As in much of postcolonial Africa, a nontraditional nobility emerged with President Mobutu after he outmaneuvered his political rivals with the backing of the military to assume the leadership of the DRC, which he later renamed "Zaire." This was after a chaotic political struggle during which the first Con-golese Prime Minister, Patrice Lumunba, and later the Secretary General of the United Nations, Dag Hammersjold, lost their lives. The leader of the Katanga province, Maurice Tshombe, whose succession bid failed, would also die in exile. Mobutu would later emerge as the absolutist ruler for over thirty years before he was driven out of office by Lauren Kabilla in 1997.

The unending crises also led to the assassination of Kabilla by his own body guard. Succeeded by his son, the legacy of violence has continued as Joseph Kabilla has continued the tradition of dictatorship. The relentless opposition to his rule has continued to prolong the state of anarchy in the Congo.

The Congolese patrimonial system is characterized by a lot of uncertainty because of the constant threat of military intervention. As an absolutist regime with a military aristocracy, the one-party system was in place to suppress any opposition to the rule of the presidential monarch to whom the political aristocracy must give an unalloyed loyalty.

Characterized by a lack of productivity, the political aristocracy has been an avenue of upward mobility in the Congolese absolutist state. Power, wealth, and prestige are obtained through the presidency. As patrimonial servants of the president, the aristocracy is heaped with rewards, honors, and riches. Without the president, they would be nothing. Consequently, the leader ensures that any incipient autonomy from him is destroyed (Callaghy 1984).

PREBENDALIZED POLITICAL ECONOMY

Like most postcolonial states in Africa, the DRC inherited an economic system in which the state could not afford to remain a passive referee for the capitalist operators. They adopted an interventionist posture that quickly went beyond the provision of physical and social infrastructures, such as roads, hospitals, railways, and schools. Although the intention of many African governments in directly productive enterprises is to be profitable, in the case of Mobutu's Zaire (DRC) the intention was apparently to keep the loyalty of his aristocracy in politics and the military. Students of development believe that the vulnerability and fragility of any state increases pari passu with the expansion of its economic activities. Indeed, this means that certain individuals in government can block, alter, or circumvent state policies to suit their own interests. Nowhere is this more apparent that in the Mobutu administration.

Mobutu's Zairenization policy allowed his government to nationalize foreign companies without compensation to the owners. Soon after the exercise, cronies became what Akeredolu-Ale (1975) called "drone" capitalists who operated state-owned enterprises for their own personal benefits. Thus, the Congolese bourgeoisie can be said to have an economic orientation and a set of priorities that have rendered it fundamentally incapable of ruling without squeezing dry the reins of the state itself (Joseph 1984). However, it is mostly in the context of a prebendalized political economy, as experienced in many African states, that such policies can exist with little or no challenge. The term *prebendal* refers to patterns of political or economic behavior that reflect as their justifying principle that the offices of the existing holder may be competed for and then used for the personal benefit of its holder as well as that of their references or support groups. In other words, a prebendal state is perceived as a cogeries of offices susceptible to individual and communal appropriation (Joseph 1984). In the case of the DRC, the political and military aristocracies do not have any obligation to their community or support group but to the leader who is the executive president of the republic—whether it is Mobutu or anyone after him.

After the nationalization of foreign firms led to the establishment of *Gecamines*, the state-owned agency, it was managed by President Mobutu's loyalists. This has since accounted for the high level of corruption and mismanagement of government economic ventures and related firms (Radmann 1978). In the light of the challenges analyzed so far, where does education come in?

EDUCATIONAL EVOLUTION

It is within the foregoing sociohistorical context that we must now examine the development of education. The education system has evolved against the background of two striking features. The first has to do with the virtual domination of education by the Belgian Catholic Mission and the second with the mission's explicit anti-elitist posture in favor of vocational and utilitarian aspirations of only a few.

Before World War II, the Belgian colonial administration assumed virtually no operational responsibility for African education (Turner and Young 1981). Eventually, when the administration took some interest in the matter, it was only by way of subsidy to the Catholic Mission that was still responsible for education. The Protestant missions that assisted did not receive any subsidy. Until the mid 1950s, primary education—the main focus—was not only utilitarian but also terminal.

The emphasis on primary education was "to ensure that the quality of elite to be selected from it." This indeed was in line with the mission's slogan, "No elite, no problems." Similar to the situation in South Africa during apartheid, instruction in Belgian colonial schools was in the vernacular language—the indigenous language of the child. Everything was done "to avoid elitist pretensions and aspirations" (Coleman and Ngokwey 1983). The avowed aim of colonial education was "to produce better Africans, and not copies of Europeans who could never be more than humans of the third category" (Hailey 1957).

Since the foreign mining companies to whom the affairs of Belgian Congo was prebendalized did not consider education beyond the primary level as relevant to their need for the African labor force, the terminative principle was applied. The same anti-elitist principle was also applied at the postprimary and higher level—a situation that has hardly changed since independence (Markowitz 1973). According to some sources, the level of neglect of education by the Congolese leaders was such that fifteen years into their administration foreign missionaries were still in charge of their schools.

Between 1950 and 1977, enrollment in secondary schools rose from 4,004 to 643,675, whereas only 13,399 had access to some form of tertiary education in the Congo. The 1990s witnessed an enrollment of six- to eleven-year olds totaling 4.9 million in primary schools, 1.3 million in secondary, and about 862,900 in teacher education programs in the DRC. The country's three universities have an enrollment of 20,100 students. The entire education system is sustained with only 1 percent of the gross national product (GNP). The fluctuation noticed in school enrollment could be attributed to the ongoing conflicts in and around the DRC. Affected areas would always shut their school doors (Microsoft Encarta 2002).

Whatever relative normalcy experienced in the 1990s in Congolese schools may have disappeared in the first decade of the twenty-first century in view of the worsening security situation in the country. Current information indicates that 11 percent of Congolese children die before their first birthday and life expectancy, as quoted by the Catholic Relief Agency, is forty-five years. The International Rescue Agency committee recently reported that over twelve hundred people have continued to die daily from effects of the ongoing conflict.

The DRC has one of the worst transportation and communication infrastructures on the continent leaving the majority of Congolese completely isolated from health services, educational opportunities, markets and information. Violent conflict also persists today in Eastern DRC. Most recently, violence flared in Katanga province where the army is fighting to put down local militia groups. Reports from international groups indicate the DRC's diverse natural resources have played a major role in funding the conflict, and undermining efforts to promote peace, stability and economic development. The United Nations has called DRC "a neglected catastrophe, a silent but deadly disaster." (Catholic Relief Services 2006)

In the light of the ongoing conflict, the school structure 6-3-3-4 or 6-5-4 as may be found in several African countries can hardly be said to be in place in the DRC. Whenever there is a lull in the fighting in some areas, the Ministry of Education, working with Catholic and Protestant churches, has tried to restore primary education through teacher training, school rehabilitation, translation and distribution of teaching manuals, and the promotion of girls' education (boys are hardly available in view of their forceful recruitment into the army or local militia).

The UNESCO International Institute for Capacity Building in Africa has provided a forum for Congolese teachers and teacher training institutions to share their experiences, research, and emerging knowledge. The capacity building of head teacher institutions in Sub-Saharan Africa is a project that evaluates the main teacher training institutions and makes recommendations for strengthening their impact.

Recent attention to HIV/AIDS education in Africa has also become a focal point in the Congo in primary as well as secondary levels. Indeed, the sparse population currently experienced at all levels of Congolese educational institutions can be traced to the instability that the country has experienced since the colonial era. The consequences are reflected at the tertiary level.

University Education

The provision of tertiary education in the Congo since the colonial era has hardly been a priority. The restriction on postprimary education would normally have considerable effect on university education. In the same way that the economy of the country was controlled by the foreign mining and agricultural firms, the Catholic Mission was also in charge of tertiary education at its inception. Their anti-elitist posture was intended to achieve a specific purpose: nurture a docile citizenry that would continue to promote the neocolonial interests of the European enterprises in the Congo. This was evident in the actions and utterances of the organizers of the education sector in general and the tertiary level, in particular. A colonial edict prohibited the Congolese from attending any European universities including the ones in Belgium. With this restriction, it is not surprising that the Congo could hardly boast of any university graduates when it achieved its independence.

As a result of the echoes of development and agitation for the establishment of tertiary institutions across the African continent in the 1960s, the Congolese citizens were inevitably drawn into the fray. At that time, the Catholic Mission took the lead in establishing the first university in Kinshasa. It was a replica of the University of Louvain in Belgium as it was mostly staffed by the Catholic teaching order and controlled by the mining companies. Until 1971, the African politicians who were in charge of the country did not interfere with the affairs of the university (La Croix 1972).

Indeed, it was the combined pressure of the Congolese *evolues* (elite) and some Belgian professors and missionaries that brought about the establishment of the three universities in the DRC.

Lovanium University, Zaire's (DRC) first University remained a veritable state within a state, a satellite of Louvain University in Belguim, whose constitution, standards, curricular content and ethos it replicated under the dynamic and dominating rectorship of Monsigneur Luc Gillon. (Coleman and Ngokwey 1983)

Thus, the DRC's premier university was staffed and overwhelmingly controlled by Belgian professors who isolated it from the state since its inception. Lovanium's founder, Guy Melangreau, stated:

We must form a Catholic elite and assure its social and political education by having it participate under our direction in colonial undertaking. ... To this elite we must open the doors of higher education, always and under the condition that this education cannot be trusted to a state agency, which under the pretext of neutrality and of freedom of choice would create only a nursery for rebels. (cited in Ilunga 1978)

Unfortunately, the concern expressed by the founding fathers of the DRC's first university turned out to be prophetic because the endless wars that have plagued the country over the years are mostly masterminded by alumni of these institutions, including Lovanium. Somehow, the freedom that was denied the students of these institutions has turned them against their country and all within their territories—to the chagrin of the international community.

The monstrosity of an uneducated citizenry dominated by a tiny political aristocracy and backed by neocolonial interests is certainly an outcome of expression let loose by the Catholic elite that the Monsigneur Melangreau did not want. Somehow, the patrimonial disposition of leaders in academia and the political sphere would certainly have left an indelible mark on the psyche of the emerging middle class now in control of the country. This has also had its far-reaching consequences on the actions of the country's students within the context of academic freedom and university autonomy. In other words, the early founders and educators of the Congo cannot be exonerated from blame in view of the conduct of the graduates coming from their institutions.

Under the principle of university autonomy, the three universities in the DRC for a while maintained a reasonable distance from state interference even though the government, at that time, was bearing about 80 percent of the funding. Under the various charters and external linkages, the principle of institutional autonomy and freedom from state intervention was vigorously affirmed in the early years. However, it would not be too long before a change occurred. Several factors including an authoritarian faculty, a patrimonial style of university administration, and a perceived Eurocentric curriculum would prompt African students to challenge university authorities. Moreover, the more favorable subsidy to the Catholic Mission would prompt a protest from the Protestant proprietors, in terms of funding. For instance, the Protestant Free University of the Congo was at that time angling for equal treatment with Lovanium University, which was run by the Catholic Mission (Hunt 1873).

Initially, African university students were comparatively quiescent politically because of the assurance of automatically gaining elite status upon graduation. As the political environment deteriorated and the economic condition was no longer conducive for Congolese students, a state of anarchy gradually emerged. This situation was further aggravated by the wave of students uprising across Africa and indeed the world in the roaring 1960s. The news of student protests against the Vietnam War in the United States and other countries was transmitted to Africa by the media, thus capturing the imagination of many African students who had never known anything but patrimonial rule at the state and university levels. At a time when East–West relations had yet to overcome the cold war of the era, the budding Marxists on the African continent were ready to make the best out of the brewing crises.

The students' central demand was an Afrocentric faculty and curriculum to reflect their economic and cultural values. They also demanded to participate in the governance of their university. University administrators who had for a long time taken refuge behind the principle of academic freedom and autonomy were now under siege. Forced to seek assistance from the political authorities, they were now willing to trade their autonomy for protection. At that point, only the state authorities had the resources and means of curbing the situation.

The threat to peace and stability was real in view of the vehemence of the student challenge.

Although government authorities were pleased to be called to rescue of the university authorities, they were also apprehensive of having to deal with an institution that many, especially the older generation, knew nothing about. Like many African communities, the mind-set of academics and campus activities of the universities in the DRC have generally been a mystery to outsiders (Ilunga 1978).

As the then-Zairian (DRC) government grappled with the student crisis, President Mobutu saw an opportunity to curb what he viewed were excesses of the academic community that had been a threat to his dictatorship. Like every other institution in the country, it was time to make the universities part of his administration's centralization process. His first line of action was to brutally crush the student protest. Then, he merged the three universities into one under the leadership of one rector who must be appointed by the president. This was followed by a decree empowering the minister of education to appoint professors and other principal officers of the university. For all intents and purposes, that sealed the coffin of academic freedom and university autonomy in the DRC.

This scenario unfortunately would be repeated in several African countries where a military and civilian dictatorship existed. Although a love–hate relationship between civil servants and academics has always existed in these countries, African dictators have generally sought to give their regimes credibility by appointing some academics to key positions in their administrations. In the case of the Congo under Mobutu, the administration was able to maintain a degree of relative autonomy because of the input of the academic community, which sometimes used its contacts with external agencies to enhance its legitimacy. A power is legitimate to the degree that by virtue of the doctrine and norms by which it is justified and its holder can call upon sufficient other centers of power as reserves in the case of need to make this power effective (Stinchcome 1968). The legitimacy of many African dictatorships has generally been a matter of concern to rulers and their regimes.

The role of the Congolese professoriate is fairly typical of other African states with similar situations. The co-optation of academics into the government has long been an artful device of many African leaders to neutralizing dissent and opposition. The participation of academics has also been a result of their positive contribution to the development of their country.

However, African academics, including those in the DRC, have also served as a voice of opposition to unacceptable government policies because opposing political parties are either nonexistent or too weak to make a difference. In a few places, the press has also played some significant roles. Trade unions, especially in tertiary institutions, have served as a platform for dissent, especially with regard to the funding of education. Although some professors have occasionally embarrassed their colleagues by supporting some dictatorial regimes, the academic community has generally stood their ground on principle to voice constructive criticism. The community has also euphemistically referred to their erring colleagues as "political prostitutes" who are hardly welcome to campus these days.

As in some African universities, the professoriate in the DRC has lost considerable prestige, emoluments, and conveniences as a result of their general disposition to oppose alienating government policies. As a result, civil servants who earned less and had less perquisites took advantage of being "loyal servants" to political leaders to catch up with, and in some cases, surpass academics in remuneration. Although many professors appointed to high political positions received a vastly higher salary and the much coveted perquisites and indeed some peculations, many have maintained their integrity while a few have succumbed to corruption, as was the case in the Mobutu regime of the Congo and Abacha's regime in Nigeria (Gould 1980). Although the material condition of African academics and prestige have been on the increase again as a result of some improvement in university funding, some observers have said the following about Mobutu's Congo:

Once at the pyramid of occupational prestige, the professoriate plummeted to a de-esteemed and degraded status in the self-image of many of its members. It became a milieu of dearth and penury in which only men of power and corruption and their associated wealth commanded the valued material conditions of life. (Coleman and Ngokwey 1983)

In view of the bleak picture painted so far of the DRC, it has long been realized that positive change is inevitable. Invariably, it must start with the people. We must accept that development—be it social, economic, or political—ought to begin with a meaningful educational process that must be pursued massively in a vigorous manner. This also would only succeed if there is a viable economy to sustain it. Again, such an improvement needs effective leadership and a more enlightened citizenry in an environment that is free of violence and instability. Obviously, the country yearns for the leadership of an educated elite that is free of corruption and committed to the improvement of the standard of living of the masses in the Congo. To a large extent, that is still a far cry in the DRC even at the turn of the twenty-first century.

CHALLENGES, CHANGES, AND REFORMS

The most significant challenge confronting the DRC has been related to the rulers of the country. For one thing, neither the social nor political structure under the ongoing instability and near absence of development has changed since the colonial era. The business community, in collaboration with the various missionary groups and the feuding African aristocracy, did not show any serious indication of altering the status quo. If education as a primary instrument of change must thrive, it must become the primary concern of all, including the international community.

Over the thirty years that Mobutu squandered the vast resources of the Congo on himself, his family, and the tiny aristocracy around him, he was thought to be the only obstacle to development and that his exit would bring positive change. After nearly a decade since his departure, difficulties have continued. The natural resources that could have been harnessed to improve the material condition of the Congolese have continued to be the flash point of the crises. Somehow, the social infrastructure he left behind has continued to be an obstacle to economic growth and educational development.

Students of development in the Congo have always argued that control of the country's economy has never really been in the hands of the common Congolese people. Under Mobutu and his successors, the Congolese aristocracy has merely gotten some fragments of the real income from the mining and agricultural activities of the country. They contend that European and other investors have continued to be the real power behind the African leadership. In view of the country's heavy indebtedness to many of them, they would not let go. For instance, in the late 1970s, when the economic condition was terribly in shambles, the United States was urged to bring an end to the Mobutu regime. In a statement, the U.S. State Department argued that it would be difficult to cause the downfall of the regime unless there was some domestically generated political change (Young 1978). The domestically generated political change sought since then has been at the center of an ongoing war that has brought more suffering to the Congolese.

The point has also been made that the international community and its agencies to whom the DRC is heavily indebted would continue to prop up the regimes in spite of their dismal record of human rights violations, including the deprivation of meaningful education to their citizens.

Critics argue that as long as debts to the International Monetary Fund (IMF), International Bank for Reconstruction and Development (IBRD), Germany, Belgium, the United Kingdom, and a host of others in the West remain unpaid, outside interference will continue to be a hindrance to development in the country. This situation has created a vicious circle and has been responsible for many Congolese fleeing their country to Europe and the United States in search of a better life.

During the Mobutu era, the creditor-nations were always focused on the price of copper and cobalt in the world market in order to move in to demand payment. Between 1977 and 1980, the DRC had no budgetary surplus, whereas its annual debt servicing payment was US$485 million. The endemic pattern of corruption, a poor budget, and the unproductive performances that created the debt situation in the first place have continued unabated. Meanwhile, massive debt rescheduling or de facto memorandum would be necessary to maintain the near collapse of the administration (Gran 1978).

Over the years the Congolese elite have acquired a mode of consumption far beyond the productive capacity of a poor country like the DRC. The direct and indirect transfer of sophisticated goods, specialized services, and applied and theoretical knowledge have created and sustained investors and multinational corporations working in tandem with the aristocracy to sap the country dry economically.

The dual economy of the Congo has never been beneficial to the natives because the foreign companies in agriculture are producing for export while the natives have continued to engage in subsistence agrarian farming that would not even provide enough food for them. Is it not baffling that the UN Food and Agriculture Organization (FAO) is providing food aid to the Congolese when commercial farmers are exporting their products abroad? It is no wonder Gran (1978) argues that aid must be linked to the structure of the Congolese government in view of the fact that bureaucrats would not allow food aid to reach the poor masses whose efforts were sometimes thwarted by incessant droughts and other disasters that plague Central and East Africa.

If less has been said about schooling in the DRC since its inception as a country, it is because the social and political situation has done very little to promote meaningful opportunity for success in its educational endeavors. One would only hope that some state of normalcy is restored to the country so that the children of the Congo can experience education as a human right as clearly recognized by international conventions. The DRC elite and government owe it to their people and posterity. The international community should also assist the country to return to the path of normalcy. For as long as the chaos continues, their difficulties will continue to have far-reaching consequences for Africa and the rest of the world. The time to act is now.

BIBLIOGRAPHY

Adelman, Kenneth L. "The Zairian Political Party as Religious Surrogate." *Africa Today* vol. 23–24 (Oct.–Dec. 1976).

Akeredolu-Ale, E. O. "Some Thoughts on the Indigenization Process and the Quality of Nigerian Capitalism." Nigerian Indigenization Policy: Proceedings of the Nigerian Economic Society Symposium, 1975.

Callaghy, Thomas M. 1984. "External Actors and the Relative Autonomy of the Political Aristocracy in Zaire." In *State and Class In Africa*. Edited by Nelson Kasfir. London: Frank Cass & Co. Ltd.

Coleman J. S. "The Academic Freedom and Responsibilities of Foreign Scholars in African Universities." *Issue: A Journal of Opinion* 7, no. 2 (1977): 14–33.

Coleman, James, and N. Ngokwey. 1983. "Zaire: The State and University." In *Politics and Education*. Edited by E. M. Thomas. New York: Pergamon Press.

Dore, R. 1976. *The Diploma Disease: Education Qualification and Development*. London: Allen & Unwin Ltd.

Glinne, Earnest. "The Congo Crisis And The Katanga Affair." *Presence Africaine* 4–5, no. 32–33 (1976).

Gould, D. 1980. *Bureaucratic Corruption and Underdevelopment in the Third World: The Case Study of Zaire*. Oxford, UK: Pergamon Press.

Gran, Guy. "Zaire 1978: The Ethical and Intellectual Bankruptcy of the World System." *Africa Today* 25, no. 4 (1978): 5–24.

Hailey, Lord. 1957. *An African Survey.* London: Oxford University Press.

Hull, G. 1973. "Government Nationalization of the University: A Case Study of the Republic of Zaire." Presented at the 16th Annual Meeting of the African Studies Assn., Syracuse, NY, Oct. 31–Nov. 3.

Ilunga, K. 1978. "Some Thoughts on the National University of Zaire and the Zairian Political Dynamics."

Joseph, Richard A. 1984. "Class, State, and Prebendal Politics in Nigeria." In *State Class in Africa.* Edited by N. Kasfir. London: Frank Cass & Co. Ltd.

Kabeya, Luabeya. "Foreign Financial Assistance and Economic Growth in Zaire." *Africa Development Quarterly* 2, no. 3 (1977).

Kanda, Ciamaki. "Elements of Blockages in the Development of Rural Zaire." *Cas Labadu, Kasai: Cashier Economiques et Sociales* 15, no. 3 (Sept. 1978): 334–71.

La Croix, B. "Pouvoirs et structures de l'Universite Lovanium." *Cahiers de CEDAF* 2–3, series 2 (1972).

Libois, Jules G. 1966. *Katanga Secession.* Madison: University of Wisconsin Press.

Markowitz, M. D. 1973. *Cross and Sword: The Political Role of Christian Missions in the Belgium Congo, 1908–1960.* Stanford, CA: Hoover Institution Publications.

Merriam, Alan P. 1961. *Congo: Background of Conflict.* Illinois: Northwestern University Press.

Microsoft Encarta. 2002.

Radmann, Wolf. "The Nationalization of Zaire's Copper: From Union Miniere to Gecamines." *Africa Today* 25, no. 4 (Oct.–Dec. 1978).

Stinchcombe, A. L. 1968. *Construction Social Theories.* New York: Harcourt Brace.

Turner, T. E., and Young, M. C. 1981. *The Rise and Decline of Zairian State.*

Verhagen, Benoit. 1978. "Les Crisis de la Reserche Zairoise au Zaire, 1967–1977." no. 10 (July 1978): 38–62.

Young, M. C. "The African University: Universalism, Development, and Ethnicity." *Comparative Education Review* 25, no. 2 (1981): 145–62.

Young, M. C. "La Faculte des Sciences Sociales a l'UNAZ: Reflexions autour d'un mandate." *Etudes Zairoises* 1 (1978): 154–80.

WEB SITE

Catholic Relief Services: http://crs.org.

Chapter 4

SCHOOLING IN GHANA

INTRODUCTION

Ghana is officially known as the Republic of Ghana. It is situated on the Gulf of Guinea, a few degrees north of the equator. It borders Cote d'Ivoire to the west, Burkina Faso to the north, Togo to the east, and the Atlantic Ocean to the south. Ghana's topography has a low coastline with sandy shores and plains that are interceded with several rivers and streams. The topography includes a tropical rain forest, lands covered by low bushes, grassy plains, and a savannah. Ghana's longest river is the Volta. Also, Lake Volta extends through the large portion of eastern Ghana. It is the world's largest artificial lake. Generally, Ghana's climate can best be described as tropical.

Ghana covers an approximate land surface area of 230,940 square kilometers (89,166 square miles); 3.5 percent is water. This puts the total extent and size of Ghana at 239,460 square kilometers (92,456 square miles). Ghana's total size can roughly be compared to the size of Great Britain or Oregon in the United States. Ghana's population in 2005 was estimated at 22,113,000, with a density of 215 per square mile. This increased in 2006 to 22,409,572, with an annual growth rate of 2.1 percent. Infant mortality was 55.0 to every 1,000; life expectancy was 58.9 percent. In 2006, the population density was recorded at 252 per square mile.

Ghana is predominately a black African state (about 98.5 percent). Its major ethnic groups include 44 percent Akan; 16 percent Moshi-Dogomba; 13 percent Ewe; 8 percent Ga; 3 percent Gurma; and 1 percent Yoruba. Europeans and other nationalities make up 1.5 percent of the total population.

English is the official language, with several other local African languages, such as Akan, Moshi-Dagomba, Ewe, and Ga. In terms of religion, 63 percent of Ghanaians are Christians, 16 percent are Muslims, while the remaining 21 percent subscribe to indigenous faiths.

The Republic of Ghana actually began as the Gold Coast. It was one of the first black African countries to attain independence from the United Kingdom on March 6, 1957. It became a republic on July 1, 1960. Current President John Agyekum Kufour of the Republic of Ghana assumed his office in 2001.

Accra is Ghana's capital and largest city. Other large cities in Ghana include Kumasi and Tamale. On the whole, Ghana has ten regions, which are further subdivided into a total of 138 districts. These regions are Ashanti, Brong Ahafo, Central, Eastern, Greater Accra, Northern, Upper East, Upper West, Volta, and Western.

HISTORY AND POLITICS OF THE PEOPLE

The Republic of Ghana is a merger of several major ancient civilizations beginning with the old Empire of Ghana, which actually existed until the thirteen century, with the Akan people as the dominant tribe. Between the eighteenth and nineteenth centuries, the Ashanti Empire took over in preeminence. Significantly though, the area later called the Gold Coast was first discovered by Portuguese traders who settled and traded with the people in 1470. These traders came in search of gold, ivory, and spices. The Portuguese were followed later by the Dutch, Danes, Swedes, Prussians, and the British. Between 1806 and 1901, the Ashanti people who were the original landowners unsuccessfully fought a series of wars to resist the British occupation. In 1901, the Gold Coast had completely come under the British Protectorate.

In 1946, to prepare the indigenous people for independence, the British allowed their participation in local governance. In 1949, an all-African Committee was appointed to look into constitutional reforms. Between 1951 and 1954, the stride towards self-governance continued. On March 6, 1957, the Gold Coast became the first Sub-Saharan country in colonial Africa to attain independence. Significantly, it was at independence that the name Ghana was adopted. It was borne out of the belief that the Ghanaians are the actual descendants of the old Ghana Empire. Following independence, by July 1, 1960, Ghana became a republic.

Kwame Nkrumah, often described as an anticolonial leader, was the first president to rule Ghana at independence. In his tenure, especially from 1960–65, he took full control of Ghana's economic, political, cultural, and military affairs. His leadership style was typically autocratic. This spurred opposition in some quarters. Thus, while he was out of the country in 1966, he was toppled in a military coup led by General Emmanuel Kotoka. What followed was a military regime under the platform of the National Liberation Council (NLC). They established their rule by decree, dismissed the civilian government, suspended the existing constitution, and finally put a ban on civilian governance.

However, in 1969, the three-year political ban was lifted and elections occurred in August of that same year. Kofi Busia formed a new government on the platform of the Progressive Party (PP) and adopted a new constitution. His two years in office worsened Ghana's economy. The military saw this as another opportunity to take over and in January 1972 the civilian government was sacked. Ghana witnessed another military regime led by Colonel Ignatius Kutu Acheampong of the National Redemption Council (NRC). Central to Acheampong's regime was his self-help program tagged *Operation Feed Yourself*. This program was typical of General Olusegun Obasanjo's *Operation Feed the Nation* during his military era in the 1980s as Nigeria's head of state.

In 1978, Ghana witnessed yet another instability in the government as General Frederick Akufo led the coup that ousted Achempong's regime. Following this, in fewer than nine months, another coup led this time by junior military officers brought Flight Lieutenant Jerry Rawlings to power. Rawlings traced Ghana's economic depression, political instability, other forms of bad governance, and mismanagement of public funds to Ghana's past leaders. He publicly carried out an execution of leaders, such as Acheampong, Akuffo, Afrifa, and their aides—the same people who saw Nkrumah's overthrow. Some others were fortunate; they were dismissed from office with ignominy. Having done this, Rawlings organized a national election as a step towards a civilian regime.

The People's National Party (PNP) won the election and Hilla Limann was installed as president. Limann and his party did not do much for Ghana as the country's economy dwindled—a situation that led to Rawlings' return to power. Upon return, he banned political parties and suspended the country's constitution. By a referendum on April 28, 1992, a new constitution was approved and Rawlings was elected president in a keenly contested multiparty election. Subsequently, he was inaugurated president of the fourth Republic of Ghana on January 4, 1993. The period from 1992–96 was quite significant because it was the first full term served by any president in Ghana without threats of a coup. After 1996, Rawlings continued for another four-year term. With Rawlings barred by law from reelection after four years, John Kuffour emerged as president. As Ghana's ninth leader, Kuffour has successfully steered Ghana to the celebration of its golden jubilee in spite of the tensions between Rawlings and Kuffour, especially during the first year of his tenure. Generally, Ghana has operated a parliamentary system of government dominated by two main parties—the New Patriotic Party (NPP) and the National Democratic Congress (NDC).

GHANA'S ECONOMY

At independence in 1957, Ghana could boast of strong national infrastructures and a buoyant economy, especially in cocoa produce. By 1960, under Nkrumah's leadership, there were massive national projects in place. Notable among these were the Volta Aluminium Company and the Akosombo Dam, which boosted the economy and aided the planned Universal Basic Education Scheme. Unfortunately, with the worldwide drop of cocoa prices in the mid 1960s, Ghana experienced some economic depression. This had a great effect on the Accelerated Development Plan for Education (ADPE), a plan for six years of free basic education for Ghanaian children. Similarly, the depressed economy also prevented the implementation of the Education Act of 1960, which focused on funding university education.

The state of the economy in the late 1980s led to increased emphasis on vocational and technical education. The aim was to equip students who completed junior secondary school with productive skills in the working world. Similarly, in 1989, under Rawlings' drive to stimulate the economy as well as afford everyone educational opportunities, he emphasized the importance of adult and nonformal education. Indeed, adult education during this period was directly linked to Ghana's economic development. Before then, in 1972, education enjoyed about 20 percent of the nation's budget.

The Ghanaian economy can be said to be fairly strong in view of its rich natural resources, coupled with about 16 percent arable land. Ghana can boast of agricultural products such as maize, millet, sorghum, rice, and groundnuts as the nation's staple food crops, and coffee, banana, palm nuts, kola nuts, shea nuts, rubber, and cotton as good foreign exchange earners. However, cocoa has remained a major source of foreign exchange. From 2000–2001, cocoa produce was estimated at about 400,000 metric tons. Importantly, the civil war in Cote d'Ivoire that began in 2002 tended to favor Ghana's cocoa export. This was so because the war destabilized Cote d'Ivoire and displaced it as the world's largest producer of cocoa. The period of economic downturn for Cote d'Ivoire brought about a remarkable rise in cocoa prices in favor of Ghana's economy (CIA 2001).

Other natural resources in Ghana include gold, timber, industrial diamonds, bauxite, manganese, rubber, hydropower, petroleum, silver, salt, limestone, and fish. Like cocoa, gold in Ghana is another major foreign exchange earner. Gold deposits in Ghana are quite significant and good investments have been made in mining since 1992. In that year, earnings from gold exports exceeded that of cocoa and remained so all until 2003. In terms of oil, Ghana is not a major producer; the country only has a modest quantity refined, mostly for domestic consumption. On the whole, Ghana's exports of gold, cocoa, timber, tuna, bauxite, aluminum, manganese ore, and diamonds were estimated at US$2.911 billion in 2005.

In more recent times, tourism has been recorded as the country's third largest source of foreign exchange. Timber, which used to be an economic growth area, is greatly on the decline due to large-scale deforestation. On the whole, the improvement in Ghana's economy is in the agricultural sector, which accounted for about 35 percent of the nation's GDP in 2001. In more recent times, it has increased to 40 percent. This sector also employed 60 percent of the workforce in 1999 and increased to 65 percent in 2001. It has continued in that trend to 70 percent.

Ghana also has done well in the industrial sector in light of its 15 percent increase in this sector with its 10.62 million workforce. Ghana's major industries include mining, lumbering, light manufacturing, aluminum smelting, food processing, cement, and small commercial ship building. Ghana has major business partnerships with such countries as Belgium, China, Germany, France, Japan, the Netherlands, Nigeria, the United Kingdom, and the United States.

Ghana, like most third-world African nations, has also suffered some economic depression. This is largely due to mismanagement of the nation's economy and misuse of public funds. Poor maintenance culture, poor road networks, transportation, and an inadequate telecommunications sector are also responsible for its setbacks. The indiscriminate spending by public officers, large wage increases in the public sector, and deficit in the government budget were also responsible for the depreciation of the Ghanaian *cedi*—its monetary unit.

Before the 1990s, Ghana would boast of over three hundred state-owned enterprises and firms. Six years later, over half of these firms had been privatized. Again, with the inflation rate hitting a peak of 70 percent in 1995, the economic sector seriously struggled for sustenance, and sought aid from the World Bank and IMF. With the introduction of a three-year Structural Adjustment Program (SAP) and the IMF's cooperation, Ghana made some economic progress. This measure would subsequently force a decline in its inflation rate to about 21 percent in 2001. Since then, Ghana's economy grew from 3.8 percent in 1994 to 4.5 percent in 1995 due to increased gold production and an increase in cocoa harvest. The economy reverted to an annual growth rate of 4.2 percent thereafter (CIA 2006).

Resulting from the economic crunch of the 1990s and borne out of several budgetary problems and IMF pressure, fees were introduced and later increased in schools. In the 1999–2000 school year, the cost of attending school in Ghana had risen by about 600 percent, especially at the tertiary level. The effect was students' boycott of classes and riots in tertiary institutions, leading to school closures. After negotiations between the government, school authorities, and the student body, fees were slightly reduced.

DEVELOPMENT OF EDUCATION

Traditional Education

In ancient Ghana, communities were small and largely rural, but self-sufficient. Education was quite informal, unspecialized, and illiterate; even at that, it cannot be regarded as defective. Traditional education in Ghana existed until the last quarter of the nineteenth century when the first signs of state-organized education emerged.

In a typical indigenous Ghanaian setting, families shared and cared for each other. Communities worked closely together. There were villages with common farm lands, and coastal villages worked on the fishing nets together. Like other African systems of education, indigenous education in Ghana had a focus and clearly defined aims and objectives. Education, though informal, was aimed at producing persons who would be useful members of society. To achieve this, children at a very young age were trained to be good citizens, endowed with character training, and taught to acquire skills that would make them productive members of society. Parents, elders, older siblings, and the community were custodians of knowledge. They would also play their roles as teachers to the younger generation, transmitting knowledge through a variety of instructional mediums—orally, with songs, proverbs, riddles, folklore, myths, and legends as appropriate ways of teaching. Body language and other forms of communication enhanced teaching and learning.

In view of the utilitarian aim of traditional education, for an individual to be a productive and useful member of society, he must firstly be trained to be a good citizen. As is the case in most preliterate societies, the home played the most vital role as an educational agency, with the family as the main agent of socialization. The expectation was that the family would play the role of imparting proper values in children. Such positive values would help display proper attitudes not only in his immediate home but also as a member of the larger society. According to McWilliam and Kwamena-Poh (1975), the role of the home is quite crucial to inculcate good citizenry in the young learner. They also stressed that "from the age of eight or nine, the boys would follow their fathers to learn some trade and be initiated into the customs and trade. Importantly, the young had to seek information about the past by listening to their elders" (McWilliam and Kwamena-Poh 1975).

Significantly, traditional Ghanaian society did not see parents as the only teachers. Elders in the family, indeed, the whole family lineage and the whole community, were responsible for instructing the child in proper values. It is important to note that an erring child was not the only one blamed, rather the child's immediate family, entire lineage, and community suffered the disgrace. Because no one wanted to suffer such dishonor, all strived hard to play their roles to inculcate positive values in children. This is aptly illustrated in a case study by Oppong (1967) of socialization among the Dagbon in northern Ghana. Oppong tried to emphasize that traditional Ghanaian society did not see a child's training for citizenship only as the immediate family's responsibility. This cultural norm stems from the Ghanaian concept of blood relationships. It relates to extended kinship and goes beyond the nuclear family to all who could trace their lineage from the same ancestry. In other words, all such relatives are held together by a common origin and a common obligation to its members, living or dead. As such, relatives were expected to work together with parents to ensure that children of the lineage would not bring disgrace to the whole family. In fact, the home trains the child in character formation. Knowledge of the history, culture, and traditional beliefs of the people was very vital to appropriate interpersonal relationships. It also equipped children for specialized occupational roles in life.

Character training and citizenship constituted a crucial aspect of education in traditional Ghana. It was imparted directly by parents and older siblings in the family. Children were mostly educated through various routines of daily activities. Legends or fables and stories were also used to impart acceptable attitudes and morals. For example, famous Ananse stories, popular among the Akan people, oftentimes ended with moral lessons. Stories and some legends told also articulated traditional values, beliefs, superstitions, and rules that formed the basis of the people's social ethics. They were imparted in young learners who were expected to appreciate them without doubting or questioning their validity. As authoritarian as this might seem, it promoted conformity to societal expectations.

Songs, proverbs, and idioms also served as mediums of instruction. They were mostly used to correct erring children's unacceptable actions. They also served as warnings and at other times praise for good behavior. Such exposure has generally helped children to grow up and become cultured and disciplined individuals. With respect to Ghanaian oral traditions, conversations, discussions, and storytelling on moonlight nights on farms and in family gatherings provide children with knowledge of the geography of the country's terrain, the history of their people, and appreciation for the value of leaves, trees, herbs, and shrubs all around them. Children are also informed of the origin of their ancestors and their cultural. Importantly, disciplined Ghanaian children in traditional settings are identified by the way they addresses their elders through utterances, actions, and gestures.

Generally, a young Ghanaian child begins to imbibe knowledge, proper attitudes, and skills in the home. At about six years old, young girls learn homemaking and motherhood skills from their mothers. Boys are oftentimes with their fathers and other older males in the family. Boys will watch and be taught how to become a man. They learn a trade and may usually pick their father's professions. They learn in the home until they are old and mature enough to take life partners, live on their own, and begin their own families. Before all of this, they are made to go through a special initiation process into adulthood. According to McWilliam and Kwamena-Poh (1975), both Ghanaian boys and girls pass through initiation, but the initiation act for boys was usually of greater significance. This is so because the circumcision ceremony that admitted boys was not just one aspect of adult life but revealed the secrets and beliefs of their community. Boys must imbibe the social norms of their people as handed down by tradition. This singular act separated boys from childhood and from mingling with or being in the company of women and children. Boys were also admitted into the military organization of their age group. After the initiation, a boy would receive gifts such as a piece of land, a wife, and maybe a gun from his father and other older males in the family. Even as a full-grown man, an adult male has not ended his education. He still learns from older family members and the community at large. As aptly put by Oppong (1967), "Parents themselves are under the control of their own parents and also under the influence of the heads of their kindred."

Finally, the traditional system of education in Ghana also recognizes that if every individual must contribute to the growth of the society, then he must be equipped with skills that would make him a truly productive member. Most skills then were home based and oftentimes inherited. These skills included artisanship, craftsmanship, and sometimes priesthood and chieftaincy.

Colonial Education

Formal education began in the Gold Coast as far back as 1752 with the arrival of Reverend Thomas Thompson who was one of the early missionaries from America. He was from the Society for the Propagation of the Gospel and settled in the Cape Coast. His arrival to the Gold Coast was primarily evangelical, but he also needed to work with the people to convert them to Christianity. To achieve this, he first learned the Fante language. During his four-year stay, he made efforts to educate the people as well as convert them.

Following Reverend Thompson and his efforts to give education priority was the establishment of a school for the children of the Cape Coast in 1788. The school was headed by Reverend Philip Quacoe. By 1820, the school was deemed old fashioned and needed new management. A new committee was put in charge that made the school flourish with an increase in staff and students. In 1830, there were seventy boys enrolled in the school.

About the same time, the Basel and Bremen Missions from Germany and Switzerland and the Methodists Missions from Britain also established their Christian missionary work, along with introducing Western education. The Basel and Bremen Missions largely worked through schools, giving greater attention to technical education. However, with time, the Africans began to reject the missions' approach to education. The complaint was that they would rather prefer an education system that produced clerks than technicians. For them, this was a more desirable result from education. In more recent times, with the growing desire for technological growth, this prejudice has diminished.

In 1882, the first education ordinance in the Gold Coast was passed. The ordinance recommended:

1. The establishment of a General Board of Education, and other local education boards. The local boards were expected to inspect schools, certify competence of teachers, and work with the General Education Board to which they were responsible.
2. The ordinance also recommended that government grants should be given to schools to aid efficiency and viability in schools and thus meet the educational needs of the citizenry.
3. The ordinance also prescribed a curriculum which included subjects like reading, writing, and arithmetic, with emphasis on needlework for girls. History, geography, and English grammar were also emphasized.
4. Importantly, the ordinance recommended that the grants given by the government should be separated. There would be one for building and school equipment, and another for salary with some conditions attached. Teachers' salary was

determined by good discipline among students, increase in school attendance, and students' performance in compulsory subjects.

On the whole, the 1882 education ordinance was not much of a success. Consequently, the mission schools found it difficult to align their education systems with the demands and requirements of the government. Notably though, the ordinance brought about two categories of primary schools in the Gold Coast: the government and the assisted schools. The former was to a large extent a government concern, while the latter was run by missions and other nongovernmental bodies.

The year 1887 saw the coming of a new education ordinance. This may have been one of such long-lasting ordinances that it formed the basis of the education system in the Gold Coast until 1925. The local education boards were abolished, and in their place, a system of managerial control was established. The management board was actually constituted by the local governing body of the religious organizations.

Following this trend of government involvement in education, in 1909 the government established a teachers' training college and a technical college, both at Accra. The missions in the same vein established their own teachers' colleges. The Bremen Mission settled for a small theological seminary at Ho in then-Togoland, while the Roman Catholic Mission built colleges at Bla in Togoland and at Amisano near the Cape Coast.

In the 1920s, another round of educational development occurred in the Gold Coast. When Governor Guggisberg assumed his office, he appointed an education committee with O. J. Oman as the director of the committee. Oman was to work with his committee to assess past educational efforts in the Gold Coast, successes, failures, and make recommendations for a new education policy. Following the outcome of Oman's committee, the following were highlighted and recommended:

- The need to introduce the English language early enough in primary school was emphasized. It was recommended as a subject, while retaining vernacular as the medium of instruction.
- Teaching was recommended as a profession. To further enhance its status, the committee emphasized the need for training of qualified teachers, as well as improving teachers' service conditions.
- Finally, the committee recommended the establishment of a secondary boarding school for boys, with a proposed site near the Achimota College.

Consequently, with the implementation of these recommendations, there was great improvement and expansion in the education sector in the Gold Coast. Generally, Guggisberg's contributions to the advancement and expansion in education between 1920 and 1927 were quite remarkable. He played quite an outstanding role in the growth of education in colonial times.

In Guggisberg's time primary school infants were properly graded in classes, and teaching was adapted to the needs of the young children.... Mission and government organizers changed the whole character of schools...the need for the education of girls was recognised. Generally...it was a time for better buildings, better equipment, better staff, and better methods of teaching brought about by cooperation between government and mission. On the whole, looking at Guggisberg's score sheet for primary education, he concentrated on increase in pupil enrolment and attendance, curriculum improvement, emphasized teachers' qualification and certification. His administration also took cognisance of government grants to schools so as to provide teaching equipment, classroom spaces and all such things that aided standards. (Harman 1975)

This may also have been the perspective from which Nkrumah's government in 1951 saw the need to introduce the ADPE. Following the Guggisberg trend, emphasis was placed on a basic six-year primary education for all children.

However, for secondary education, not much impact was made. Instead, the concentration was on primary graduation statistics (Ward 1969). The trend in the growth and expansion of secondary schools in the Gold Coast revealed that in 1902 there were sixty-five pupils in secondary schools; by 1938, there were 919 pupils in four assisted secondary schools (including Achimota College) with over 2,000 others in unassisted secondary schools, many of which were of low quality. By the end of 1948, there were ten assisted secondary schools with 2,225 pupils and the unassisted schools had almost as many. Even in pre-independence Ghana in 1955, there were thirty-one government-assisted secondary schools with 7,711 pupils. These schools were also noted to have had a staff of 238 graduate teachers and 265 nongraduate teachers. What can be deduced is that secondary education in Ghana beginning from colonial times until the onset of independence lacked quality attention.

However, it was noted that the Guggisberg administration may have put more effort in the founding and expansion of the Achimota College—an educational experiment borne out of the recommendations by the Phelps-Stokes Education Commission. Guggisberg saw Achimota College as the pride of the Gold Coast and one that would eventually attain the status of a university. The government was responsible for the recurrent expenditure of this institution. In 1930, its control was transferred to a council of governors, thereby making it independent from government control but at the same time enjoying financial support from the government at the expense of other secondary schools.

In 1943, a commission under the chairmanship of Walter Elliot was appointed to ascertain the possibility of a higher institution in British West Africa, with the elevation of Achimota College to that status. By 1944, the British government was not yet certain about the status of Achimota as a higher institution. At that time, what was foremost in the British plan for higher education was to locate one in Nigeria. In the light of this, the British government urged the Gold Coast to make Achimota College function as a feeder college to the proposed University in Nigeria. This did not go over well with the Gold Coasters. The British government had no option but to establish university colleges in both Nigeria and the Gold Coast in 1947. The University College of Gold Coast was located near Achimota. Following closely in 1951, a

College of Technology was also established. The establishment of these higher institutions in the Gold Coast in this period was accelerated by grants from the United Kingdom.

Notably, a university college during this era was usually modeled after Cambridge University in England. Standards were set according to the customs and traditions of Cambridge University. Even some of the buildings at the Legon Institution were a reflection of the Cambridge college system.

After Guggisberg, some notable progress was recorded under the governorship of Sir Alan Burns who assumed duty in 1942. Despite the shortage in human and financial resources that came as an aftermath of World War I, Burns made some effort to advance education. He began by rebuilding the schools ruined by the war and established new primary schools. In 1944, he worked out a financial scheme to provide scholarships for training teachers for secondary schools. Significantly, with the assistance of the Scottish missionaries, schools were established across the Gold Coast for the blind, the physically challenged, and the mentally retarded.

A new turn in the development of education, otherwise termed "accelerated development," began in early 1950. It was actually intended to set the stage for independence and self-rule. This came with the victory of the Convention Peoples' Party (CCP) in the country's first general elections in February 1951. Paramount in the CCP's campaign was the promise of education for all. There was also the main intention of bridging the education gap between the north and south. Before then, parents from the north resisted enrollment for their children while many in the south were interested in formal education. This may have been connected with the long presence of missionaries in the south.

With the CCP victory, Nkrumah emerged as the first indigenous president. He appointed Kojo Botsio as the country's first minister for education. For them, the most urgent issue was education for every child of school age. Indeed, their foremost goal for Ghana, in preparation for self-rule, was an accelerated development plan for education. The emphasis was on six years of free basic education of all Ghanaian children of school age. There was also a major campaign to teach adults to read and write—first in their indigenous language, then in English. The ADPE also focused on increased enrollment in teacher training colleges, improved salaries for teachers, and scholarships for students who wished to proceed to secondary schools. McWilliam and Kwamena-Poh (1975) have affirmed that, although the facilities for middle school, secondary, and technical education were greatly increased, the rapid expansion of primary education was the most striking feature of the ADPE. Indeed, the Universal Primary Education Scheme was central to the whole plan. Essentially, children enjoyed access to education. Even though parents assisted with buying books for their children, they were relieved of the burden of tuition fees. Classrooms were expanded to accommodate the teeming increase in enrollment. By 1957, at the attainment of independence, a statistical report showed that there were over 450,000 children in primary schools, which was about twice the figure recorded in 1951 (Education Statistics 1957). It was also noted that there were about 15,000 teachers employed to teach in this scheme. The ADPE also took cognizance of secondary education. Secondary schools were expanded and standards were improved. One significant achievement for secondary education in this plan was the introduction of the sixth form: a two-year pre-university course for secondary school graduates.

Postindependence Education

On attainment of independence in March 1957, Ghana had the development of education on its priority list. In the first few years of his presidency, Nkrumah was busy with the review and development of educational policies laid down in the decade before independence. In view of this educational development, one slight flaw was noted. As is peculiar with most Sub-Saharan African nations, more progress was recorded for primary education than at the secondary education level. In Ghana, an outstanding figure of about half a million was recorded as provisions were made to absorb children of primary school age in the ADPE. The ideal plan would have also been an increase in vacancies to accommodate primary school graduates. However, that was not the case; the amount of same attention was not given to secondary education in terms of growth and development. This lopsidedness was, however, remedied in the 1962–63 school year. The government increased the number of secondary schools and enrollment intake so much so that as of 1966, there were 105 public secondary schools with a total enrollment of 42,111 students (Ministry of Education 1971).

Even though Ghana witnessed rapid expansion in education from 1961–66, the same cannot be said of educational standards. It was more like mass education than qualitative education. Around 1966, there was high decline in performance in primary education in the northern part of Ghana. This was not quite noticeable in Ashante and southern Ghana because of the presence of private schools that thrived there.

The overthrow of the CPP and Nkrumah's government in 1966 brought in a new government with new educational ideas and policies for the Ghanaian populace. The new government blamed the deterioration in education on poor management, corruption, and a poor economy. It instigated a rejuvenation of the country's education system. This began with an immediate halt in the rapid expansion of primary schools and the so-called policy of compulsory education. The result was the closure of some public primary schools that were assessed to have suffered degradation.

The turning point in Ghana's education system and policies at this stage of independence was the appointment of an Education Review Committee by the new government under the NLC. The committee, under the chairmanship of Professor Kwapong, had a major goal to perform a comprehensive review of Ghana's education system at all levels. Importantly, educational problems were to be examined and addressed, and recommendations made. The focus was also on excessive spending and financial waste in education. The committee's findings included an increase in the falling standard in education, decline in academic achievement, lack of quality in teaching and learning, inefficiency in school supervision, inadequate staff accommodation, lack of teaching equipment, and poor norms of discipline and behavior among students (Education Review 1967). The committee also noted that while Nkrumah's Plan may not have been a bad idea after all, it lacked focus. There was the tendency toward expansion without taking cognizance of the need for available qualified teaching staff and adequate teaching equipment, among other issues. The result was a breed of mediocre school graduates without an adequate educational background.

This same problem of the dearth of an educational plan and administration (of which Nkrumah's regime was guilty) was again condemned by the PP in September 1969. In this administration's development plan, it blamed the CPP for weakness in administration, planning, and coordination of educational development. Also, imbalances in the structure of education were evident in the unequal distribution of facilities, low-quality instructional materials, and other facilities. The administration was also blamed for the relationship gap between the school and its curriculum, in relation to the demands of work and life after school (Ministry of Information 1971).

The Educational Review Committee of 1966–67 was also concerned with the medium of instruction employed in schools. It recommended that a Ghanaian language be introduced as the medium of instruction for the first three years of primary schooling. The change to English as a medium of instruction was recommended in the fourth year of primary education, while a Ghanaian language would continue to be studied as a school subject. For schools located in urban areas and in the metropolis where children were easily exposed to spoken English, the change to English as medium of instruction began earlier than the fourth year of learning. Again, it was recommended in experimental schools where English was a familiar language (as a medium of instruction and a subject), a Ghanaian language should be taught throughout the course of training. The importance of the language of instruction to the Committee may not have been unrelated to their insistence that children found it easier to learn in their mother tongue and quite readily expressed themselves, their ideas, and reactions in the same language. This view was again revisited and upheld in 1971 when the Ministry of Education in its curriculum innovation of elementary education stated:

It is now Government Policy that the main Ghanaian languages at present provided for in the curricula of primary and middle schools should be used as the medium of instruction in the first three years of the primary course and, where the subject makes it possible, in the next three years as well. In any upper primary or higher classes where English is the teaching medium, the appropriate Ghanaian language(s) will be properly taught as a school subject. (Ministry of Education 1972)

The committee also noted the importance of quality and trained teachers, as well as an increase in the number of teachers needed to instruct the expected number of school-age children. Therefore, in its recommendation, the Committee urged the government to raise the "academic and professional levels of teacher education, and offer the teachers conditions of service that compare very favourably with other types of employment." The expectation was that teachers with improved status would in turn help to raise the standard of education in Ghana as well as give teachers job satisfaction. The government in its bid to achieve this goal embarked on a reduction in the number of colleges of education. The idea was to make teacher education a postsecondary course that would produce quality teachers of academic and professional standards. In the same vein, the Committee also recommended that teacher educators should be professionals who would produce quality teachers.

Regarding secondary schools, the Education Review Committee of 1966–67 recommended that:

no secondary school should be built or opened until all schools are properly housed and have expanded to their optimum size of three streams.

It further noted that since the inception of the CCP government, there had been an urge for secondary school expansion without taking cognizance of the facilities to go with it. It recalled the instance of the 1971 increase in secondary school intake, which was borne out of the same lapses made by the PP government to have a secondary school in every district. Moreover, as prescribed by the government of that time, secondary schools were expected to fulfill such requirements as "to produce the bulk of the middle level manpower of our economy" and "to produce potential top-level manpower for university courses" (Ministry of Education 1969).

Furthermore, the Committee suggested that there was need for equal emphasis in the curricula for the sciences and humanities. Similarly, the need for the inclusion of business education in secondary schools was intended to train and produce more competent office personnel like secretaries. Therefore, there was a need to maintain a five-year duration for secondary school. This would lead to a school certificate of the same standard as the ordinary level of the General Certificate of Education examination (GCE). For those who wished to continue, provision was made for a two-year, sixth-form course leading to the General Certificate of Education Examination at the Advanced Level (GCE A/L).

Besides secondary and teacher training education, the Review Committee on Education recognized the need to emphasize technical education. It suggested at that period of the nation's development, there was a need to pay some attention to technical and commercial training to serve as midlevel education. Before then, it had been noted that the education system in Ghana was quite lopsided because of the emphasis given to secondary and grammar schools at the expense of technical and vocational educations. The plea, therefore, was for a reorientation of the importance of technical education in an advancing nation. Specifically, an adequate supply of technicians and skilled craftsmen meant greater productivity in the economic sector.

In the light of the above suggestion, the government gave more attention to the technical and commercial schools. There were technical colleges for the secondary and tertiary stages of education. Three major polytechnics were established in Accra, Takoradi, and Kumasi. They provided advanced-level crafts and technical courses and courses in domestic and other commercial subjects. Students who succeeded at this level proceeded to the University of Science and Technology in Kumasi for further studies. There was also the Tarkwa School of Mines, which offered pre-university technical diploma courses in mine surveying, mining, or mineral dressing. Additionally, the Teacher Training Institute at Mampong trained technical teachers for middle schools, while the Technical Teachers' Training College in Kumasi was more of an advanced college that trained teachers for higher technical institutes and polytechnics. The recommendation that the government should take over private commercial schools was accepted. Thus, the thirteen private commercial schools in Ghana were incorporated and brought into the public education system under the Ministry of Education. Following this development, for the first time, the government in July 1971 conducted the Ghana Business Certificate Examination both at the ordinary and the advanced levels. The examinations were conducted by the West African Examinations Council (WAEC) on behalf of the Ministry of Education.

Finally in terms of the management, organization, and control of schools, the Committee opted for total decentralization of education. Another commission was immediately set up to work on the reorganization of the Ministry of Education. The Mills-Odoi Commission made the following recommendation: "We have proposed that the management of schools and training colleges should be decentralized and removed from the Ministry of Multi-Purpose, Regional and District Authorities." This recommendation was welcomed by the government and incorporated into the 1970 one-year development plan. Below is the outcome of the plan on management and organization of schools (see figure 4.1).

Also significant in this period of educational review in Ghana is the current educational structure for pre-university education that replaced an old one.

In their analysis of Ghana's educational plans and structure for the period beginning from September 1975, McWilliam and Kwamena-Poh (1975) have identified some basic principles that are reminiscent of Guggisberg's educational proposals for the Gold Coast some fifty years before. These are:

1. Every child should be given the opportunity to obtain a preparatory formal education before eighteen to twenty-four months.
2. The need for formal education for children at age six.
3. The duration of basic formal education should be nine years and it should be free and compulsory.
4. The inclusion of a practical program as an essential aspect of education, especially in the acquisition of skills.

Figure 4.1
Structure of Ministry of Education and Ghana Teaching Service Pre-University Division

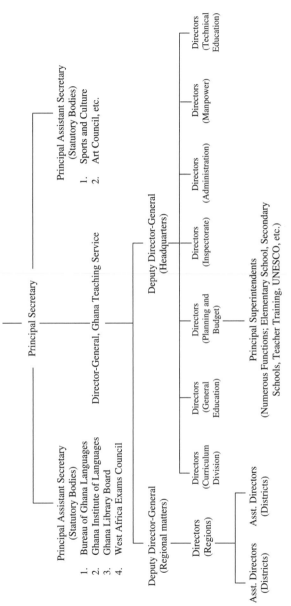

Commissioner (Minister) for Education, Culture and Sports

Principal Secretary

Principal Assistant Secretary
(Statutory Bodies)
1. Bureau of Ghana Languages
2. Ghana Institute of Languages
3. Ghana Library Board
4. West Africa Exams Council

Principal Assistant Secretary
(Statutory Bodies)
1. Sports and Culture
2. Art Council, etc.

Director-General, Ghana Teaching Service

Deputy Director-General
(Headquarters)

Deputy Director-General
(Regional matters)

Directors
(Curriculum
Division)

Directors
(General
Education)

Directors
(Planning and
Budget)

Directors
(Inspectorate)

Directors
(Administration)

Directors
(Manpower)

Directors
(Technical
Education)

Directors
(Regions)

Asst. Directors
(Districts)

Asst. Directors
(Districts)

Asst. Directors
(Districts)

Principal Superintendents
(Numerous Functions; Elementary School, Secondary
Schools, Teacher Training, UNESCO, etc.)

Source: Ministry of Education (1967a).

Figure 4.2
Structure of Education

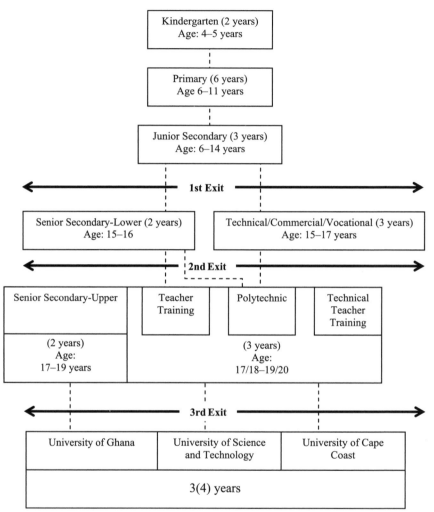

Source: Ministry of Education (February 1974).

5. Emphasis throughout pre-university education on:

    (a) the development of practical activities and the acquisition of manual skills;
    (b) the development of the qualities of leadership style, self-reliance, and creativity through the promotion of physical education, sports and games, cultural and youth programs; and
    (c) the study of indigenous languages, science, and mathematics.

6. The emphasis on teacher education and its relevance in the realization of the stated principles and objectives of the new reforms.
7. The drive for making most institutions day schools.

Generally, from the late 1960s through the 1970s, education in Ghana thrived and enjoyed some stability. Beginning in the early 1980s, Ghana's education system began to suffer some setbacks. This may not be far-fetched considering the economic hardship that was experienced and heightened by a series of military coups and their attendant instability in governance. However, in 1988, Rawlings' military government came up with another new structure and content of education for Ghana with the acceptance of the Dzobo Report on education. The reforms concentrated on pre-university education (see figure 4.2). It found the seventeen-year pretertiary education to be time-consuming, limited in scope, unproductive, and expensive to both government and parents. It also found that access was limited and the curriculum content overemphasized grammar school types of education. In its place was a slight modification to a 6-3-3 education system: six years in primary school, three years in junior secondary school, and another three years in senior secondary school. Also emphasized in this ongoing reform was the need for adult and nonformal education. Essentially, the education reform can be summarized as follows:

1. Reduce the length or duration of pre-university education from seventeen to twelve years.
2. Increase access to education at all levels, particularly at the basic and secondary prevocational training levels, and in general skills training.
3. Ensure proper administrative, management, and financial management of the education sector.

Notably, at the early stage of implementation, much was achieved in terms of reducing school duration. However, in terms of teaching and learning quality, not much success was made. Significantly, access to education was not yet improved.

Consequently, in his return as a civilian president, Rawlings continued his education reforms. He began with the implementation of the Free and Compulsory University Basic Education (FCUBE). Its focus was on providing compulsory, basic, and quality education for children in Ghana.

The FCUBE was launched in October 1996 by President Rawlings. Its implementation was for a ten-year period aimed at fulfilling the Fourth Republic Constitution. The Constitution in part stated:

government shall within two years after parliament.... Draw up the program for implementation within the following ten years for the provision of free compulsory Universal Basic Education. (Chapter 6, Section 38, subsection 2)

Among other issues, the implementation of FCUBE was also aimed at addressing the shortcomings of the 1987–88 education reforms. Thus, the focus in relaunching FCUBE was:

1. expansion of access to good quality basic education;
2. promotion in the efficiency in teaching and learning;
3. improvement of teachers' morale and motivation through incentive programs;
4. to ensure adequate and timely supply of teaching and learning materials to schools; and
5. to improve and create a more healthy teacher-community relation.

To effectively achieve this, the government of Ghana, through its Ministry of Education, with the assistance of nongovernmental organizations and the community at large, put in place other subprograms. The programs included the following:

1. The QUIPS program. This was aimed at improving quality and maintaining standards in primary schools. To attain this, focus was on producing competent teachers, educational managers, and planners in a conducive learning environment. This program was supported by the United States Agency for International Development (USAID).
2. The Child School. This community program in education, otherwise known as *Child Scope*, was sponsored by UNICEF. Its aim was to improve reading, writing, and number skills among primary school learners.
3. The Performance Monitoring Test (PMT) and the School Performance Appraisal Meeting (SPAM) were programs introduced in 1998 to test children in English language and mathematics in public schools. The results were then discussed at SPAMs—a forum created for parents to discuss and analyze their children's performance. Thereafter, SPAM would work out strategies for improving performance and helping schools achieve set targets. So far, the programs have proved quite effective in view of the close monitoring and assessment of teaching and learning outcomes in basic schools.
4. The District Teacher Support Team (DTST) was more or less an anchorage for the improvement of teaching and learning at the district level. It was aimed at providing support to schools in the area of professional practice in literacy, numeracy, and problem solving.
5. The Whole School Development (WSD) program is a Ghana Education Service (GES) strategy for assessment in the development and achievement of the aims of the FCUBE program. To fully monitor this achievement, zonal coordinators are appointed to serve as links between the preservice and in-service programs. The whole school development program also tries to create a link between district and regional management personnel to teacher training colleges.

Since the implementation of the above program and interventions, Ghana has recorded a marked improvement in its education system. There have been improved standards in education, quality in teaching and learning, as well as invigorated curriculum content. This period has also witnessed an increase in enrollment in primary and secondary schools in the public and private sectors. Under the reform program, Book Scheme for basic schools, supplementary readers and other teaching materials were distributed to public schools. The scheme also extended its goodwill to public junior and senior secondary schools, as well as some private schools. Ghanaian children in schools enjoyed the benefits of Book Scheme from June 1995 until December 1999.

The community's input in this education reform is also noteworthy. Community groups such as District Education Oversight Community, District Education Planning Team, and Parents-Teachers Association were put in place. All of these groups in their own way played roles in the smooth functioning of education in Ghana. All the 110 district assembles in Ghana established district education funds to assist school projects in their districts.

Generally, the various levels of education were given all kinds of encouragement by way of assistance. For instance, by way of strengthening science education in senior secondary schools, science resource centers were established in schools and textbooks in various subjects were also provided. The emphasis on technical and vocational education was made popular with the establishment of public technical schools. Private investors were also encouraged to own technical and vocational schools. To also improve quality in communication technology, a curriculum was developed for information communication technology (ICT). Students in secondary schools are trained in this subject with access to the Internet. They are even made to sit for the senior secondary certificate examination in this subject. Teacher education programs were also given special attention in this scheme. Existing teacher colleges were rehabilitated and teacher education programs were reorganized to produce quality teachers. Teachers were generally motivated to enjoy all of their job incentives.

Of importance to this reform scheme was girl-child education. In 1997, Ghana's Education Service (GES) established a Girls' Education Unit. Its aim was to increase girls' enrollment with a projection to equal boys' enrollment by 2005. Although considerable progress has been recorded at all levels of learning since the 1990s, the target has yet to be met. Before then, the Ministry of Education had instituted the Science Technology, Mathematics Education (STME) clinic for girls. It was also meant to encourage girls to develop interests in mathematics, science, and technology-related fields. To further increase girls' zeal to learn, Ghana Educational Service launched a Girl-Child Scholarship program in 2001. The government, in its education reforms and through its Ministry of Education, was able to create some awareness on the need and importance of girl-child education. In addition to the emphasis on girls' education, the government had a major task of eradicating illiteracy in Ghana by the year 2011. Thus, in 1991, a nonformal and adult education division of the Ministry of Education was established. The functional literacy program has had the support of the World Bank.

Finally, education reform in tertiary education was launched in 1991 with a government white paper on a university rationalization committee report. The focus was on a redefinition of higher education to include universities, polytechnics, and teacher training colleges. The report's major aim included expanding access, improving the quality of teaching and learning, as well as providing the needed infrastructural base for accelerated manpower development, especially in technical fields of studies that would sustain the nation's economic sector. In 1991, Ghana had thirty-eight teacher training colleges, ten polytechnics, and six universities. Additionally, there were ten accredited private universities, nine accredited tutorial professional colleges (that prepare candidates for examinations of recognized professional bodies), and two distant education learning centers that represent accredited universities outside Ghana.

Success in the reform on tertiary education meant an increased enrollment in both public and private universities. Academic programs were made more qualitative and the physical structures of many institutions were considerably improved. In all of these, one thing seems clear from the education reforms of Rawlings' government: Ghana has realized its need for quality education as a crucial tool for reshaping the economic sector and, indeed, the whole of Ghana's society.

Education in Ghana under John Agyekum Kufuor's government has further improved. In recent times, Ghana has about 12,630 primary schools, 5,450 junior secondary schools, 503 senior secondary schools, twenty-one teacher training colleges, eighteen technical institutions, two diploma-awarding institutes, and five universities serving a population of over 20 million people. Generally, Ghana operates a 6-3-3 system for pre-university education and three to four years for tertiary learning. In other words, a total of six years is spent in primary school, three years in junior secondary school, and another three years in senior secondary school. Significantly, the six years of primary education added to the three years of junior secondary education gives a total of nine years of basic education. Basic education is free and mandatory for all pupils. Ghana's system for pre-university education has a total duration of twelve years, of which the first nine years are free and compulsory. The duration of tertiary education is a minimum of three years, depending on courses of study. Entry into tertiary institutions like universities, polytechnics, teacher training colleges, and other higher training institutions is essentially very competitive because of the difficult examinations and other entry requirements.

STAGES OF THE EDUCATION SYSTEM

Preschool Education

Preschool education in the Gold Coast dates back to 1843 when the Basel Missionaries established a kindergarten. However, government participation in early childhood education can be traced to 1951. Their involvement was borne out of the need to provide custodial care for children while their parents were away at farms, the market, or work. Thus, the government, through its department of social welfare and community development established nurseries. These were opened six days per week. These pioneer nurseries were situated in large urban centers like Cape Coast, Accra, Sekondi, and near markets. The nursery schools were run by private individuals and voluntary organizations with the government playing a supervisory role.

In 1965, nursery education was separated from other early childcare programs like *crèches* and day care centers. The Ministry of Education was responsible for nursery education, while the department of social welfare continued its supervisory role in running *crèches* and day care centers.

The reforms in the 1970s gave more recognition to preschool education in Ghana. Nursery education was encouraged by the reform in which eighteen to twenty-four months of nursery education was considered not only a good idea but also crucial in preparing children for entry to primary school. Again in 1979, the legal basis for organizing and operating preschool education was established.

Generally, preschool education in Ghana is encouraged, though not compulsory. Less than 50 percent of children of preschool age are in nursery and kindergarten schools. The small number of available nursery schools may be one of the reasons for low enrollment in nursery education. In essence, there are few available nursery schools in Ghana. They are mostly owned by private individuals, groups, communities, churches, NGOs, etc. However, in more recent times, there have been a few model nursery schools in the districts and regions that are owned and run by the Ghana Education Services (Ministry of Education).

Primary Education

Primary education in Ghana is basic and compulsory. It is emphasized as the foundation on which other levels of learning are built. The entry school age is six years old, with a six-year course duration.

The aims and objectives of primary education are as follows:

1. Numeracy and Literacy Skills. This includes inculcating in the learner the ability to count, use numbers, read, write, and count effectively.
2. Lay the foundation for skills in inquiry and creativity.
3. Developing sound moral attitudes and a healthy appreciation of Ghana's culture and identity.
4. Developing the ability to adapt constructively to a changing environment.
5. Lay the foundation for the development of manipulative and life skills that will help the individual pupil function effectively to his own advantage, as well as that of society.
6. Inculcate good citizenship education as a basis for effective participation in national development. (Ministry of Education 1976)

To achieve the above objectives, the Ministry of Education prescribed the following subjects as the primary school curriculum:

1. Mathematics
2. Science
3. Social Studies

4. Ghanaian Languages
5. English Language
6. Agricultural Science
7. Life Skills
8. Physical Education

At the end of primary education, the pupils are encouraged to proceed to junior secondary school after having taken a primary school certificate examination.

Junior Secondary School

Education in junior secondary school is tuition free and mandatory. This stage of learning can be described as the junior level of secondary education. The program was implemented in 1987 under the new education reforms. The junior secondary school as the premier stage of secondary education accommodates pupils who have completed primary education. Its duration is three years of academic, prevocational, and technical training.

The aim of junior secondary education as stipulated in the education reforms of 1987 is to give pupils a broad education that includes a predisposition to technical and vocational subjects and basic life skills. This is intended to enable students to

1. discover their aptitudes and potentials so as to induce in them the desire for improvement, and
2. help them appreciate the use of their hands as well as the mind, thus, helping them become more creative and employable.

Subjects in the junior secondary school curriculum are

1. Mathematics
2. Integrated Science
3. Social Studies
4. Cultural Studies
5. Ghanaian Languages
6. English Language
7. French (optional)
8. Agricultural Science
9. Life Skills
10. Physical Education
11. Technical Drawing
12. Basic Technical Skills
13. Vocational Skills

It is important to note that the Ministry of Education approved twelve vocational and technical subjects for junior secondary schools. However, each school has the option of selecting any two. The selection is done on the basis of availability of teaching and learning materials, which are usually locally produced.

At the end of the junior secondary school, the students take a Basic Certificate of Education Examination (BCEE). This qualifies them to proceed to senior secondary schools. For others, with the technical and vocational skills acquired, they may decide to go into the working world.

Senior Secondary School

Senior secondary education is designed for students who have completed junior secondary school and the nine years of basic education. The duration of education at this level is three years. The objectives of senior secondary education as prescribed by Ghana's education policy include

1. to reinforce and build on knowledge, skills, and attitudes acquired at the junior secondary level of learning;
2. to produce well-developed and productive individuals, equipped with leadership qualities, and capable of fitting into a scientific and technological world; to contribute to the socioeconomic development of their immediate environment and the country at large; and
3. to increase the relevance of the content of the curriculum to the cultural and social problems of the country.

To effectively achieve the above-stated objectives, the following subject offerings are prescribed. They include seven core subjects and other electives, namely core subjects:

1. English Language
2. Mathematics
3. Science
4. Agricultural and Environmental Studies
5. Life Skills
6. Ghanaian Languages
7. Physical Education

There are three optional subjects from a wide range of specialized courses. These include

1. Agricultural Science
2. Business Studies
3. Technical Education
4. Vocational Education (Home Economics and Visual Arts)
5. General (Arts and Science Education)

At the end of senior secondary school, students take the senior secondary school examination and the West African School Certificate Examination.

A pass in these examinations earns them certificates as a prerequisite to higher education.

Generally, primary schools, junior, and senior secondary schools in Ghana are both public and private. Public schools enjoy government-funded supplies of teaching equipment and generally subsidized education. In effect, public schools are tuition free because of government subsidies. Private schools do not receive government grants. They depend on tuition paid by the students to sustain the school. However, teaching in private schools may be more qualitative and interactive with the number of students in classes compared to public institutions.

Higher Education

After completion of senior secondary education, candidates may take a qualifying entrance examination to any of the universities in Ghana. Some others may opt for higher education in polytechnics, higher technical institutes, or teacher training colleges. Importantly though, there is no age limit for admission into tertiary institutions. There are various types of courses and programs offered in higher institutions. Courses offered in the universities include

1. The first degree course
2. Higher degrees; for example, the master's degree, and PhDs
3. Subdegree diplomas
4. Subdegree certificate courses
5. Programs for mature students

The National Council on Tertiary Education (NCTE) is the implementation arm responsible for higher education in Ghana.

Adult and Nonformal Education

Adult education in Ghana dates back to 1951. It was introduced by the government of the then-colonial administration as part of the ADPE. The aim was to prepare everyone—the young and the old—for self-government. This mass literacy campaign of 1951 was designed as a community development program. Its major aim was to teach adults to read and write in their own language as well as in English. This was what was obtained as adult education all through the 1950s until the 1970s when an extensive literacy campaign was launched by the country's Ministry of Labor and Social Welfare. This afforded adults more literacy opportunities. In that same year (after the launch), the UN estimated about 70 percent of the nation's inhabitants about the age of fifteen years were illiterates. Even at that, the figure was a 5 percent improvement over an estimated 1960 adult literacy rate of 25 percent (Quarterly Digest 1984).

The government was dissatisfied with the low-level literacy rate and established the Institute of Adult Education at the University of Ghana. The

Institute spread its program to different parts of the country. Significantly, in the activities of this Institute were the annual new year school activities. It was attended by leading educators, government officials, and numerous social welfare organizations. On such occasions, the Institute's achievements as well as future plans for adult education were subjects of deliberation. On one such occasion in 1989, then-President Rawlings emphasized the importance of adult education especially in relation to economic development and nation building. This may have prompted the establishment of the nonformal education division of the Ministry of Education in 1991. Its major aim was to work towards a total eradication of illiteracy by the year 2011. In 1982, the literacy rate improved, with 40 percent of the total population literate in comparison to 30 percent recorded in the 1970s. However, it was also noted that of the 60 percent that was illiterate in 1989, 57 percent were women. In response to this gap between males and females, the Ghana National Council of Women blamed women's low literacy rates on the high dropout rate, especially at the elementary level. The Council called on the government to articulate girl-child education to create greater awareness. This call was heeded in 1997 with the establishment of the Girls Education Unit as an arm of Ghana's Educational Services.

On the whole and in more recent times, beginning with President Rawlings' administration and in keeping with the economic reform program, there were fundamental changes in Ghana's education system. Some recent reform measures have made curricula at all levels a little more relevant to the economic needs of the people. Thus, the government's pursuit of increased enrollment, quality education, and the introduction and implementation of the two phases of secondary education were intended to enhance the nation's economic sector. On the whole, it can be said that the reforms and implementations served as a stepping stone to greater heights in Ghana's education system—much of which President Kufuor's administration seems to have been reinforcing since 2001.

REFORMS IN EDUCATION

Like in most developing nations, there are always problems, obstacles, and difficulties in the development of education. These problems can always be solved through constant reforms. In the forty-fifth session of the International Conference on Education held in Geneva in 1996, Ghana identified educational problems that needed urgent attention. They included

1. poor teaching and learning outcomes;
2. lack of management efficiency; and
3. inequitable access and participation in education.

In terms of teaching and learning outcomes, student achievements have been recorded as quite low. Even with the introduction of the Criterion Referenced Testing (CRT) through the assistance of USAID, not much improvement has been achieved. However, possible causes of poor academic achievement have been identified. Lack of basic instructional equipment—even where available, they are not adequately used by teachers. High rates of absenteeism on the part of teachers and pupils have oftentimes resulted in poor teacher–pupil contact hours. Also, lack of adequate in-service training for teachers and poor incentives tend to give the teaching profession a low and unattractive status.

It was also observed that the width and depth of the curriculum content tends to make teaching and learning quite burdensome for both the teachers and pupils. This is further heightened with the controversial issue of the language of instruction. English, the official language, is far from being spoken and written, especially by those in the rural and deprived areas. This has made communication in the teaching of core skills quite difficult. This problem exists in primary and secondary schools.

Another major problem presently pervading educational development in Ghana is the lack of effective management at the various levels of the education sector, especially as it concerns the full implementation of basic education. There are management challenges that involved a conflict with responsibility and authority, administrative inadequacies especially in postings, transfers, and discipline on the part of teachers. There is the issue of incompetence on technical matters, such as planning, budgeting, and data gathering for educational development. Also, overstaffing in urban schools and understaffing in rural schools tend to characterize education at the primary and secondary levels. These problems undoubtedly are crucial management challenges. Finally, poor community participation, gender disparity, and poverty due to harsh economic conditions have generally led to high level of dropouts, especially at the basic level and even at the secondary and tertiary levels. Parents with low income find it difficult to provide education for their children and wards.

However, in more recent times, the government through its Ministry of Education has identified the above problems and has been working towards their eradication. Hopefully, this will afford Ghanaian children full participation and access to education. Most of these problems seem to pervade and inhibit implementation of the FCUBE program. Since 1994, the Ministry of Education has been working with the district education oversight committees and school management committees to work out modalities where the district authorities and local communities would be encouraged to assume ownership of schools and participate fully in their functions.

Also, with the present reforms, the number of secondary schools has increased, even though many are located in rural areas. The aim, however, is to expand access to secondary education as well as improve their quality.

At the tertiary level, much has been done to expand and increase access. Ongoing reforms indicate the opening of new universities and other higher institutions; for example, there is the new University of Development Studies in the northern part of Ghana. In Winneba, the government established a University College of Education. Polytechnics and other teacher training colleges have been redesignated as tertiary institutions. It is hoped that with all these reforms and with time, access will be greatly expanded and Ghanaians can also boast of quality education at all levels.

BIBLIOGRAPHY

CIA. 2001. *World Factbook*, Washington, D.C.

CIA. 2006. *World Factbook*, Washington, D.C.

Graham, C. K. 1971. *The History of Education in Ghana: From the Earliest Times to the Declaration of Independence*. London: Frank Cass Publishers.

Harman, H. A. 1975. "Education in the Gold Coast, 1910–1935." In *The Development of Education in Ghana*. Edited by H. O. A. McWilliam and M. A. Kwamena-Poh. London: Longman.

McWilliam, H. O. A., and M. A. Kwamena-Poh. 1975. *The Development of Education in Ghana*. London: Longman.

Ministry of Information. 1967a. *Report of the Commission on the Structure and Remuneration of the Public Service in Ghana*. Accra, Ghana.

Ministry of Education. 1967b. *Report of the Educational Review Committee*. Accra, Ghana.

Ministry of Information. 1969. *Ghana Official Handbook*. Accra, Ghana.

Ministry of Education. 1971a. *Digest of Educational Statistics 1971–72*. Accra, Ghana.

Ministry of Education. 1971b. *Educational Statistics, 1968–69*. Accra, Ghana.

Ministry of Education. 1972. *Pre-University Education in Ghana*. Accra, Ghana.

Ministry of Education. 1974. *The New Structure and Content of Education for Ghana*. Accra.

Ministry of Education. 1996. "The Development of Education 1994–1996," National Report from Ghana presented to the 45th Session of the International Conference on Education, Geneva, September 30–October 5, 1996.

Oppong, C. "The Context of Socialization in Dagbon." *Institute of African Studies Research Review* 4, no. 1 (1967): 13.

Whyllie, R. "The New Ghanaian Teacher and His Profession." *West African Journal of Education* 8, no. 3 (1964): 175.

Chapter 5

SCHOOLING IN IVORY COAST

INTRODUCTION

The wave of social and economic turbulence that swept through the political landscape in Africa in the 1960s was somehow avoided in the Ivory Coast (*Cote d'Ivoire*). It was not until the end of the millennium that the country started to experience some instability. Compared to several developing countries, the Ivory Coast, though one of the smallest countries in Africa, excelled in economic development, which has also enhanced its educational development. The country's relative success could be attributed to the strong and yet rational leadership of its first president, Felix Houphouet-Boigny. All things considered, the contribution of France, its former colonial overlord, can be described as mixed. The French legacy for some years facilitated some political stability and economic growth but did too little to develop the educational potential of the Ivorian people.

The Ivory Coast, which for nearly three decades had one of the best, but restricted, education systems among many developing nations has in recent times experienced paralysis in view of the current political turmoil that has engulfed that region of West Africa. According to a recent UNESCO report, some secondary school students have been unable to take their final year certificate examinations due to the closure of schools. Because such chaos is not typical of this once-peaceful and prosperous oasis in Africa, it is hoped that this is only a passing phase in the attempt to establish a democratic system.

The economic capital of the Ivory Coast, Abidjan, sits along the shoreline of the Atlantic in the south while the entire country itself is sandwiched between Liberia and Guinea in the southwest and Ghana in the east. Yamoussoukro, its relatively new political capital and seat of government, is a growing metropolis with one of the largest Catholic cathedrals in the world—courtesy of the late

President Houphouet-Boigny, a Christian, who was able to sensibly manage the religious conflicts occasionally experienced in a country where Muslims and practitioners of traditional religion constitute the majority of its population, especially in the northern region. Between 1975 and 2005, the population of the country grew from 6.1 million to 16.4 million, comprising about 60 ethno-linguistic groups spread across a land area of 300,000 square kilometers. Administratively, the country is divided into forty-nine districts and administered by an appointed prefect and an elected council. Each district is further subdivided into 183 prefectures. Until recently, when oil was discovered along with gas off its shorelines, the country depended mostly on agriculture for its economic sustenance. The economy was very strong in the 1970s in spite of occasional price fluctuations of export commodities in the world market. With such export crops as cocoa, palm produce, rubber, groundnuts, pineapple, and timber, the Ivorian economy was very buoyant. Their recent discovery of iron ore, diamonds, and more petroleum in the Bangoro province has brought more diversification of its economy in favor of manufacturing.

In 1999, exports totaled US$4,007 million while imports totaled US$3,270 million, most of which came from France—its major trading partner, the United States, and Nigeria. With an annual growth of 7 percent for a little over twenty-five years, the economy raised the per capita from US$145 to US$450 during that period. It soon rose to US$1,000 in the 1980s (Library of Congress 2006). This phenomenal growth from the 1980s has been on the decline as a result of the political situation in the country. The conflict in the Ivory Coast has forced a decline in the amount spent on education from 25 percent to 5 percent of the GNP and the country's per capita from US$1,000 to US$670 in 1996 (Berthelemy and Bouguignon 1996). In spite of the difficulties of the last decade, the Ivorians have managed to keep education as a priority. Even though the economy has also been bruised by the political struggle among the politicians, it has continued to be reasonably well managed.

While the political instability currently experienced in the Ivory Coast has some ethnic and religious underpinnings as in most African countries, the situation has generally been contained as a result of the elite's nationalistic tendencies and sense of moderation cultivated but somehow subdued during the colonial era. Because their material condition was also not as harsh as experienced by those in the Democratic Republic of Congo and other former colonies, they have tended to be more refined in handling their political differences. The legacy of honesty and transparency of their patriarch, President Houphouet-Boigny, has instilled in the leadership some principle of freedom sought among different factors.

Although the Houphouet-Boigny administration was seen by some critics as dictatorial, it brought a measure of stability while he was alive. For one thing, he forestalled all coups planned against his administration even though he was not a soldier. Unlike his Zairian colleague, President Mobutu Seseseko,

President Houphouet-Boigny's leadership style though authoritarian was perceived to be generally humane and less alienating of the citizenry.

As a result of the leadership's favorable disposition toward education, the Ivorian government spent more in that sector to raise primary school enrollment from 33 percent in 1960 to 55 percent in 1975 (Chinery 1978). All other sectors of education including secondary, technical, teacher, and tertiary levels received as much as one third of the entire national budget in 1985 (Library of Congress 1985). The solid foundation laid in the area of education due to the country's sound economy was sustained by the African elite created by the French during and after their colonial sojourn in West Africa.

Apart from the effective leadership by the first generation of African politicians, the country was fortunate to have a reasonably honest and transparent elite, with a reasonable sense of patriotism and good educational backgrounds. The Ivorian success was further buttressed by a favorable natural environment free from drought, flooding, and poor soil condition. Indeed, the agricultural products opened more avenues for manufacturing and other areas of the economy to fund elaborate educational programs when things were favorable in the 1970s (Berg 1960).

The Ivorian authorities also heeded the World Bank's advice about a possible trade-off between growth and distribution of income and were, therefore, inclined to emphasize the former without neglecting the latter in their development strategy. They were further commended for a policy orientation that focused on growth and oriented development outwardly rather than inwardly as a success strategy (Chinery 1978).

The rosy picture painted so far would not last for long because the economic strategy comprising good managerial and skilled labor was indeed imported from France and neighboring countries. The near absence of most Ivorians in the boom of the 1960s was soon to be blown wide open. For a while, the influx of people from other countries did not seem to be a problem because the GNP and per capita were initially unaffected adversely. Not too long after, such factors as falling prices of export commodities, the widening gap in income between urban and rural dwellers, and heavy reliance on foreign workers began to take their tolls on the economy. The worsening political climate in the country would soon bring the boom of yesteryears to a burst. The factors have no doubt had an adverse effect on Ivory Coast's educational development since the turn of the new millennium.

SOCIAL AND HISTORICAL CONTEXT

Although the Ivory Coast is one of the smallest countries in West Africa, its people are known to be part of several large ancient African kingdoms of Ghana, Mali, and Songhay. Their ancestors migrated from Ghana in the southeast and Mali in the northwest. It is well known that as part of these ancient kingdoms they were well established by the eighth century AD and were

Mande-speaking Africans. The Ghana kingdom extended almost to Timbuktu in the east, the Upper Niger in the southeast, and the Upper Senegal in the southwest. Between the thirteenth and seventeenth century, the Mali kingdom flourished in commerce and scholarship (Fafunwa 1962). Not too far from the Ivory Coast, the ancient Songhay Empire spanned part of the present Niger Republic and part of northern Nigeria. The Songhay Empire reached the height of its glory, power, and prestige in the fifteenth and sixteenth centuries AD. The Benin Kingdom from which migration was also known to have taken place extended from Lagos to the Niger delta region, all along the shores of the Atlantic in West Africa.

Located near the busy centers of the old slave trade settlements, namely Liberia and Sierra Leone, the Ivory Coast received some returnees from the Americas and part of Europe. As the obnoxious trade folded up, some of the returnees quickly settled down to develop plantations of their own in the Ivory Coast, which also thrived in such crops as cocoa, coffee, and other commodities including ivory—from which the country derived its name, The Ivory Coast.

In the early 1800s when the Europeans returned to West Africa as traders of ivory and farm commodities, they encountered competition from some African middlemen and plantation owners who would not allow them to penetrate the hinterland for direct trade with the natives. Moreover, tropical diseases, such as malaria and others transmitted by mosquitoes and tsetse flies, caused the death of many European adventurers. Thus, diseases played a great role in preventing penetration to the hinterland. Unlike South Africa and East Africa, the climate of the West African Coast, especially around the equator, was generally too hot, humid, and hostile for the foreigners and as such was responsible for the very small number of European settlers in the region (De Lusignan 1969).

On arrival in the Ivory Coast in 1807, the aim of the French was to add the country to its list of colonies. However, in the course of their negotiations with African chiefs and leaders, there were difficulties as the African leader's authority was undermined. Moreover, their trade policy was biased toward their African competitors, one of whom was Houphouet-Boigny, a Baule chief, farmer, and doctor. As a result of several negotiations on trade and administration of the country as one of France's colonies, it became necessary for Chief Houphouet-Boigny to start an association of African planters to serve as a pressure group. Initially, the association was not intended to be a political party. Over the course of time, issues pertaining to the French's unfairness in trade and a need for a more united nationalistic posture transformed the association into a political party under the leadership of its founder, Houphouet-Boigny, in 1949.

The action of the African leaders prompted a hostile reaction and confrontation that was later resolved through negotiation. The demand for self-rule within a loose confederation of other French colonies in West Africa was granted. The idea of a confederation was to pool the resources of all the colonies together in order for the rich ones, such as the Ivory Coast, to be able to assist the poorer ones and thus leave France relatively free from bearing the burden of those countries. As expected, export from the colonies would keep the factories in France running. Of course, the prices of their commodities were dictated by the mother country—France.

In principle, the French colonial policy implied a theory of assimilation that was based on the assumption of equality of all men who should be treated alike. The policy rightly condemned slavery and colonial exploitation. In reality, this lofty ideal was hardly practiced in trade and the administration of the colony, especially in all areas of education. For example, formal schooling was restricted to a small number of pupils on whom a very sophisticated system was lavished. The theory of assimilation was such that the product of the system would become a "black Frenchman" with no less privileges and taste as his counterpart in France, in terms of culture, cuisine, and fine wine (Mortimer 1969). To top it all, a mastery of the French language ought to be such that the African elite in that class of graduates could hold their own—favorably, in Paris or elsewhere in Europe. To those who had attained such education, the citizenship of France was conferred (Foster and Clignet 1960).

Some critics of the assimilation policy believe that the French were less than honest, in view of the slow pace and restrictive nature of the educational programs in the Ivory Coast, especially at the postprimary level (Blakemore and Cooksey 1981). At the time of self-rule in 1958, there were only a few qualified Africans to fill top-level civil service jobs. Thus, although primary education increased sixfold between 1947 and 1957, there were only 150 graduates with baccalaureates in 1958. Indeed, most of the graduates were not even Ivorians; they were foreign students, most whom were Europeans. As a result of this anomaly, most European administrators retained their positions after independence and many modestly qualified African civil servants were upgraded to more senior positions (Blakemore and Cooksey 1981). For all intentions and purposes, the Europeans were still in charge of the private as well as public sectors in the entire French West Africa, including the Ivory Coast.

Compared to many African countries, the Houphouet-Boigny administration was largely successful in utilizing its well-managed economy to raise the level of education in the country. What was deficient was the focus on a small proportion of the school-age children on whom he lavished expensive programs. Although they would later become enlightened elite, the rest of the country's children remained illiterate, thus widening the gap between the poor and the new rich. The leadership's continuation of the colonial policy indeed created a crop of African elite that has carried on French administrative practices and served as intermediaries between the government and citizens. The fact that their orientation was heavily influenced by France has prompted some critics to view the situation as neocolonialist (Fafunwa 1980).

Just as the French have been commended for the political stability experienced in the former French colonies in West Africa, they have also been blamed for aspects of their legacy in these countries. It would be simplistic to blame France or its former colonies for the series of coups that later swept through old French West Africa in Togo, Benin, Burkina Faso, Guinea, and now the Ivory Coast. First, the level of education or sophistication in these countries was too low to sustain democracy as practiced in Europe and America. Second, the level of poverty among the populace was such that power was viewed as a means of getting out of poverty; hence, politics or military coups were a matter of life and death. Third, France obviously did not want to be seen as continuing to interfere in the affairs of countries to whom self-rule had been granted. Fourth, the reality of ethnic and religious conflicts was too strong in African polity for any one entity to be held responsible for not stopping the chaos. Finally, even a benevolent dictator like Houphouet-Boigny who for a long time maintained a measure of stability was blamed for not doing enough to prepare a better succession.

Consequently, much of the problem may be put on not extending educational opportunities to more Ivorians. The best tribute that any one can pay to founding father Houphouet-Boigny of the Ivory Coast is to refocus education on all the citizens of the country, especially the young.

When the political situation in the Ivory Coast is viewed within the social landscape of African polity, it is pertinent to observe that leadership is not for the lily-livered because of the diversity of the population. The problem of legitimacy and acceptance has always been a bone of contention in African politics because many of the conflicts can generally be traced to the rejection of either the leader or the group he represented—be it religious or ethnic. Therefore, it is pertinent to take cognizance of this reality in assessing how much can be expected from a leader within the context of an evolving democracy in Africa. Such peculiarity may not always be compatible with Western norms or expectations. When all is said and done, democracy means different things to different people. For most African societies, it takes someone with a patriarchal stature and disposition to lead and tackle the multifarious challenges of development confronting the region—and the Ivory Coast is not excluded. Ever since their patriarch and founding president left the scene, change in leadership has occurred more than three times within a decade. What is important to note is that this has not taken place through a democratic process.

The recurrent problem of political instability in Africa, of which the Ivory Coast was spared for a long time, can be traced to the low level of transparency, fairness, and equity on the part of many leaders in the distribution of scarce resources among its numerous and diverse ethnic groups. The emergence of a leader has generally been viewed by his group as their chance to have a larger share of what is euphemistically referred to in Africa as "the national cake." With that in mind, competition for key positions of power has generally prompted a do-or-die struggle usually based on ethnic lines. When the contest is over and the winner is perceived to be fair minded (as was the case of a few past leaders), they usually gain the acceptance and loyalty of most people. That was the case for Houphouet-Boigny who was, though from the small ethnic group of Baule, a Christian and yet ruled the predominantly Muslim Ivory Coast for nearly three decades.

President Houphouet-Boigny belonged to a small class of benevolent-but-tough African leaders including Julius Nyerere (Tanzania), Leopold Senghor (Senegal), Jomo Kenyatta (Kenya), Tafawa Balewa (Nigeria), and Nelson Mandela (South Africa) who served their countries selflessly. The antitheses to this group are SeseSeko Mobutu (Zaire), Idi Amin (Uganda), Eyadema (Togo), Haile Mariam (Ethiopia), and all the military dictators across the continent who emptied their countries' treasuries and left their nations in ruins.

DEVELOPMENT OF EDUCATION

Within the constraints of its colonial experience, the Ivory Coast's political leadership developed its education considerably well. Favorable economic conditions coupled with France's cooperation gave education in the country a comparative advantage over other African countries. The involvement of France in the overall development of education in its former colonies in West Africa has received mixed ratings. It was commended for facilitating qualitative education for a small group of Ivorians and criticized for leaving most of the population illiterate. As a member of the confederation of former French colonies, the Ivory Coast was constrained to abide by rules governing the union of these countries by accepting an influx of foreign students and workers, which for a while was an advantage before the economy collapsed.

When the Ivory Coast achieved its independence in the late 1950s, it had been under French rule for nearly six decades during which more could have been done to increase the spread of education. Unfortunately, less than 30 percent of school-age children were in school when France granted Ivorians their freedom. With most citizens of the country left illiterate, it was not surprising that top civil servants of European origin had to be retained to carry on their work in the new nation, including the schools. Somehow, the African leaders spent a lot of money on education that was limited to a small number of beneficiaries, many of whom were foreign students. According to a World Bank profile, the agricultural laborer in the Ivory Coast had only one year of schooling; Ivorian workers in commerce had an average of one and one-half years in school, while 70 percent to 80 percent had no education; and workers in industry had four years, while those in government had about six years (World Bank 1996).

Equally striking is the share of foreigners—mostly French expatriates in top positions in the economy. Almost 80 percent of managerial jobs and 50 percent of administrative jobs in modern enterprises (public and private) in the Ivory Coast in 1980 were filled by non-Africans (Berthelemy and Bourguignon 1996).

What is interesting about the World Bank profile is that this same institution in 1978 cautioned the Ivory Coast government against what it called "rapid numerical growth in the system of formal education in view of its cost" (Chinery 1978). The high cost of education referred to could be attributed to the country's reliance on expatriate teachers and learning materials imported from Europe to provide sophisticated educations for the small number of elite being educated. At the same time, the government was providing generous scholarships for this group in select high schools and universities inside the country and abroad. Educational television provided to many schools also added to the cost of education. Although the government planned to introduce universal primary education in order to reach more children, it was not implemented. Indeed, such a move would have brought a more rapid expansion of educational access to a larger number of children in the Ivory Coast.

Since the 1970s, the Ivory Coast has spent between 18 percent and 36 percent of its annual budget on education—a situation unmatched by any other country in the world (Chinery 1978). The small number of university graduates turned out has constituted the elite who have dominated the political as well as academic life of Ivorian society. The high cost of training the elite prompted the World Bank to suggest that "part of the social cost of university education and part of secondary education be passed on to students." Such suggestions have generally been received with skepticism because those decisions would be made by the beneficiaries who themselves are generally in government and would not make rules that are against their interests.

The premium put on the costly Eurocentric orientation to education for the elite in the Ivory Coast was such that recurrent expenditures in the sector were doubling every four or five years within the first fourteen years of independence. During the same period, the recurrent spending at all levels of schooling and training was at an annual rate of 17.5 percent, while the total recurrent public revenue was only 12.5 percent. Of some 69 countries compared with the Ivory Coast in 1973, the country spent a larger proportion of 32.6 percent on education (World Bank Comparative Education Indicator 1975). If, indeed, the high cost of education was prudently expended on only Ivorian children and not on foreign nationals and expensive technical assistance programs, which later proved to be more expensive, the country would have been better off. In view of the way education has been handled in the country, it would appear that control of the situation was entirely not in the hands of the citizens because the machinery of the government was still in the hands of the foreign interests who controlled education during that period.

If, indeed, the control of some essential institutions, such as education and commerce, was externally determined as claimed by critics, there must be a reason that can be found in the French policy of assimilation. For instance, only a few well-assimilated Africans would be granted French citizenship. Education and economic successes were ways of limiting the number of Africans to which such rights and privileges would be granted. Therefore, it was not intended that the door to these institutions would be opened to too many people who might flood the streets of Paris and other European capitals (Clignet and Foster

1966). This is where African leadership failed and may be held accountable for underdeveloping the country. Although they may not have received the best technical assistance or advice, they were still responsible for the lapses in the system. Their expressed desire to Africanize the school curriculum and make their programs less Eurocentric was not executed as stated. To say the least, the entire situation was a disservice to the African culture and development in every way.

EDUCATION STRUCTURE

The Ivorian education structure has three stages: primary school is for six years, leading to a certificate; secondary school is for seven years and has a three-year junior program and a four-year senior section, which is a little above secondary school in the United States. On completion, the baccalaureate is awarded to facilitate entry to a university or secure a job. The duration of a degree program is between three and six years, depending on the type of course studied and the entry qualifications. Other types of tertiary institutions also offer courses and training that lead to certificates for admission to a degree program in any of the three universities—the University of Abidjan is the leading institution. In schools and commercial houses, a good number of technical and teacher education institutions are responsible for the essential midlevel manpower needs of the country. Adult education activities were promoted in the 1980s to reduce the illiteracy level among the adult population.

The public schools in the Ivory Coast are tuition free and have been so since independence. The only fees charged are for entrance examinations and the purchase of school uniforms for pupils. No less than 14 percent of primary and 29 percent of secondary students are in private schools that are run mostly by the Catholic mission. The State pays all teachers including the ones in private schools. The private schools are allowed to charge modest fees. The State is responsible for the supply of learning and teaching materials. The government also grants generous scholarships to secondary and university students. Recipients of such awards are expected to serve the government for a specified period on completion of the courses.

Primary Education Curriculum

As far back as the mid 1980s, the Ivory Coast had no less than 1.5 million pupils in its primary schools. Of this number, 75 percent were boys and 50 percent were girls aged fifteen years and younger. School enrollment accelerated between 7 percent and 9 percent per annum and later took a nose dive to only 2 percent when the country's crisis began. The state was unable to sustain its usually generous and expensive programs in education as political and economic conditions grew worse.

The entry age into the six-year primary program remains at seven or eight years old. Preparatory, intermediate, and elementary make up the three stages of primary education. With French as the language of instruction, the children are taught reading, writing, and arithmetic, with some rudiments of natural science, physical education, music, and art at the first two levels before they are introduced to history and geography at the higher level. Gardening and agriculture are emphasized in the rural schools. They receive a certificate (*certificate d'etude primaries elementaries* or CEPE) at the end of this stage. It is significant to note that over two thirds of entire lessons taught to sixth graders in the Ivory Coast were devoted to France—the homeland (Ki-Zerbo 1961).

Most of the teaching and learning materials used in Ivorian schools were imported from Europe and as such were irrelevant to life in Africa, especially in the rural areas. Although some urban schools were generally well supplied with materials, transportation and other obstacles prevented rural schools from access to such materials. Even when textbooks meant for European schools were adapted, the children still experienced difficulties because of the lack of familiarity with objects and situations that were alien to them. Ironically, children at the higher levels of schooling in the Ivory Coast knew the history, geography, the fauna, and flora of Europe more than the ones of their country, at least theoretically (Farine 1969). At that level, the realization that such knowledge would open more doors of opportunity was a propelling force.

Like many African countries, life in rural communities in the Ivory Coast is particularly difficult, especially for pupils who have to walk a long distance to the nearest school where teachers are hardly available due to high absenteeism. Teachers prefer urban schools for obvious reasons; some inducements are generally offered to attract teachers to village schools. In general, curriculum in Ivorian schools tends to be modified in favor of intellectual development in anticipation of entering a secondary school.

Secondary Education Curriculum

In view of the restrictive nature of admission into Ivorian secondary schools, an average of only 10 percent of primary school graduates enter the College or *Lycee*, which used to be fairly different institutions due to their emphasis on either the arts, sciences, or commercial and technical subjects. The *Lycee* was administered by the central government while the municipality controlled the college, although both were centrally funded. For a seven-year program, students would be admitted into the first cycle of four years, after which those who earned a certificate (*breve d'etude du premiere cycle* or BEPC) were allowed to proceed to the College or *Lycee* or enter a teacher education institution or seek employment.

Midlevel manpower training is available in colleges of agriculture, commerce, and technology. Ninety percent of Ivorians are farmers, fishermen, foresters, and hunters, but training in these vocations does not attract many young people because they offer little income and prestige. Young people are mostly interested in white-collar jobs in urban areas. The government has not done much to change this situation, which has accounted for urban migration and its attendant problems of unemployment and increases in crime and other social problems (UNECA 1965).

Culturally, Ivorian secondary school places its graduates between the French and African ways of life. An Ivorian minister of education stated the following:

The school does not integrate the child into his traditional and natural milieu, but gives him the means to escape from it; the school, far from being a factor of development in accordance with its role, that is, the advancement at one's individual and collective, has finished by becoming a source of disintegration and break up of the society. (Tanoh 1965)

By the minister's own admission, the school system has failed to achieve its stated objective of transmitting and reinforcing African culture among its students while improving its midlevel manpower needs. According to the government official, the ruralization policy "has remained theoretical and approached cautiously" (Tanoh 1965). The dilemma of the African elite in the Ivorian government is their desire to be African and French at the same time. This state of anomie experienced in the schools has done more damage to the reputation of a generation of African elite that are generally considered to be honest and transparent in terms of corruption. Therefore, it is not enough to admit their failure; they should act to correct the anomaly in the interest of succeeding generations.

One way to achieve the needed change is to gradually reduce the number of personnel in foreign technical assistance programs and intensify the training of more Ivorian teachers using a revised curriculum that is more culturally relevant to Ivorians. That way, students and teachers can experience what Farine calls, "the psychology of the young Africans based on their concept of life and their traditional values as well as the moral values of our times" (1969).

Tertiary Education

In the last decade, the number of universities in the Ivory Coast has risen from one to at least three due to the government's approval of private universities. The University of Abidjan, patterned along French universities, used to be the only one available to the small number of secondary school graduates who aspired to attend it. Still heavily dependent on French assistance, the University of Abidjan has faculties of law, sciences, and letters, and schools of agriculture, public works, administration, and fine arts. Other tertiary institutions known as *grandes en les* award certificates in specialized fields in cooperation with the national university. Only 100,724 were admitted and matriculated during the 1997–98 school year. Out of this number, 81 percent were in public institutions while the rest ended up in private ones; 18 percent were in institutions not funded by the state while 6 percent were attracted to schools of technology. At a time when Ivorian teachers were in great demand, enrollment in teacher education institutions dropped from 1,500 to 200 in 1987 (Houenou 2003).

Tertiary institutions in the Ivory Coast, like many French universities, have several categories of teachers whose activities cover primary, secondary, and tertiary institutions. These range from the professor teaching at the secondary or university level, the assistant professor at the secondary school level, and instructors and monitors at the primary level. Their insistence on quality at all levels has prompted the focus on how well students perform from the primary to tertiary level. This has its limitation because there is only a small number who can be catered to.

Like some African countries, the enrollment of females in tertiary institutions is mostly in the areas of the arts, social sciences, and health-related fields, such as nursing and pharmacy. The sciences, technology, and medicine are gradually attracting more females. Males more or less dominate engineering and science-related professions. Forestry and agriculture, which the government is interested in as a means of a foreign exchange source, has yet to attract sufficient Ivorian students.

EDUCATION REFORM

Although education in the Ivory Coast had an encouraging beginning shortly after independence, difficulties arose as a result of some misplaced priorities. The realization that an expensive quality education would reduce access for a large number of children came a little late. Not only were many Ivorian children excluded from the system but also vital areas of teacher and technical education also could have been given more attention. Due to financial constraints, the cost of sophisticated programs, such as educational television and generous scholarships for the fortunate few in their secondary and tertiary institutions, had to be reviewed to allocate more funds to primary education and adult literacy programs.

Even though considerable lip service was paid to ruralization and Africanization of the Ivorian curriculum, school authorities in the country could have done a little more to reduce the emphasis on Europe in general and France in particular. Although not rejecting the promotion of French language, it ought to be studied along with African culture and languages for the benefit of Ivorian children.

In view of some errors that have been experienced in the past, the advice of some international agencies ought to be scrutinized and weighed against local conditions and circumstances. For instance, when the country needed to have more children in school at all levels, the following advice was offered:

There is a sharp divergence between the net private benefits and net social benefits from education. Although powerful incentives are given to individuals to continue school, the cost to society for additional schooling may be excessive. An important objective of educational policy should be a closer correspondence between private and social benefits and costs. (World Bank 1978)

In the short run, private benefits may not seem to match the cost to society, but in the long run, the entire community benefits from the education of the individual child who in one way or the other becomes an asset not only to his family but to the entire country. For a multiethnic African society, it is not only necessary to educate all, it is most expedient to do so in order to achieve fairness and equity. Sooner or later, the benefit becomes apparent. However, this is not to say that appropriate authorities should not prioritize their use of available resources in the education sector.

Education reform in the Ivory Coast ought to focus on the universal primary education that should be compulsory and available to all Ivorian children. The State was at one time committed to such an endeavor when it stated:

Currently, the country is embarking on a reform of technical and vocational education that will not only expand the whole system, but will render it more efficient and more closely related to the needs of the economy in terms of skills and training. (Chinery 1978)

It is also anticipated that agricultural education is promoted through curriculum changes, in view of that sector's importance to the economy. The perception of farming as associated with poverty and ignorance must be changed by a deliberate government policy. If greater realism and resourcefulness are injected into agriculture and young Ivorians are motivated through mechanized farming, as was the case with educational television, the chances of agriculture making a positive impression on the youth would increase.

Similarly, the desire for technical and vocational training would also have to be promoted by providing well-equipped workshops for trainees in carpentry, masonry, electrical work, and more. More than ever, theoretical approaches to education ought to be complemented with practical experiences to give it proper grounding. For example, mathematics must be related to buying and selling commodities on the market in order to remove it from the realm of abstraction in children's minds.

In conclusion, the Ivory Coast must go back to its original zeal of using education to promote industrial development as was the case in the 1970s. Like Nigeria and Zimbabwe, agriculture was deliberately utilized to stimulate the economy with education as the engine behind the revolution (Peaslee 1971). Even though young Ivorians were inclined to white-collar jobs, there was enough interest in agriculture to make its earlier success a reality (Peaslee 1971). In spite of its recent difficulties, the Ivory Coast on the whole has done considerably well in its education reform for the development of the country.

BIBLIOGRAPHY

Berg, Elliot J. "The Economic Basis of Political Choice in French West Africa." *American Political Science Review* 54, no. 2 (1960).
Berthelemy, J. C., and F. Bouguignon. 1996. *Growth and Crisis in the Ivory Coast.* Washington D.C.: World Bank.

Blakemore, K., and Brian Cooksey. 1981. *A Sociology of Education for Africa*. London: Allen & Unwin.

Bolibough, J. 1964. French Educational Strategies for Sub-Sahara Africa: Their Intent, Derivation, and Development. PhD diss., Stanford University, 1964.

Chinery, Hollis. 1978. *Ivory Coast: The Challenge of Success* (a World Bank country economic report). Washington, D.C.: John Hopkins University Press.

Clignet, R., and P. Foster. 1966. *The Fortunate Few*. Evanston, Ill.: Northwestern University Press.

De Lusignan, Guy. 1969. *French Speaking Africa Since Independence*. New York: Frederick A. Praeger.

Fafunwa, A. Babs. 1980. *New Perspective in African Education*. London: Macmillan Education Ltd.

Farine, Avigore. "Society and Education: The Content of Education in the French African School." *Comparative Education* 5, no. 1 (1969).

Houenou, Pascal V. 2003. In *African Higher Education: An International Reference Book Handbook*. Edited by D. Teferra and Philip G. Altbach. Bloomington: University of Indiana Press.

Ivor, Morrish. 1978. *The Sociology of Education: An Introduction to Society, Identity & Continuity*. London: Allen & Unwin.

Jalloh, A. A. 1973. *Political Integration in French-speaking Africa*. Berkeley, CA: Institute of International Studies.

Ki-Zerbo, J. "The Content of Education in Africa." Final Report, United Nations Economic Commission for Africa/UNESCO, conference of African States on the Development of Education in Africa, Addis Ababa, May 15–25, 1961.

Morgenthau, R. S. 1964. *Political Parities in French-Speaking West Africa*. Oxford, UK: Oxford University Press.

Mortimer, Edward. 1969. *France and the Africans (1944–1960)*. New York: Walker and Co.

Peaslee, Alexander L. 1971. "Primary School Enrollments and Economic Growth." In *Education in Comparative and International Perspectives*. Edited by K. I. Gezi. New York: Holt, Rinehart.

Sik, Endre. 1970. *The History of Black Africa*. Vol. 1. Budapest, Hungary: Akademiai Kiado.

Taba, H. 1962. *Curriculum Development: Theory and Practice*. New York: Harcourt.

Tanoh, M. A. "Rapport de M. A. Tanoh. Minisg del'Education National devant le congres du P.D.C.E." *Education et Techniques* no. 31 (1965): 8–9.

United Nations. 1966. *E.C.A., African Agricultural Development*. New York.

World Bank Comparative Education Indicator. (Oct. 15, 1975).

Chapter 6

SCHOOLING IN KENYA

INTRODUCTION

When non-East Africans think of Kenya, the images often invoked are those of the Mau-Mau warriors led by Jomo Kenyatta against the European colonialists and Kenyan young men and women easily winning the annual marathon races in Boston, New York, and across the world repeatedly. Of course, the games and wildlife parks are also a great attraction for the would-be visitor to the country. However, there is more to Kenya than these outward perceptions.

In terms of the physical description of Africa as a whole, one cannot lose sight of the almighty Mount Kenya (5,199 meters) and Mount Kilimanjaro (5,895 meters) in Tanzania—both with the continent's highest points. With Lake Victoria covering a total area of 83,000 square kilometers, Kenya can also boast having the largest lake in Africa. With such bodies of water in Africa and others, including Lake Tanganyika in Tanzania, the Congo River, the Senegal River, and the Niger River, easy access and navigable links between and within regions to the interior are provided in the continent. These waterways have considerable hydroelectricity that has yet to be fully tapped.

Kenya, an East African country, is bordered on the north by Sudan and Ethiopia, on the south by Tanzania, on the east by Somalia and the Indian Ocean, and on the west by Lake Victoria and Uganda. Kenya is a former British colony that gained independence in 1963 and became a republic a year later. Nairobi is the country's capital and largest city.

At the beginning of the twenty-first century, the population of the African continent was estimated at 818 million (2001). Of this population, Kenya has a population of about 28.7 million people. It has a density of about fifty to one-hundred inhabitants per square kilometer, with less than 35 percent in the urban areas. The life expectancy of an average Kenyan is fifty years while its infant mortality rate is estimated to be seventy five to one hundred in every 1,000 live births. The overall health statistics in Africa since the inception of the twenty-first century reveal that infant mortality is about 88 percent, of which malaria accounts for 9 percent. In 2001, AIDS claimed as many victims as 2.2 million in the whole of Africa. Invariably, this has drastically affected life expectancy in the continent. In Kenya alone, the number of cases recorded living with HIV/AIDS was estimated at fifty to two hundred per 1,000 people. The situation was even made worse by its poor medical services. There are only about five to twenty doctors per 100,000 in Kenya. Notwithstanding, this has its effect on the economic and educational life of the country.

A majority of Kenyans are black Africans, with a few Arabs, Asians, and Europeans in the minority. The black population comprising over forty ethnic groups has three major ethnolinguistic groups, namely, the Bantu, the Cushitic, and the Nilotic. During the colonial era, the administrators grouped people according to their ethnic origins and assigned them to specific areas of the country. Only people of a particular ethnic identity were allowed to reside in such locations. This pattern of ethnically based settlements persisted in Kenya before independence to the present day. With little success, the apartheid regime in South Africa attempted to do this with their homeland program. Even though economic and political development tends to have increased mobility and urbanization among the country's citizens, ethnicity has remained a key factor in the country's polity. Kenyan's official languages are English and Swahili, both of which are widely used in communication. However, nearly each African ethnic group also has their own indigenous language thus making for considerable linguistic diversity in the country. Most Kenyans speak an average of three languages: the language of one's ethnic group, Swahili, and English. In terms of religion, about 70 percent and 6 percent of Kenya's population are Christians and Moslems, respectively. Other faiths include Hindus and Sikhs (a relatively small number).

Economically, Kenya is relatively similar to South Africa and Egypt, and better than most African countries. Kenya's per capita GNP is over US$2,000. Essentially, Kenya has a diversified economy that includes manufacturing, industries, and tourism, which is a major income earner for the country. In the agricultural sector, Kenya has livestock. Like other East African countries such as Malawi and Uganda, Kenya is a leading producer of coffee and tea. Collectively, these countries produce 14 percent of the world's export. In the same vein, Kenya, Tanzania, and Madagascar produce 19 percent of the world's sisal. Kenya also produces a little over 200,000 tons of fish, for export and local consumption. This is a bit of an irony in that Kenya, like other East African countries, have experienced food shortages through drought and other disasters. Consequently, they sometimes have had to rely on aid and imports of food to supplement their needs. Kenya is one of such African countries that suffer this fate.

Concerning regional integration, Kenya is a member of the Commonwealth, the African Union (AU), and the UN. It is also linked economically and politically with the community of East African nations, including Tanzania and Uganda, and other neighboring countries. Kenya holds membership in the East African Development Bank (EADB), Common Market for East and South Africa (COMES), Indian Ocean Regional Association for Regional Cooperation (IOR-ARC), Africa-Caribbean Pacific Countries Association (ACP), and East African Community (EAC).

As an independent country since 1963, the Republic of Kenya has been one of the most developed countries in Sub-Saharan Africa. With Kenyatta elected as its first president, his fifteen-year presidency brought relative prosperity. On his death in 1978, Vice President Daniel Arap Moi succeeded him. The ten years that followed witnessed corruption, political intolerance, and widespread poverty. Kenya's booming economy was weakened in the 1980s as a consequence of a rising trade deficit. This compelled the government to adopt the structural adjustment program imposed by the IBRD and IMF. In the early 1990s, Moi was battling with his citizens' dissatisfaction borne out of the harsh economic situation that was imposed on them. However, in 2002, Moi was compelled to step down, a situation that opened wider doors for political changes in Kenya. However, the economic damage from the 1980s had wiped out the economic progress of the 1960s and 1970s. Without question, this has had a negative effect on the general advancement of Kenyan society, especially in the education sector.

TRADITIONAL EDUCATION

Much of the progress or drawbacks in schooling may be attributed to the indigenous education that the average Kenyan child was exposed to at birth. Kenyans, like most traditional African societies, place great importance on family and the values and responsibilities associated with it. Kenyan families tend to be large and households often include many members of the extended family. Polygamy has continued to be away of life to the present day among every social class and ethnic group. Many of Kenya's rural dwellers live on small farms, while others are nomadic livestock herders. With a higher standard of living, city dwellers live in modern houses except in the slums where most of the poor live.

Essentially, in traditional Kenyan society, education was carried out in the family system by members of both nuclear and extended families. The purpose was to ensure that children were provided with adequate love, care, and security in their early years. The aim of education was to cater to children's intellectual, social, emotional, and physical needs. The method of training and learning was mostly oral. The underlying philosophy of traditional education was to help children acquire appropriate skills for an occupation. Children were also taught their roles in life. Male children had the responsibility of carrying on the family name, while females were expected to bring wealth to the family through marriage.

Another important feature of education in traditional Kenya is manifested in the initiation ceremonies and formal training for adulthood. In Kenya, much of peer group socialization was achieved through the age group system. Traditional socialization processes equipped young ones with appropriate knowledge, skills, ideas, attitudes, and patterns of behavior needed for survival in a rural setting. Through tribal legends, riddles, and proverbs, the Kenyan's cultural heritage was transmitted and their origin was established in the minds of their youth. In other words, in spite of the oral tradition employed, rural traditional Kenyan community had an organized way of teaching its youth. Knowledge was imparted through succeeding stages of initiation from status to status in traditional Kenya and among the Kikuyu people (Kenyatta 1965). The assumption of each status was accompanied by a sequence of rules and organized instruction of one sort or another. Oral information is gathered at various levels of indigenous education in Kenya (see Table 6.1).

In the same vein, girls had a similar system of grading according to rites performed. Following the age range and status (like that of the males) the grading for girls included *Rukenge, Mwana, Karigu, Muumo,* and *Muhiki.*

Of great significance in the above system of education is the change in status from boyhood or girlhood to fully identified adolescents. This means passing through the stage of initiation and circumcision is quite crucial to attaining manhood for boys. Circumcision was viewed as a rebirth and as such would be aptly described as "being born again." Thus, one who has passed through the childhood stage into full adolescence should no longer behave like a child. He should be able to discern right from wrong. Buttressing this view, Kenyatta

Table 6.1
Kikuyu Rites of Passage for Boys

Age in Years	Status	Kikuyu Name	Sign
1–3	Infant	*Rukenge*	None
4–5	Child	*Mwana*	None
6–12	Boy	*Kahii*	Piercing of the earlobes
13–17	Uncircumcised (adolescents)	*Kihii*	Piercing of the outer edge of the ears
18–20	(i) Newly circumcised warrior	*Muume*	Circumcision
	(ii) Warrior married with child	*Mwanake Muthuri wa mucii*	None
	(iii) Elders (Juniors)	*Kamatimu*	None
	(iv) Elders (Seniors)	*Kiama kia maturanguru*	None

Source: Furley and Watson (1978).

(1965) has said that the initiations were such that the instructed were supposed to know what is "right" from "wrong," alongside a host of other beliefs and customs of their people. They were also made to bear pain without showing signs of distress. This was a proof of manliness and a quality of mind worthy of being possessed as men in their society. It is against this background that one can understand the level of endurance seen in Kenyan runners in marathons races.

Another important aspect of Kenyan indigenous education is discipline. A vital aspect of general home training came directly from home discipline, especially for the younger generations. The Kenyan child, especially the male, was taught to be disciplined in and outside the home. He learned discipline in various ways through games: wrestling for physical strength and stamina, spear throwing and archery for accuracy, and hunting for physical fitness, stealth, and the development of tracking abilities. A boy who could not withstand pain, especially that of circumcision, brought untold shame to his family. It was an indication of parental training and such a boy was considered a coward for life. Respect for elders was also stressed.

Indigenous education as found in Kenya is typical of most traditional African societies. It was quite rich in songs, stories, proverbs, riddles, myths, and legends. They formed a literary heritage and a reflection of the people's customs, culture, beliefs, and philosophy of life. Significantly, this formed the basic foundation in Kenyan indigenous education and a means of transmitting knowledge, skills, and attitudes to its young. The Kikuyu people are quite rich in stories; each conveys a specific message and meaning. Kenyan children even to this day are told stories of the origin of their people and great battles fought. Such stories usually have underlying morals and lessons. For example, the story of the moon and the sun is quite familiar among Kenyans. It aims to teach children why the moon shines at night and the sun during the day.

Like stories, songs served various purposes in Kenya's indigenous education. Traditional songs and lullabies were a means of teaching the local dialect as well as correct pronunciations. Other songs were mainly ceremonial. Children were taught songs and their meanings on appropriate occasions. There were seasonal songs for harvesting and in periods of famine. There were also songs conveying the deeds of great heroes and ancestors. Ogot (1963) explains: Among the Luo people of Kenya, songs were used as a means of teaching history and recalling with pride the past achievements of great people. He cited the first of such songs as one that traced back ten generations. He describes the song as being truth and self-evident, especially when migratory people are facing foes in larger numbers. The song says:

Eee, one child is not enough, one child is inadequate
Eee, when the war drums sound "tindi!" "tindi!"
Who will come to your rescue?
—one child?

The message of the song is quite clear. Kenyans, like other Africans, have generally believed in a large family. This was subtly inculcated in every young learner through songs.

Indigenous education in Kenya also featured stories, proverbs, and riddles that were quite useful in transmitting morals, truth, and values to young learners. These were more or less direct oral instructions which were used to instill and reinforce positive behavior in children and wards. It was commonplace to hear a Kenyan father emphasize to his son that "men have spears." In effect, the message to his son is that he, like all men, was born to fight. Similarly, the Tanzanians would caution "haste has no blessing," which means more haste less speed.

Dances cannot be ignored in indigenous education in Kenya. From his early years, the Kikuyu child learns words, music, clapping hands, and making simple bodily movements from his mother's lap. As he grows older, these bodily movements become more rhythmic. He develops new and distinct dance steps with added facial expressions. The learned dances are intended to celebrate special rituals and occasions ranging from new births, initiations, marriage, and even death to seasons of harvests and other celebrations. Through dances and perfected rhythmic movements, opportunities are created to assert the masculine self or the feminine gait and touch—a handsome face is displayed as well as a show of strength. For females, beautiful bodies are adorned with ornaments. These rituals prepared them for their roles and natural cycles of life from courtship to marriage and procreation.

Without gainsaying, the variety of educational experiences was quite crucial to the Kikuyu people as vehicles for transmitting knowledge and positive attitudes. Furley and Watson (1978) suggested:

More research needs to be done into such stories, riddles, proverbs, songs, prayers, poems and dances of East Africa, before they are lost. They contain so much valuable information about African literary education and culture.

We will find that in today's education in Kenya, stories, songs, and poems are still featured on school timetables, especially at the elementary stages of learning. However, they may not be as effectively transmitted as they were in traditional settings where full meanings and appreciation are better felt.

Finally, religion is another essential aspect of indigenous education in Kenya. As the average child develops, he imbibes beliefs and a disposition for invocation to ancestors while responding to given instructions in taboos, sacrifices, and ritual worship. He is sometimes taught how to make charms and practice divination as well. He learns early enough the structure of the African hierarchy, so he knows the position of the omnipotent God, the gods and deities, the clan, the family, etc. He is taught respect and obedience bearing in mind where he fits into the hierarchy, tradition, religious beliefs, and practices. Traditional Kenyan society believes in the existence of an almighty creator as well as in an all pervading spiritual force. This is evident in their daily prayers, worship, praise, songs, and incantations. Consequently, children in the home imbibe such religious education through these rituals until it becomes a natural part of their lives.

EDUCATION IN THE COLONIAL ERA

The family's role in educating children was supplemented by formal education with the coming of modernization and urbanization in Kenya. Western education was introduced by missionaries in the mid 1800s. They taught the people elementary reading, carpentry, and gardening. By 1910, about thirty-five mission schools had been founded. The aim of missionary education in Kenya was for citizens to be able to read and understand the Bible and spread Christianity. This stems from the belief that the most rudimentary knowledge of the 3Rs was crucial for converting people to Christianity.

It is also important to mention that Kenyans did not warmly accept education from the missionaries initially because they were quite hesitant and conservative about accepting Western education or its influence in their lives. Krapf, an early missionary in East Africa, stated in his memoirs that the first few pupils at Rabai Mpya, near Mombasa in Kenya, insisted that they be paid by the missionaries for attending school (Datta 1984). However, it was not long before the advantages of Western education became clear to them. LeVine and LeVine (1963) have asserted that among the Gusii of Kenya, during the colonial era, the popular perception of the material benefits of education was more of a myth. For example, Gusii elders told the story of a prophet whose forecast before the advent of the Europeans was that white men would visit the Gusii, take away their children, and give them white mushrooms. This prediction was later interpreted to mean that the Europeans would set up schools for the Gusii children and education obtained would pave the way to earning more Kenyan shillings.

About the same time that missionaries were struggling to make their impact felt, colonial administrators arrived to make treaties with African leaders. In the course of such negotiations they would need some clerks to carry out the jobs. Consequently, they thought only a measure of literacy was necessary but even at that they were able to modify what the missionaries had started—a task they undertook in stages.

Beginning with early childhood education, the first signs of education existed in the 1940s. The first of such institutions were established in urban centers by European wives to cater to Europeans and, later, Asian children. However, with time, some others were established in urban areas in African locations, and on tea and sugar plantations for African children. The main aim of preschools during this period, especially as it pertained to the Kenyans, was more of custodial care and security services. There was little or no emphasis on formal learning. These institutions for African children were more or less "away from home" centers. They were organized by mothers who took turns caring for children while others worked on the tea and sugar plantations. Such centers were also organized in emergency villages during the Mau-Mau war of the 1950s.

Typical of most African nations, the birth of the Kenyan African Anti-Colonial Movement (KANU) directed against European control occurred in tandem with Kenyans appreciating the relevance of education as an agency for effective communication with and mobilization of the masses. In other words, education was seen as a means of bringing about economic development, cultural awareness, and political self-assertion as part of the struggle for independence and emancipation from colonialism. This resulted in a great demand for mass education in the 1930s. Ward (1967) states, "In countries like Ghana and Kenya, the graph of attendance at primary and middle schools had been rising slowly over the several decades, but now it suddenly rocketed upward at a steep angle." Godfrey (1966) affirms that between 1963 and 1964 Kenya had put in 13.3 percent of her total spending on education. This was quite an incredible figure as compared to past expenditures on education.

Hailey (1957) opined that colonial education in British dependencies in Africa was not only limited quantitatively but also marked by a heavy stress on primary education. Moumouni (1968) stated that, in 1937, Kenya could boast of only two junior secondary schools, both run by missionary societies. According to Hailey (1957), there was indeed a resultant effect due to the neglect of secondary school needs during the colonial period. In the year 1952—the beginning of the last decade before decolonization—enrollment in Kenya's secondary schools came to less than 2.1 percent of the total primary school enrollment.

A comparative analysis of colonial education with that of the missionaries in Kenya can be said to characterize both by their Eurocentric bias. This is reflected in their curricula and medium of instruction. The emphasis in curricula was on the liberal arts with little or no attention to instruction in vocational, technical, science, and professional areas. English language was their favored medium of instruction. It is important to mention here that even though Kenya and Tanzania are both East African countries and British dependencies, Tanzania insisted on Swahili (their local language) as their school medium of instruction.

On the whole, education in Kenya was dually controlled by the colonial administration and missionaries. Even then, the education provided may be described as quite minimal in quantity and quality. However, one cannot say that Kenya in the colonial era did not have the advantage of exposure to education.

EDUCATION: POSTCOLONIAL KENYA

Having attained independence, educational development in Kenya was aimed at the following goals:

1. Expansion of education at all levels;
2. Provision of qualitative education;
3. Revision of colonial education and curriculum diversification to include technical, vocational, and professional components; and
4. The Africanization of the curricula as a whole. (Datta 1984)

It was on the basis of the above that postindependence Kenya witnessed a restructuring of its education system. It consists of eight years of primary education, four years of secondary education, and four years of college or tertiary education. Simply output, Kenya operates the 8-4-4 system of education.

Before 1980, almost all education in Kenya was provided free by the government. However, all through the 1980s the deteriorating Kenyan economy, the huge IMF loan repayment, and reduced foreign aid resulted in fewer funds for qualitative education. In 1986, the Kenyan government took another step to revise the primary and secondary school structures and their curriculum content. This indirectly increased the financial demand on schools' limited resources. If quality education must be maintained, the alternative was to charge school fees. Thus, public schools that had been free began to charge fees. However, such school fees varied depending on school location. Schools located in poor and rural areas charged far less than those in wealthy, urban neighborhoods. If nothing else, this was expected to afford access to a good number of the population access. Unfortunately, government support could hardly sustain staff salaries, administrative maintenance, school supplies, and books. Hence, the schools that charged low fees had to work harder to sustain themselves. What eventually evolved was a situation where children from poor homes had to drop out of school. To help stem the growing trend of falling education standards in Kenya, there was the urgent need for private alternatives. The government's call for the establishment of private primary and secondary institutions was spontaneously responded to. By 2001, the number of private schools had grown considerably. All public schools in Kenya are controlled by the Ministry of Education, while private schools are supervised by district education boards. Curriculum development is done by Kenya's Institute of Education, a semiautonomous agency of the state.

The language of instruction is English; it is also the official language. Swahili is also widely spoken in Kenya. However, in some cases, the indigenous language or local tribal languages are used in the first three grades in primary school in state and local levels. Although Kenya's education system is on an 8-4-4 structure, preschool education, which is still evolving, is also considered an important organ of the system.

PRESCHOOL EDUCATION

Since the attainment of independence, the number of preschool centers has greatly increased with the government taking a keen interest in initiating and promoting its growth. This zeal in the establishment of preschool program actually began in response to the Kenyan government's call for *Harambee*. *Harambee* is in a way similar to the Tanzania philosophy of *Ujama! Harambee* is a slogan as well as call for self-reliance and social responsibility of all citizens towards the building of a united Kenya. Before 1980, preschool in Kenya was partly a government concern. Preschool also referred to as nursery school and in most cases was privately owned with the Ministry of Culture and Social Services playing a supervisory role.

Since the 1980s, preschool programs became the responsibility of Kenya's Ministry of Education, Science and Technology, with private investors as partners. Such private bodies who are mostly financial and material resource partners include the local parent-teachers associations and churches—notably the Church of the Province of Kenya, the Catholic Church, and the Presbyterian Church of East Africa. Other private sponsors include firms, cooperatives, state corporations, women organizations (for example, the Young Women's Christian Association), and all such voluntary organizations.

Essentially, preschools are available to children aged three to six years old. The school duration is about three years by which time the children are ready for serious academic work in primary school. Preschool is more of an early socialization program for preschoolers with the provision of custodial care. Also, there was a desire to give the Kenyan child a head start in formal schooling. In keeping with this policy, the preprimary program has taken cognizance of the physical, socioemotional, mental, and special needs of growing children. In the same vein, Kenya's government has the following stated goals for preschool education:

- provision of an informal education aimed at developing the child's mental capabilities and physical growth;
- provision of opportunity for learning and living through play;
- development in the child for an appreciation of his culture and customs;
- helping the child to form right habits for effective living as an individual and member of a group;
- fostering in the child spiritual and moral growth;
- developing the child's imagination, self-reliance, and his thinking skills; and
- helping to enrich the child's experiences in a way that would enable him to cope better with primary school life. (Kenyatta Foundation 1984)

Kenya, like most independent African nation, is working hard at Africanizing its curriculum and teaching materials, thus making them quite culturally relevant. Educational planners as well as curriculum experts in Kenya have also deemed it necessary to begin the refinement of the system from the early childhood stage. In doing this, they have taken into consideration the cultural, geographical, and linguistic diversity of the nation. To come up with a suitable yet standard model curriculum and teaching materials, workshop participants cut across preschoolers (themselves), preschool teachers, parents, teacher educators, and the community. At the government level, seminars were also organized. UNICEF has also assisted in such workshops. Regarding teaching materials that are quite crucial to early childhood learning, the following are considered culturally relevant to teaching and learning in Kenya's nursery schools:

1. Things such as clay, sand, wood, water, etc., are basic play materials because they are found in and around the child's environment.

2. Simple concrete materials, like wooden toys, abaci, wooden letters and numbers, and building blocks are easy to make and quite affordable, too. Teachers and their children in class can produce such materials as class projects and are sold to parents.

3. Elementary graphic materials like workbooks, drawing books, coloring books, and reading books are produced by young Kenyans.

4. Also, elementary literature, story books, poems, rhymes, songs, etc., of Kenyan tradition, in various languages with familiar Kenyan names, jokes, plays, games, etc.

5. Teaching guides, educational guidelines, manuals, and syllabi drawn to suit the Kenyan child.

6. Finally, with modern technology, the use of videos and compact discs, films, tape recorders, computers, cassettes and satellite television are being used to popularize stories, songs, rhymes, games, and dances in the various local dialects in Kenya. (Ministry of Education, Science and Technology 1984)

Administration and Control of Preschool

As previously highlighted, Kenya is an African country where early childhood learning has not been left solely in private hands. It is more of a partnership venture between government and parents, local committees, churches, voluntary organizations, and other private investors. The government, through the Ministry of Education, Science and Technology, is responsible for curriculum development, registration of schools, inspection, supervision, and provision of policy guidelines for all necessary school programs. While all other partners are mostly involved as financiers, the administration of nursery education is handled at the preschool headquarters section in the Ministry of Education, Science and Technology. Its responsibilities include registration of schools, coordination of government grants and funds, other external financial sponsorship and donations, and the provision of policy guidelines. The Ministry's inspectorate division monitors professional standards of all preschools in Kenya. This division also coordinates the inspection and supervision of preschools as well as organizes preschool teacher education programs and administers preschool teacher education examinations.

Kenya's National Centre for Early Childhood Education (NACECE) is situated in the curriculum development center of the Institute of Education. As a professional body, NACECE implements government policies on early childhood education. This center has a network of subcenters called District Centers for Early Childhood (DICECE). The district centers serve as facilitators and trainers in the development of early childhood programs. The first nine of such centers was established in January 1985 and by 1987 six more were added (Institute of Education 1987).

These agencies have collaborated with government and early childhood education sponsors, such as the Bernard Van Leer Foundation, UNICEF, and Aga Kahn Foundation. They have worked together to set up more district centers across the country and conducted early childhood education programs for parents and their communities. Such organized programs are supervised by experienced teams of school district inspectors and preprimary supervisors from the country and the municipal councils. Also in the hierarchy of the early childhood education administrative cadre is their National Implementation Committee that is appointed by the director of education and plays an advisory role as well as helps to implement national and district programs on early childhood education.

PRIMARY EDUCATION

Primary school in Kenya is compulsory. Its duration is eight years with a minimum entry age of six years old and exit age of fourteen years old. At the end of eight years, the pupils are expected to take the Kenya Certificate of Primary Education (KCPE) as a prerequisite for secondary education or a basic minimum certificate for the working world. Significantly, the primary school curriculum is quite broad with a focus on functional and practical education. This is designed to cater to Kenya's children who may not go beyond primary school. Even more important, the primary cycle is expected to prepare children for the secondary stage of learning.

The aims and objectives of primary education are to help the young learner:

1. acquire literacy, numeracy, and manipulative skills;
2. develop the self in terms of expression and discipline, and be self-reliant, fully utilizing his senses;
3. develop an ability for clear logical thought and critical judgment;
4. acquire a suitable basic foundation for the working world, especially in the context of the nation's economic and manpower needs;
5. experience a meaningful course of study that will lead to enjoyment, successful learning, and a desire to continue learning;
6. appreciate and respect the dignity of labor;
7. develop desirable social standards and positive attitudes;
8. grow into a strong and healthy person;
9. develop a constructive and adaptive attitude to life based on moral and religious values and responsibilities to his immediate community and entire nation;
10. appreciate one's own as well as other cultural heritages, develop aesthetic values, and make good use of leisure time; and
11. grow toward maturity and self-fulfillment as useful and well-adjusted members of the society. (Ministry of Education, Science and Technology 1987)

Primary Education Curriculum

Kenya's national curriculum for primary education that has existed for a few decades is British oriented. Its aims include providing students with adequate intellectual and practical skills for useful living. Its three broad principles include

1. a revision to improve quality content, and relevance so as to meet the needs of the pupils, some of whom will proceed to secondary school and others whose formal education may terminate at that point;
2. make primary education available and compulsory for all; and
3. a diversified curriculum aimed at competence in a variety of skills.

Primary school subjects include

1. Business and creative arts: arts and crafts, music, and physical education
2. Languages: English, Swahili, and mother tongue
3. Mathematics
4. Religion: Christian and Islam
5. Agricultural science
6. General science
7. Home science/domestic science
8. Health science
9. Social studies: civics, geography, and history.

Pupils must take final examinations to be awarded the KCPE. The aims of the examination include

1. candidate ranking according to their attainment of knowledge, skills, and attitudes; and
2. feedback to facilitate improvement of primary schools. The examination can be used as a prerequisite for selecting candidates for secondary schools and other postprimary institutions.

In 2001, the Kenyan president declared the need for free and compulsory primary education. The idea of a universal basic education for Kenyan children was actually muted in the mid 1980s with assistance from the World Bank. The government then set up in six zones boarding primary schools in the regions. The implementation took effect in 2001 when public primary schools no longer charged school fees. The aims of this reform measure were

1. to restore fairness to the education system and reduce inequality between rich and poor schools
2. expand access to quality education and
3. promote efficient teaching and learning beginning with the primary level.

As of January 2002, the government had already begun working on full implementation of the Free and Compulsory, Universal Basic Education program (FCUBE)—a commendable effort in an African country.

SECONDARY EDUCATION

Secondary education in Kenya is quite expensive and affordable only by middle- to upper-class citizens. Parents pay up to Ksh30,000 per student per year (*The Economist 1998*). The secondary grades are called *forms* and the curriculum emphasizes academic subjects, especially the sciences and vocational subjects at the upper secondary level. The academic standard of the national and provincial schools is higher than that of the *Harambee* schools in local communities. Similarly, the quality of education in private schools is better than standards in public schools. Kenyan secondary schools have a four-year duration. The entry and exit ages are between fourteen and eighteen years old.

At the end of secondary education, candidates take the second national examination called the Kenyan Certificate of Secondary Education (KSCE). Candidates are graded on a twelve-point scale from A to E. This forms the basis for admission into tertiary institutions and the world of work.

Before the 1980s, Kenya's primary and secondary schools were mostly government owned. Education provided in these public schools was free, but in the 1980s, with their economy deteriorating and government funding to schools reduced drastically, fees were gradually introduced in 2001. Even with that, the fairly high quality of education provided earlier in public primary and secondary schools could hardly be sustained. To revamp the academic standards of schools, the government called for private sponsorship and ownership, the response of which was quite encouraging. Bauer (2002) expressed, "By 2001, there were 700 primary and 300 secondary private schools throughout Kenya." These private schools were quite attractive because of their provision of adequate facilities, laboratories, athletic facilities, and other amenities. Moreover, the quality of education given was quite impressive. According Bauer (2002), the best private primary schools have led the nation in KCPE scores. Although the general public may have been slightly unfamiliar and uncomfortable with the concept of private schools at their inception, it is now readily accepted that private schools can provide superior education. The *Kenyan Star* noted in a January 12, 2002, editorial that since the inception of private schools, especially in urban areas, they have dominated their public counterparts in performance on national examinations. They have turned out to be the shrines of quality education in Kenya churning out top achievers year after year. However, this does not mean that all private schools are of high standards. The quality of private schools in Kenya varies. The Ministry of Education, which issues licenses for the establishment of schools, takes time to inspect such schools. Generally, it can be said that since the year 2000 private schools have gained greater acceptance in Kenya. Table 6.2 shows the number of private and public schools in Kenya as of December 2000.

SPECIAL EDUCATION PROGRAMS

The government of Kenya takes cognizance of its physically challenged citizens. Various educational services are rendered to them and others who are disabled through the Ministries of Education, Health, and Culture and Social

Table 6.2
Private and Public Schools in Kenya

Type of School	Number of Schools
Public primary school	18,000
Private primary school	700
Total	**18,700**
Public secondary school	3,400
Private secondary school	300
Total	**3,700**
Public universities	6
Private universities	7
Total	**13**
Public teaching colleges	21
Private teaching colleges	8
Total	**29**

Source: Ministry of Education, Science and Technology (1987).

Services. Statistics from these ministries show that in 1987, special education programs within the Ministry of Education catered for about 8,000 children in fifty-six special schools and forty-six other integrated programs. Likewise, the Ministry of Culture and Social Services had in place ten vocational and rehabilitation centers.

Essentially, Kenya's special education centers and programs take care of children who are visually impaired, hearing impaired, physically challenged, mentally retarded, maladjusted, and all such children with multiple impairments. It is important to note that this special education program also forms an integral part of each level of formal schooling. Consequently, the educational goals of special education at each stage of learning are as follows:

1. provision of skills and attitudes aimed at rehabilitation;
2. identifying, assessing, and providing early intervention in correcting disabilities, and rehabilitation;
3. promoting awareness of the needs of the disabled and proffering methods of alleviating the effects of various disabilities;
4. promoting an integration of the disabled to formal education and training; and
5. promoting the provision and use of specialized facilities and equipment and suggesting and promoting measures to prevent impairment to limit the incidence of disabilities.

As of 1987, the State had put in place organized special schools and other integrated programs at all schooling levels. Statistics have revealed that between 1985 and 1987 there were about six special residential primary schools and a secondary school for the visually impaired. There is also the Machakos Trade Training Centre and a few others run by voluntary organizations.

For those with hearing impairment, twenty-two residential schools with two units each exist in regular primary schools and two vocational centers. On the average for that period, Kenya was taking care of 2,190 children with hearing disabilities, spread across 245 special training centers and forty integrated regular schools. Those with serious physical disabilities were kept in special homes run by voluntary organizations and other government-assisted voluntary organizations. Others with minor physical disabilities attended integrated schools from home. Finally, mentally retarded children had access to education in sixteen special schools and thirty-two other special units in regular primary schools. Others with multiple impairments attended schools such as the School for the Deaf and Blind at Kabaranet in the Rift Valley Province of Kenya.

Since 1964, Kenya has always had great teacher training plans. The Kenyan Institute of Education was established in 1964. Members of the Institute were pulled from teacher training colleges, the Ministry of Education, the university college, voluntary bodies, and the Kenya National Union of Teachers. The major aim of establishing the Institute was to make it a center of activities for the teaching profession, educational research, and for advisory services to the government, especially in educational matters. In 1968, a research wing was added to the Institute. The research wing was developed to become the Center for Curriculum Development and Research, which has been involved in the planning of various aspects of education such as languages, mathematics, science, and general methods. It also concentrated on the evaluation of teaching materials; new courses and programs; in-service training for teachers; producing, assessing, and evaluation of textbooks; conducting teaching practicum, etc. To date, this Institute has maintained a close link with the Ministry of Education and, in more recent times, tertiary institutions in Kenya.

PRESCHOOL TRAINING PROGRAM

In Kenya, every stage of learning has its specialized teachers. The aim is to produce qualified teachers to achieve the set goals for each cycle of learning. For the preschool level, Kenya's National Centre for Early Childhood Education (NACECE), based at the Curriculum Development Center in Kenya's Institute of Education, works in collaboration with the District Centers for Early Childhood Education (DICECE) to train preschool teachers and develop the curriculum and the syllabi for teachers' courses. Programs for preschool teachers run for two years after which recipients are awarded teacher's certificates. Prerequisite entry for this teacher education program is Kenya's Certificate for Secondary Examination (KCSE). However, sound untrained teachers who are already in the field (working as classroom teachers) and possess a minimum of Kenya's Certificate for Primary Examination (KCPE) are offered in-service training opportunities. The intention of the Kenyan government is to completely phase out untrained teachers in all learning cycles.

BASIC TEACHER EDUCATION PROGRAMS

Teacher education programs for primary school teachers are in-service courses mostly organized by the Ministry of Education, with grants-in-aids from the Bernard Van Leer Foundation, UNICEF, and the Aga Khan Foundation. The training of these teachers is for two years at the end of which candidates are expected to acquire skills and techniques in the teaching of various subjects as well as acquire academic proficiency in the thirteen subjects taught in primary schools. Significantly, a greater part of the training is spent on pedagogy while the other is on content, learning, and practicum. Recipients of the education program are awarded a certificate for any of three grades—P1, P2, or P3, depending on their performance in centrally-set examinations.

SECONDARY TEACHER EDUCATION PROGRAM

Teacher education programs for secondary school teachers are carried out at two levels. There are teacher training colleges where candidates earn a diploma in education in two years. There is also training at the university where students are taught for four years before earning a bachelor's degree in education. For some other graduates who are nonprofessionals in education, they undertake a one-year postgraduate diploma course in education. Importantly, the duration of training is expected to produce quality teachers with proficiency in pedagogy and content. They are expected to teach secondary school students.

PROFESSORIATE IN TERTIARY INSTITUTIONS

Teachers in higher education may not have special training in teacher education but must have a good first-class or second-class (upper) degree in their areas of specialization to teach at the university levels. It is noteworthy that this is the pattern in all former British colonies. In pre-independence Kenya, like other British colonies, universities were supposedly autonomous but at the same time attached to London University and colleges. These institutions had the same entry qualifications and the same curriculum except for some variations that were actually negotiated. However, consensus must be reached with London in terms of examinations and external degree requirements. Such examinations must be supervised by London's external examiners. In other words, the emphasis was more or less on academic qualifications of European or international standards rather than local standards even when such may not have necessarily been suitable for some aspects to African life at home. The struggle to make an African degree acceptable and equal in status to a European degree came much earlier in the West African territories than in East Africa.

Table 6.3
Kenyan Students Abroad in 1963

Africans	1,823
Arabs	12
Asians/Indians	1,477
Europeans	436
Total	**3,748**

Source: Furley and Watson, 1978.

The colonial universities started out as very expensive institutions for upper-class students. Their high academic programs differ very little from those of the typical British university and were considerably divorced from indigenous influences. In effect, research was not linked with the local needs of Africans. Instead, the Eurocentric curricula were unacceptable to African academics who also criticized them.

However, with time in the historical development of higher education in Africa, a period came when Africans who yearned for something more indigenous were able take courses from the Makarere College (earlier affiliated with London). This college actually grew from several existing African colleges. It was open to all Africans from Central Africa, Sudan, and East Africa. Thus, Kenyans were afforded access to higher education. Furley and Watson (1978) noted that in spite of the establishment of a tertiary institution in Nairobi, Kenya, there was a remarkable increase in the number of Kenyans and East Africans generally moving out to overseas universities in their thirst for higher learning (see Table 6.3).

The numbers who went abroad in the early 1950s increased rapidly... to take Kenya in 1947 there were 13 African students from Kenya in Britain, and by 1950, there were 350 Kenyans abroad, either in Britain, America, India or Pakistan. In the late 1950's, the number going overseas from Kenya for higher education rose quite remarkably. Surprisingly too, even with the establishment and expansion of the Royal College in Nairobi, by 1963, the number of Kenyans abroad rose even higher. It was noticed that the African students exceeded the Asians in number. (Kenya Ministry of Education 1961–1963)

Similarly, Symonds (1966) affirmed that between 1961 and 1963 Kenyan Africans abroad doubled from 914 to 1,823. He further asserted that in 1962 there were about 3,800 Kenyans overseas, but four years later there was a decline to 3,600. Furley and Watson (1978) have said that even with this trend in decline, the Ministry of Education was not quite convinced that the development of the secondary school sixth form and access to the nation's university would fully quench the Kenyan thirst for higher education overseas.

However, with the 1966–1970 Development Plan in Kenya, the policy of bonding students in government service may have brought the desired change. The policy states:

Scholarships and bursaries offered by foreign governments could be accepted by the government of Kenya only if they are relevant to Kenya's needs. Students chosen for those awards will be treated in the same manner as students at the University of East Africa, and on their return to Kenya, will be similarly engaged in work in the national interest in Public Service, the Teaching Service or other approved occupations. (1966)

In the final analysis, Kenyans and indeed East Africans were beginning to appreciate their own tertiary institutions and academic programs. The Royal Technical College in Nairobi and Mombassa Institute of Muslim Education were the first institutions to offer higher education in Kenya. The establishment of these institutions also saw the decline of Kenyans in the Makarere College. In 1961, two higher institutions in Kenya were established. The Kenyan Polytechnic in Nairobi offered courses in mechanical, electrical, and civil engineering. Other courses included building, commerce, science, printing and institutional management, and drawing. These programs were offered on full-time, part-time, and even as "sandwich" basis (that is, one semester per year). In 1966, financial assistance came from UNESCO and USAID loans. It expanded the program in terms of equipment and infrastructure and the number of students grew rapidly to about 1,550. The program even incorporated trainees from industries as part of their evening programs. The Kenya's Institute of Public Administration at Kabete commenced at about the same time. It offered courses in administration especially in the training of administrative and executive staff for the civil service, local government, community development, and cooperative service. Other courses included secretarial studies, managerial studies, and the training of district magistrates in public law. In Symonds' (1966) words, "The institute offered the first full professional training in Africa for community development officers."

Today, as a developing African nation, Kenya can boast of more tertiary institutions for its populace. There are about six public universities that have been granted a royal charter by the Commission for Higher Education (CHE) and thirteen private universities mostly owned by religious bodies. Many are affiliated with larger U.S.-based universities whose degrees are also being awarded in the country.

Education in tertiary institutions in Kenya has generally attracted good enrollment. In the public and private universities, enrollment can be roughly estimated at 80 percent in public universities and 20 percent in private universities. Table 6.4 shows statistics of undergraduate enrollment in both public and private universities between 1996–1997 to 1999–2000.

The statistics show private universities have generally maintained a good trend in growth in keeping with public policy on tertiary institutions in relation to opportunities available to Kenyan students. In spite of such growth, the yearning for opportunity in such institutions is largely unsatisfied in view of the limitation. Other reasons that could be adduced for the steady growth of private universities in Kenya are the need to complement government-

Table 6.4
Undergraduate Enrollment in Kenyan Public and Private Universities

	1996–97		1997–98		1998–99		1999–2000	
	M	F	M	F	M	F	M	F
Public Universities								
Nairobi University	10,102	3,558	9,347	3,232	8,976	3,449	8,489	3,440
Kenyatta University	5,520	3,054	4,530	2,613	4,738	3,020	4,189	3,007
Jkuat University	1,818	417	2,556	452	2,471	621	2,512	625
Egerton University	5,445	2,340	5,705	2,331	5,654	2,519	7,132	2,841
Moi University	0	0	3,588	1,363	3,705	1,418	4,136	1,649
Maseno University	1,739	859	1,860	949	2,687	1,312	2,044	1,211
Subtotal	24,624	10,228	27,586	10,940	28,231	12,339	28,502	12,773
Private Accredited								
Daystar University	559	691	565	727	720	961	861	1,417
Baraton University	489	433	470	372	498	454	537	507
Catholic University	569	638	0	0	742	660	807	810
U.S.I.U.	852	901	868	940	902	999	928	1,032
Scott Theological College	65	13	68	14	80	16	84	19
Subtotal	2,534	2,676	1,971	2,053	2,942	3,090	3,217	3,785
Other Private Universities								
Nazarene University	116	82	230	159	200	119	264	154
NEGST	45	39	67	28	68	40	44	46
East	124	15	112	23	106	25	77	20
PAC	90	12	80	13	73	24	85	26
NIST	39	16	53	18	20	9	43	22
KHBC	52	23	37	21	42	27	47	36
St. Paul's T.C.	92	9	92	13	84	15	83	17
Methodist University	0	0	0	0	74	33	103	56
Subtotal	558	196	671	275	667	292	746	377
Total	27,716	13,100	30,228	13,268	31,840	15,721	32,465	16,935

Source: Ministry of Education, Science, and Technology, Statistics Section (2000).

maintained higher institutions and the interest of religious organizations to provide citadels of learning for their adherents.

Funding of Universities

Before the 1970s, university education especially in government-owned institutions was basically free. Thus, all funding came from government. Beginning with the 1991–92 academic year, the government introduced annual fees by way of cost sharing. Besides the bulk from the government, funding of public universities now came from tuition fees, catering, and other incidental charges.

The private universities did not receive any grants-in-aids or funding of any sort from the Kenyan government. They generated substantial income from their institutions, which are mostly profit making. In effect, fees are charged strictly in accordance with standards and quality of education and on the basis of full cost recovery.

Administration in the University

At the helm of university administration in Kenya is the University Council, chaired by a government appointee and other government- and university-appointed members. The University Council is charged with the responsibility of policy formulation guiding faculties and departments, and the appointment of the university's vice chancellor. The University Senate is responsible to the Council in matters pertaining to academics and administration of the university. The University Senate is presided over by the vice chancellor and is dominated by professors and heads of departments who are appointed by the vice chancellor. There are also other appointees representing various boards and interests in the senate. Under the senate, faculty boards and departments oversee and also administer examinations. Except for deans of faculties who are elected by faculty staff and are also members of the university senate, representatives on university councils and all other officers are appointed. Full professors are automatically members of Senate. It is important to note that this pattern is typical of universities in former British colonies like Nigeria and Ghana.

Research and Publication

Besides teaching, which is a major role of the university, Kenyan universities also conduct research and publication. On record, between the 1970s and early 1980s, a great volume of research was carried out at the oldest and biggest public university, the University of Nairobi. The focus of their research work was developmental trends in Africa. One of the biggest constraints in the growth of research and publications in Kenya's university system is a lack of adequate research funds and grants. However, most postgraduate research works enjoy grants (though minimal) from local donors and international organizations. Meanwhile, one can say in terms of qualified researchers, Kenya is still growing.

Other tertiary institutions include six teacher education (diploma-awarding) colleges, twenty other teacher training (certificate-awarding) colleges, four national polytechnics, seventeen institutes of technology, and twenty technical training institutes. All of these are spread across Kenya. A number of government ministries also offer three years of professional training at the diploma level for their midlevel manpower requirements.

The three stages of university programs are

1. *Bachelor's Degree.* Various tertiary institutions offer bachelor's degrees, which are prerequisite for master's and doctorate degrees. At the University of Nairobi in Kenya, bachelor's degrees with honors are obtained in four years, with the exception of veterinary medicine, medicine, and architecture, which span five to six years. The minimum requirement for entry into the bachelor's program is the KCSE (with a minimum of C+ in ten subjects).
2. *Master's Degree.* This is the second stage of tertiary learning. At the University of Nairobi, this program takes one to three years (which is typical), while Kenyatta University offers a two-year master's degree.
3. *Doctorate Degree.* At the University of Nairobi, holders of the master's degrees can obtain a PhD with a minimum of two years' course work, research, and a thesis.

Other university courses grant postgraduate diplomas and certificates or ordinary diplomas and certificates.

An important development in the financing of universities has been the introduction of cost sharing in recent times. In this plan, all Kenyan nationals who are undergraduates in the university are entitled to an annual maximum loan of Ksh1,025, repayable when the student starts working after a grace period. This loan helps to sustain the student while schooling.

NONUNIVERSITY POSTSECONDARY EDUCATION

The institutes of technology provide training for students attaining the KCSE. Education attained here equips the recipient find employment in medium- and large-scale industries. The government also supports educational institutions whose duration of courses range from two to four years. Courses offered include construction, engineering, business studies, textiles, agriculture, accounting, etc. Polytechnics also offer similar programs at the end of which certificates, diplomas, and higher diplomas are earned.

NONTRADITIONAL STUDIES

Kenya, like Tanzania, is aware that a nation cannot wait for its children to become educated before development begins. In line with this thinking,

President Nyerere of Tanzania implemented his mass literacy campaign to raise the literacy rate among adults, as well as the emphasis on formal and nonformal education. It is in the same manner that the Kenyan government laid its own foundation of adult and nonformal education. As far back as 1966, Kenya's government established a Board of Adult Education. The aim was to coordinate the various agencies involved in the adult literacy campaign, such as the East Africa Literature Bureau, the College of Social Studies at Kikuyu (which was renamed the Adult Studies Centre in 1966), and the Extra-mural Department of the University College. In 1967, with the help of UNESCO experts, a renewed literacy campaign began. Thirty-one out of Kenya's forty-one districts were used for the pilot study. About thirty to forty trained literacy teachers were sent to each district. The products were tested in reading passages written in English and Swahili. Success was recorded in this campaign. In 1969, 80,000 students were enrolled in the mass literacy and adult education scheme. By 1970, the scheme was planned to cover the country's remaining ten districts with a total enrollment of 100,000. The major objective was to prevent the isolation of older people who did not have the same advantage of education that their children did. The program was described as one of Kenya's most outstanding efforts (Furley and Watson 1978).

Today, Kenya has not relaxed in her bid to provide educational and literacy opportunities to all. Kenya has distant learning education programs at various levels. Other nonformal education centers include

1. Community Education
2. Continuing Education
3. Cultural Programs
4. Information and Public Relations Programs
5. Leadership and Management Training.

Instruction in these programs is mostly administered by University of Nairobi and Kenyatta University. Postgraduate diplomas and certificates are awarded by the latter.

GIRL-CHILD EDUCATION: INDIGENOUS AND MODERN

In traditional Kenya, parents vehemently denied education to their girls. A major reason for this reluctance is the economic roles played by females. Leaving the home for school would put a big burden on the economic sustenance of the homestead. Another reason for refusing females access to education was the expectation that the missionaries would implant in their girls the idea of monogamy. That too may cause them to reject polygamy. In the opinion of some Kikuyu elders, this Christian idea could further weaken the economic structure of the traditional society. In effect, a home with many women increased not just the number of children in the family, but also the hands available to perform farm and house work.

However, between 1873 and 1913, the Catholic Mission and some Protestant groups pitched their tents in East Africa. Their aim was to introduce and promote education for Kenyan girls. Teaching in their schools was quite practical with a strong bias towards domestic science. The education of girls would prepare them for marriage. The curriculum content included lessons in cooking, sewing, home crafts, and laundry work. Significantly, the curriculum aim was a reflection of the economic aspect of indigenous education for girls. Even at that, the local people opposed it strongly.

Between 1913 and 1917, the missions had made their mark in the Nyanza area of Kenya, even though the number of boys was more than that of girls. Generally, embracing education for the Kenyan girl-child may have been quite slow and hesitant at the beginning, but with time, the Arab and African races took a greater interest in sending their daughters to school for training in Western ways. Old customs die hard with the Kikuyu people; it took time and patience to allay their suspicion that Western education would not destroy their old ways.

At the turn of the twentieth century, the growth of mission schools especially in the densely populated areas of Kikuyu and Nyanza had increased tremendously. The Church Missionary Society and other religious organizations had established over 250 central and out-station schools. There was also a girls' boarding school at Kahukua that was described by the Phelps-Stokes Committee as "the best-planned institution for native girls in East Africa" (Phelps-Stokes Commission).

In the late 1920s to early 1930, Kenyans were becoming more appreciative of the need for formal education as was evident in the establishment of more schools. In their demand for this, the Kikuyu Association in 1923 sent a memorandum to the Hilton Young Commission. Their request was for the establishment of schools in every area of Kenya so that more Kenyan children could attend. This would include their female children. As explicitly put by the Kukuyu, "There has to be sufficient educated girls to be wives to these educated boys." This enthusiasm may have been borne out of the fact that, at this period, there were more Asian and European girls than African girls in Kenyan schools. The indigenous Kenyan parents then realized the need to change their stiff opposition because their young daughters ran to the mission schools solely for shelter and escape from their parents' persecution. Education for these escapees was generally secondary. In time, many became comfortable with schooling.

However, with time and increased grant-in-aids from the government and local councils, the missions expanded girls' education in Kenya. In 1928, the church of Scotland Mission at Kikuyu had on its attendance roll fifty-six girls in their boarding schools; by 1930, the number had increased to ninety-six. The program was quite elementary and lasted four years. They were taught homemaking, mother crafts, needlework, cookery, and hygiene. At the end of the program, girls who excelled took another year of advanced study for training as teachers. As of 1931, statistics showed a total of 40,000 Arab and African girls in schools all over Kenya. However, this figure, especially for African girls, diminished as a result of the revolt of the indigenous people against the missionaries. They accused the mission schools of preaching and teaching against Kikuyu traditional practices of female circumcision. This led to mass withdrawal of African members from churches and their children from mission schools. The renewed demand for schools was directed at government schools. There was indeed an obvious disparity in the attendance of boys and girls. This disparity led Phillip (1936) to cry out that "tragic results will follow if the education of the African woman does not develop on parallel lines with that of her husband." Somehow, this was not the case with other East African countries like Tanganyika (Tanzania) and Uganda. Those countries did not allow financial constraints or any other hindrance for that matter to mar their girls' access to education.

The trend of low enrollment of girls in Kenyan schools continued. Following the recommendations from the Phelps-Stokes and the Binns reports, which identified the long-standing problem of the low female population in Kenyan schools, there was only a mere endorsement of the efforts that were already being made. No new initiative was made.

Again in 1961, at the request of the governments of Kenya and Great Britain, IBRD undertook a survey of Kenya's economic development. Girl-child education was one of the problems revisited. The low enrollment of girls in schools was again identified. However, in Skinner's critical review (1963), the World Bank survey may have done a good job with the compilation of statistics, thereby making the survey a useful reference source, but it failed to integrate studies of the various sectors of the developing economy into a cohesive plan. In other words, the World Bank survey provided a description of past accomplishments rather than a dynamic prescription for the future. Thus, the problem of female access to education in Kenya suffered yet another setback and feasible recommendation.

Even in more recent times, the issue of low female enrollment in Kenyan education is still a major problem. In his assessment of gender imbalance at the tertiary level, Ngome (2003) has recognized that the proportion of female enrollment declines as they move up the ladder. As a result, female students make up about 30 percent of the total enrollment in public universities. In other words, female students in Kenya's public universities are underrepresented. Ngome goes on further to affirm that gender parity is more evident in all accredited private universities. He put the total percent of enrollment between 1999 and 2000 at 54.5 percent. His assessment of this figure is relatively high when compared to the situation in public universities. What this shows is that most females enroll in private universities because they fail to secure admission in the public universities.

Generally, the campaign for increased female enrollment in education and the imbalance against the girl-child's access to education is a contemporary problem in Kenya. For example, a recent campaign in 2003 on "Hands up for Girls' Education" contributed immensely to increase girls' enrollment in the Kibera schools in Kenya.

MAJOR EDUCATION REFORMS IN KENYA

Education in Kenya is based on an 8-4 system. This has been in existence since the late 1980s. The Kenyan child is expected to have eight years of primary education, followed by four years of secondary school, and four years of tertiary schooling in a college or university.

In 1963, the Kenyan government promised free education to its people. This promise became feasible in 2003 with the arrival of the National Rainbow Coalition Government. With free basic education, classrooms became overcrowded and teachers conducted classes outdoors. Statistics have shown that the teacher-to-pupil ratio was 1:80 and sometimes 1:90. Even though this has increased the workload of teachers, it is obvious from statistics that about 1.7 million Kenyan children who hitherto had no access to primary education were enrolled in 2003. In a statement by Kenya's Education, Science and Technology Minister, George Saitioti (2005) stated that since the introduction of free primary education, the number of pupils who took certificate of primary education exams increased from 587,961 to 657,747—that is, a 12 percent increase. This, he claimed, is the highest increase to be recorded in past decades.

The question now is: In addressing one educational problem of introducing free basic education for all Kenya's children, has the government not created another problem? For one thing, Kenya's secondary education is not easy. This is because public secondary schools are few and private ones are quite expensive. These are not easily affordable by most families. In fact, the initial intent was an eight-year duration in primary school that would be terminal for most pupils. Recent government statistics indicate that since the introduction of free primary education, pupils who graduated from the 17,600 government-run primary schools could not get accommodated in Kenya's 4,000 public secondary schools. Consequently, most recipients of the primary school certificate were unable to enter the few available secondary schools. They have therefore abandoned formal schooling at the end of their primary schooling. Parents, who were financially able, sent their children to private fee-based secondary schools.

The government has recognized the new challenge created by the free primary education scheme and is seriously working on further reforms for addressing the issue of providing more secondary schools. Francis Ng'anga, the secretary general of Kenya's National Union of Teachers, stated, "It is in our interest to see every Kenyan child complete primary education and get a chance to get access to secondary education." A plea was also directed to parents to assist in the establishment and expansion of secondary schools. In other words, Kenyan parents have been asked to actually play a major role in building more secondary school facilities. This would enable their children complete primary educations and facilitate entry to the secondary schools automatically in the same premises, if possible. However, the government is aware of the high poverty rate in Kenya, where nearly half of the population lives below the poverty line. Most families have just enough to meet their basic needs with little or nothing extra to spare. It is in recognition of this that the Kenya government has taken on the huge financial commitment of providing teachers instructional materials, salary subsidies, and other financial grant-in-aids. It has also called on communities to help in the provision and expansion of secondary schools.

At the tertiary level, the Kenyan government has revisited the status of polytechnics. They have come to realize that part of the solution to postsecondary education is to popularize polytechnic education. There is indeed the urgent need to give polytechnics an enhanced status and prestige. This would include a review of the polytechnic curriculum to give it a new meaning and direction. For one thing, most Kenyan parents are quite reluctant to send their wards to polytechnics because those institutions are seen as inferior. They are of the opinion that polytechnics teach mere practical skills rather than the prestigious academic courses. The fear is that their wards may end up in blue-collar jobs.

So far, the reform in this sector centers on making the polytechnic curriculum more attractive. In terms of prestige, it is hoped that it will entice people to acquire skills, earn good income, and make their graduates self-employed. Also, there is the need to improve some decaying infrastructural facilities and introduce computer technology to polytechnic programs.

Another educational issue earmarked for urgent attention is in the university sector. Although Kenya has its own public and private universities, most parents still send their children abroad for tertiary educations. This is a result of the high demand for higher education. There are few public universities and most are inadequately equipped: many have poorly equipped laboratories, fewer computers, and other teaching aids. These facility inadequacies have made the private universities more attractive and thriving for those who can afford their fees.

All the same, even though Kenya's government may be slow in its educational reforms, especially when one considers the poor economic state the country is in, the government still strives hard to improve its education system. Presently, with some functional support from the government of the United Kingdom, primary education is gradually attaining a more qualitative status and becoming accessible to most Kenyan children. Such financial aid has also improved health programs in schools; helped with the purchase of school books and other learning equipment, and facilities including some reconstruction of class rooms; and helped provide water and better sanitary conditions for children in public primary and secondary schools. More financiers' investments in the expansion of secondary and tertiary institutions has been undertaken. Hopefully too, with the financial support from other advanced countries and organizations, Kenya will continue to improve its institutions in order to raise the economic and social lives of its people.

BIBLIOGRAPHY

Anderson, J. E. 1970. *The Struggle for the School: the Interaction of Missionary Colonial Government and Nationalist Enterprises in the Development of Formal Education in Kenya*. London: Longman.

Datta, A. 1984. *Education and Society: A Sociology of African Education*. New York: St. Martins Press.

Furley, O. W., and T. Watson. 1978. *A History of Education in East Africa*. New York: NOK Publishers.

Godfrey, E. M. "The Economics of an African University." *Journal of Modern African Studies* 4 (1966): 436.

Hailey, L. 1957. *An African Survey*. London: Oxford University Press.

Kagia, J. *Integration of Education, Health and Care for the Total Development of the Child*. Paper presented at a seminar on Early Childhood Education in Kenya: Implications on Policy and Practice, Mombasa, Aug. 31–Sept. 4, 1987.

Kenya Ministry of Education. *Triennial Survey, 1961–1963*.

Kenyatta, Jomo. 1965. *Facing Mount Kenya: The Tribal Life of the Kikuyu*. London: Secker and Warburg.

Kipkorir, L. I. *Innovations in Early Childhood Education and Care—The Kenyan Experience*. Paper presented at a Seminar on Early Childhood Education in Kenya: Implications on Policy and Practice, Mombasa, Aug. 31–Sept. 4, 1987.

LeVine, R. A., and B. B. LeVine. 1963. "Nyansongo: A Gusii Community in Kenya." In *Six Cultures; Studies of Child Rearing*. Edited by B. B. Whiting. New York: John Wiley and Sons.

Ministry of Education, Science and Technology. 1984a. *Republic of Kenya: Early Childhood Education Programme. The DICECE component, 1985–1989*. Nairobi, Kenya: Ministry of Education.

Ministry of Education, Science and Technology. 1984a. *Under Lines for Preschool Education in Kenya*. Nairobi, Kenya: Jomo Kenyatta Foundation.

Ministry of Education, Science and Technology. 1987. *Education in Kenya, Information Handbook*. Nairobi, Kenya: Jomo Kenyatta Foundation.

Moumouni, A. 1968. *Education in Africa*. London: Andre Deutsch.

Ngome, C. 2003. "Higher Education in Kenya." In *African Higher Education: An International Reference Handbook*. Edited by D. Teferra and P. C. Altbach. Bloomington: Indiana University Press.

Ogot, B. A. "British Administration in the Central Nyanza District of Kenya." *Journal of African History* 4, no. 3 (1963).

Phelps-Stoke Commission Report.

Prewitt. 1971. *Education and Political Values: An East African Case Study*. Nairobi, Kenya: East African Publishing House.

Sheffield, J. R. 1973. *Education in Kenya: A Historical Study*. New York: Columbia University, Teachers' College Press.

Ward, W. E. F. 1967. *Educating Young Nations*. London: Allen & Unwin.

Chapter 7

SCHOOLING IN NIGERIA

INTRODUCTION

By virtue of its population, size, and material resources, Nigeria stands out as a leading African nation in many ways. In spite of its mixed record as a democracy, it has played a leading role in mediating several political crises in and outside Africa. Economically, its record of success is maximally low and hence some have euphemistically referred to Nigeria as the sleeping giant of Africa (Iyoha 2005).

With a population of about 150 million occupying a land area of about 922,768 square kilometers endowed with rich mineral and agricultural resources, the country has yet to maximize its huge potentials to the benefit its citizens in terms of overcoming poverty. It has been claimed that every fifth African in the world is a Nigerian. It is also true that Nigeria is currently the sixth oil-exporting country in the world. The country is endowed with mineral resources such as coal, bauxite, and tin, while its agricultural products include cocoa, rubber, groundnuts, palm oil, rice, and other crops produced for local consumption and export. "Indeed, it is estimated that over US$300 billion has been earned by Nigeria from oil over the last thirty years. ... Recently, it has been said that private wealth of Nigerians in overseas accounts is of the order of US$107 billion or more" (Anya 2003). Yet nearly 70 percent of Nigerians are estimated to be poor and each living on US$1.00 per day United Nations Development Programme ([UNDP] 1998).

The state of the Nigerian economy has been blamed on the poor quality of political and public service leadership. The outcome of the mismanagement of the economy has accounted for the high unemployment and poverty since the 1970s when an atmosphere of criminality and social vices became the hallmark of military rule in Nigeria (Anya 2003).

Occasionally, sectarian violence has erupted in different parts of the country between Christians and Muslims. Such incidents have led to a sense of insecurity among the people, many of whom have suffered some losses, including lives and property. Religious fundamentalism, not unrelated to the high illiteracy among the masses, has been blamed for this social malaise. Even though some leaders of Christian and Muslim communities have generally tried to resolve their differences when these disturbances take place, the causes generally have had some political undertone. The educational gap between the predominantly Muslim north and the mostly Christian south has been a sore point in relations. It has its roots in the historical evolution of Nigeria. Unfortunately, the trend has not abated as more children are in school in the south than in the north.

Politically, Nigeria has had a checkered history of political misadventure initiated by the first line of political leaders whose corrupt practices shortly after independence led to military intervention. After several decades of military autocracy, Nigerians have concluded that their country, like India, would have been better off politically without a dictatorship. The social and political instability coupled with its economy malaise could be put squarely at the doorstep of the military politicians who institutionalized corruption and political instability in a state of affairs that has continued to bedevil the nation to date. The most unfortunate aspect of this misadventure in governance is the involvement of some academic politicians whose debased connivance with the military in their misrule is equally reprehensible. These military apologists are hardly welcome in Nigerian campuses these days. To say the least, the marriage of the military and academic elite in the governance of Nigeria is at the root of the country's problems.

In the light of this, where does education come in? In view of the paradoxical situation in which Nigeria has found itself, we are prompted to raise the question about what difference education really makes within the context of the enigma called man (Omatseye 2003). If the Nigerian elite who criticized the colonial administrators of underdeveloping their country have been part of a failed system of governance in terms of leadership, the value of education is inevitably called into question. Education as cultural and intellectual heritage ought to bring out the best in us in terms of social and economic advancement of the society.

Although the literacy rate in Nigeria is about 70 percent, Nigeria can boast of a large pool of highly qualified professionals in all fields of study at home and abroad, although some of these Nigerians have generally excelled more abroad than at home. Former U.S. President Bill Clinton once described Nigerian professionals as excellent. When some have attributed these problems to a so-called Nigerian factor, what this really means is nothing but nepotism. Things would really have improved if the right persons were put in the right positions in spite of their ethnic or social backgrounds.

If natural and human resources were not in short supply in Nigeria, something else must be missing to account for the country's seeming retrogressive or slow pace of development. A strong-willed leadership in the political and moral spheres, backed and nurtured by appropriate education, can certainly be identified as the missing link. Consequently, the neglect of education (not mere literacy) by the country's political leaders is an offshoot responsible for the state of underdevelopment. Somehow, some economically less endowed countries in Africa have realized the power of education in relation to economic development and have done more than Nigeria. Such is reflected in their budgetary allocation to education when compared to Nigeria.

Beyond the regional differences in the growth of education, there is also a wide gap between the very rich and the very poor in Nigeria. The implication is that lower-class and middle- to upper-class children end up in different schools. In general, the poor children find themselves in government schools with dilapidated classrooms, poorly motivated staff, and ill-equipped facilities with little or no materials to work with. However, children from affluent homes attend the high-brow, fee-based schools with state-of-the-art equipment and highly motivated teachers whose salaries and other incentives are better.

The good federal government secondary schools otherwise called "Unity Schools" that for decades provided some succor for all bright children, including those from lower socioeconomic backgrounds, are gradually out of reach for the poor, whose performances in the government entrance examinations are no longer a match for the rich children from private primary schools. With a drop in funding to these special schools, spread all over the Nigerian federation, the quality is not what it used to be. Indeed, as the gap between the affluent and the poor grows wider in Nigeria, so does access to quality education for the less privileged.

With state funding becoming insufficient, each family is constrained to pay for whatever quality of education they can afford for their children. The agitation for resource control by the oil-producing states against the federal government can be traced to the high level of poverty among the people of that region. It is an irony that fewer educational opportunities are available to the children from whose backyard the nation's wealth is produced.

It is not surprising that the situation has now led to insurgency in the Niger Delta area. Although the Nigerian government bears a good portion of the blame, the multinational corporations would seem not to have done enough to satisfy the yearnings of the host communities in terms of improving their educational facilities and providing jobs to raise their standard of living. What is most reprehensible is that many of these oil-producing communities lack water supplies and electricity because of the negligence of the state and multinational corporations who tap their gas and petroleum resources. To the extent that effective leadership and the spread of economic opportunities remain a hindrance, educational development in Nigeria will continue to be slow.

SOCIAL AND HISTORICAL CONTEXT

After almost a century of forging unity among the various ethnic and linguistic groups that make up present-day Nigeria, the task has proved most daunting. Before amalgamation, most ethnic nationalities were part of the old Mali, Ghana, and Songhai Empires and then the ancient Benin and Warri Kingdoms, which date as far back as five centuries. From North Africa down to the south of the Sub-Saharan regions, each of these empires had their own system of government, not unlike that of ancient Egypt from which some of them had historical links or drew inspiration or inheritance. These kingdoms were administered by a hierarchy of princes and chiefs whose citizens were exposed to traditional African education before their contact with Europeans in the south and the Muslim invasion from North Africa. Although various cultural artifacts constitute Africa's documentation of trends in the absence of any written scripts, the oral tradition was efficient and reliable at the time. Therefore, it was surprising to the early European explorers to meet a fairly sophisticated system of governance in the "dark" continent in the sixteenth century during their visit to the Benin and Warri Kingdoms in the south.

After one hundred years, when the European missionaries came back shortly after the industrial revolution in Europe and the end of the slave trade, the kingdoms were still in place and better organized to do business with them around 1807. Missionary activities, followed by commercial and colonial adventures, were propelled by the 1885 balkanization of Africa by European powers—an action that later led to the amalgamation of many ethnic nationalities from these kingdoms and empires that were already being broken into several countries, one of which is present-day Nigeria. Out of the current fifty-three countries in Africa, only five—Egypt, Ethiopia, Liberia, Libya, and South Africa—were not under colonial rule in 1955. The European countries that profited from the balkanization of Africa were Britain, Belgium, France, Portugal, and Spain. For nearly sixty years, Nigeria, like the rest, fought for its independence before it was achieved in 1960.

Before the amalgamation of the then-northern Nigerian territory with the south in 1914, Islam had taken hold in the north, which resisted the influence of missionary education. The gap created as a result of the rejection of Christian education in the north has not only remained but also has worsened the situation. This imbalance has remained a bone of contention between the two regions. The implications are social and political. The recent wave of Islamic fundamentalism has not helped the situation as more schooling at all levels in the south is perpetuating the imbalance, while the north is still moving slowly. It must be said that the effort of some northern elite to promote education beyond the Quranic school level has been met with strong cultural resistance backed by religious fundamentalism. It is against this background that three types of education—traditional, Muslim, and Western—have existed in Nigeria.

TRADITIONAL EDUCATION

Traditional education precedes Muslim and Western education in the life of the African child because he is born into it. When he is eventually introduced to Muslim or Western education, the process of blending begins. The average child has the advantage of being taught in their mother tongue; that is, the language of the ethnic group spoken in rural communities where 70 percent of Nigerians live. In addition to that, pidgin English (an adulterated form of the English language) is spoken mostly in the urban areas, along with Yoruba in the southwest, Igbo in the southeast, and Hausa in the north. Although English remains Nigeria's lingua franca, there are over two hundred other languages and dialects spoken in the country.

Like most African countries, whatever cultural differences exist cannot be viewed as major because of the blurring effect of such diversity by the educational process and urbanization. For as one pundit puts it, in old Africa, the warriors, the hunter, the noble men of character, or anyone who combined the latent features with a specific skill was adjudged to be a well-educated and well-integrated citizen of his community (Fafunwa 1974). Education in the traditional African society is never considered an end in itself but a means to an end. Hence, functionalism has generally remained the most reliable yardstick for determining the usefulness of education.

Within the context of African cosmology, the homogeneity of being does not allow for the fragmentation of an institutional relationship as long as a positive outcome is achieved. In other words, the social, political, economic, and religious institutions are inseparably intertwined with education (Omatseye 1978). This pragmatic concept of human relations makes social responsibility, justice, fairness, and equity the hallmark of African communalism. To that extent, participation in group activities is mandatory in traditional education because the African child is expected to learn through communal activities. Such activities as ceremonies, recitation, demonstration, fishing, and farming are only a few of the numerous initiation activities that he must be involved with to move from one level of traditional education to another until he graduates into manhood. The same is also true for girls, though in different activities defined by the community.

Indigenous education has been defined as … the aggregate of all the processes by which other forms of behavior which are of positive value to society, a process of transmitting culture for continuity and growth, dissemination of knowledge to ensure social control or a rational direction of society. (Fafunwa 1974)

Due to the extreme importance that African tradition places on succession and inheritance, childbearing is a cardinal aspiration of the family. The absence of a male child in the traditional society is viewed as a bad omen. Inasmuch as the girl child is appreciated, the fanfare that characterizes the celebration and merriment in the naming ceremony of a child, especially a male, speaks volumes of the values attached to children. The meaning as well as significance attached to inheritance dates back to the time of ancestral worship—a situation that even Western education has not altered significantly. Indeed, childlessness can still be viewed in African society as a vacuum in one's life.

Age Grouping

For the purpose of effective education and skill acquisition, grouping of children according to their age has importance because seniority confers social and economic privileges on individuals in the community. Old age in Africa is assumed to confer wisdom on the elderly. As a sage, the oldest man in any community automatically assumes the headship. Symbolically, he must therefore be consulted by other leaders about important decisions concerning the people. As children grow older, they move from one age group to another in the hierarchy after meeting certain conditions through educational processes; usually, ritual ceremonies characterize their upward mobility toward manhood or womanhood.

Traditional Curriculum

With the multilateral objective of producing an honest, respectable, skilled, cooperative, and conforming individual, the curriculum of traditional education is complex. It consists of physical training, character development, respect for elders and peers, intellectual training, interest in poetry and prophetic skills and oracles, vocational and agricultural training, and community participation and promotion of cultural heritage (Fafunwa 1974). Because these activities take place in formal and informal settings, all adults in the community are considered teachers in the system. It is every adult's obligation to teach every child what he or she needs to know. Aspects of the traditional African curriculum include:

1. *Physical Training.* The set of outdoor activities that takes place is characterized by playful exercise of sensory and motor apparatus resulting in the adaptation of the individual child to his environment. Imitative play consisting of the representation of adult daily activities focuses on the social aspiration of the child toward adulthood. Competitive games that test the physical, intellectual, and social qualities of the child rounds up this component of indigenous education. (Raun 1940)

2. *Character Development.* The moral aspect of life as a well-sought virtue is imbibed from the environment of the child's home and community. This aspect is exemplified more in adult behavior than it is taught. Adults who must live exemplary lives would have less to say because their lives ought to speak louder than their voices to the children. Elders in the community have a responsibility to impart their code of morals, manners, and decorum to the young. Adults who fail to comply are considered a source of shame to their families and will lose the respect of the young ones. Children are also taught to respect age or seniority in their relationship with others. Hence, greeting and salutations among ethnic groups like the Yoruba and Hausa tend to be elaborately respectful. Indeed, Africans have different types of greetings to match every occasion, be it resting, working, eating, or having fun.

3. *Mental Development.* An adult African who is well grounded in his language would hardly make a speech, short or long, without injecting a proverb or an

adage or metaphor into it. This is learned from childhood by listening to the elders during conversation. Riddles, storytelling, poetry, recitations, and a host of other forms of instruction are learned by children in the course of growing up in the community. Africa's oral tradition is replete with these intellectual activities, which Western education has yet to integrate into the school curriculum.

4. *Human Resource Development.* Vocational training in traditional African education through the apprenticeship system is at the heart of all activities in the community. Before the advent of Western education, the average male child was an apprentice to his father in whatever trade or vocation he engaged in. Therefore, it was usual for a family to lay claim to the secret of certain trades or crafts such as hunting, carving, smith work, brass making, herbal medicine, and a host of other skills and expertise.

5. *Social Cultural Heritage.* In the context of the oral tradition, African cultural heritage is transmitted from generation to generation through religious rites, burial rites, marriage ceremonies, and different annual festivals. A Nigerian educator once described this cultural heritage as exemplified more in behavior than taught. (Fafunwa 1974)

ISLAMIC EDUCATION

Although Islamic education predates Western education in Nigeria, the influence of the former, especially in the north, has done very little to reduce the high illiteracy rate in that region. In contrast, the early influence of Christian or Western education in the south has accounted for the higher literacy and educational development of the region. The educational imbalance between the predominantly Muslim north and the Christian south has been a constant flash point in Nigerian political relations.

The difference in worldview held by the two faiths is such that education is considered subservient to religion in Islam while Christians tend to view education as an instrument for understanding and enhancing their faith. According to Von Grunebaum, an Islamist, education is primarily intended "to pilot man toward salvation rather than self improvement" (El-Garh 1971). Much of what constitutes the purpose of education in Islam, as derived from various interpretations of the Holy Quran, has to do with what man must learn for the good of his religion and shun what is not required. Although this interpretation is disputed by some Islamic scholars, it appears to have had some negative effect on the literacy rate among the country's Muslim population. The current drive is to integrate Quranic studies in Arabic into a Western-type education to bring about a reasonable balance in the Nigerian mainstream.

In spite of the politics of Islamic education, especially in the North, many northern leaders since independence have fought hard to persuade their citizens to embrace Western education to enjoy the social and economic benefits associated with such attainment. Shortly before independence, the first prime minister, Sir Abubakar Tafawa Balewa, took on the emirs in the north whose cooperation was lacking in sending children to school in that region. He also challenged his people to allow their daughters to attend the few available schools. Part of the resistance of most northerners at the time was the fear that their children would be converted to Christianity (Omatseye 1978). Although the illiteracy rate is higher in the north than in the south, the situation is even worse among Muslim girls and women, many of whom are hardly allowed out of their homes. Although the situation is now better than what it was, there is much more to be done in this regard.

It is quite encouraging to know that many state governors in the north have started to offer free education to girls in the region. The increasing number of girls in their classrooms is a radical departure from the past when only boys were allowed to attend the Quranic schools where learning consisted mainly of copying and memorizing selected texts of the Quran. Although it is considered that Nigeria's governance has been dominated by the northern elite since independence, it is difficult to understand why the education imbalance between the south and the north continues to exist. The only possible rational explanation would be the strong impact of Islam and Islamic culture. A leading politician of the north once told a gathering of stakeholders in education how his father opted to go to prison than allow him to go to school. It was preferred that he become a herdsman tending his father's cattle. Almost in tears, he told his audience that his two daughters had respectively graduated in medicine and law that year. Therefore, one is hopeful that some change is taking place, though slowly. As more states in the north integrate Quranic studies into the mainstream, Islamic education like traditional education can provide added value to the overall development of education in the country.

WESTERN EDUCATION

In Nigeria's history, Christian education was equated with Western education. For one, Christian missionaries initiated formal schooling with the sole aim of converting natives to Christianity. Literacy was needed to enable converts to read the Bible and serve as priests in the churches. When the British later took over the governance of the country, the purpose of education was modified in order to turn out clerks, interpreters, and lower-level manpower for their administration and commercial ventures. From the very beginning, care was taken by the colonialists not to overeducate the African who might then aspire to higher civil service positions. The focus was on primary education only because it was cheap and easy to operate.

Because the acquisition of some literacy was the primary objective of colonial education, vocational, scientific, and technical skills received little or no attention. Whatever practical skills were available to the Nigerian child during the colonial era were incidental and limited in scope. When a few educated African political leaders realized that they must take their own destiny in their hands, they used the limited opportunity available to them to provide some skills needed by their people. The inclination toward the arts was due to its less expensive nature. It was cheaper to teach religious studies, history, or literature than science and technology, for which a laboratory, workshop, and equipment would be needed. Leach observed:

Missionaries had to come with [L]atin service—book in hand and the [L]atin grammar in another hand. Not only had the native priest been taught the tongue in which his services were to be performed, but converts...had to be taught elements of grammar before they could be taught elements of religion. So the grammar school became in theory, as much in fact, the necessary anteroom, the vestibule of the church. (1969)

Although Christian education initially opened up opportunities for Nigerians in terms of social mobility, the missionaries' shortcomings may not have been deliberate compared to the colonial administrations who were bent on keeping out from civil service the few educated Nigerians that they saw as potential rivals. The paucity of secondary school education and the rarity of opportunity in tertiary institutions were viewed as evidence of this unwritten but obvious policy in education. As Nigeria gravitated toward independence and obstacles to upward mobility were disappearing, the European administrators bowed to the inevitable.

The European, seeing his position of dominance crumbling, challenged at every turn, is visibly frustrated at his own inability to prevent a downward revision of his position in the new structures, he may resort to excessive and bitter criticism of Nigerians, often for faults which he is unwilling to recognize in himself. (Smyth and Smyth 1960)

What the missionaries and the imperial powers had in common was the notion that elements of African culture, as evident in indigenous education and its system of governance, were not worth incorporating into Western education to which Africans were exposed. Fernandez has referred to this phenomenon as "the spiritual imperialism of Christian missionaries" (1964). This lack of respect for "the savage pagan who must be converted, baptized and saved against his own will" did not do any credit to the missionaries. It is also speculated that the element of coercion in the conversion of some Africans in Christian schools was not imitated by British administrators who took over from the Christian workers.

Advent of British Education Ordinance Number 3 of 1887 for the Colony of Lagos gave Nigerian education a formal statutory status. Proclamation Number 19 of 1903, based on the English education system, became applicable in the Protectorate of Southern Nigeria. These and similar legislative acts provided the framework for the development of education in Nigeria before its independence in 1960.

Although the foundation of formal education was established by Christian missions, Nigeria has no state religion. Its deliberate policy of the separation of state and religion does not make it an irreligious state because the church and mosque have generally provided the spiritual ennoblement of the nation by insisting that fairness, truth, and justice, guided by divine ethics, be part of the educational experience in Nigeria.

EDUCATION FOR SELF-DETERMINATION

As Nigerians anticipated their political emancipation in the 1950s, three political parties emerged to control the three regional governments in addition to the central one in Lagos. The Northern People's Congress (NPC) (a Hausa-Fulani party) took control of the northern region while the Action Group (AG) and the National Council of Nigeria and Cameroon (NCNC) were in charge of the western and eastern regions, respectively, in the south. The two regional governments in the south placed the highest priority on education. In 1955, the government of the western region introduced a free universal and compulsory education, otherwise named the Universal Primary Education (UPE). The proposal included a massive teacher-training program and facilities for modern secondary schools. Six years after the introduction of this scheme, enrollment rose from 36 percent to 90 percent with nearly all children of school age in school.

Two years after the introduction of UPE, the government of the eastern region introduced free education as well but with less success due to financial constraints. It was later modified to make the first three years of primary school free and the last three for fee based. In both regions, secondary schools charged very modest fees. While the two regional governments in the south carried on their competition to offer free education, the north was unable to join in due to financial constraints. They were more concerned about promoting education in the rural areas and adult literacy than with universal primary education.

The imbalance in educational spread between the two major regions of Nigeria was due not only to the acceptance of Western education in the south but also to the north's inability to participate in the competition started in the south. Indeed, the competition still has not stopped because more universities are springing up in the south today than in the north. The number of applicants for the university spaces is also greater in the south.

CHALLENGES, CHANGES, AND REFORMS

As a multi-ethnic country, Nigeria has always grappled with the challenges of disunity especially on political and economic issues. Although education is viewed as a force of unity, it has not always been successful as a way of overcoming cultural differences in the country. The outbreak of its civil war towards the end of the 1960s was an indication of the constant threat to the country's survival as a nation. It was against this background that many stakeholders in Nigerian education gathered for the country's first national curriculum

conference. The aim was to provide a framework for the review and harmonization of existing curricula, policies, and educational practices in all the states of
the federation. Occurring at the time when the Nigerian civil war was raging
against the then-Biafran rebels, the conference adopted "national unity" as its
theme.

Among other recommendations, a national policy on education with a 6-3-
3-4 structure was adopted. A student would spend six years in primary, three in
junior secondary, three in senior secondary, and four years on a typical bachelor's degree in the university. Other courses in some professions would usually
take a maximum of six years. Colleges of education and polytechnic certificate
and diploma courses take between two to four years.

In all government primary schools across the country, no fees are charged
except in private schools (and are relatively expensive in view of their quality).
A recent government policy has extended basic education to cover all junior
secondary schools. This means that fees are no longer charged in government
junior secondary schools. As usual, modest fees are still charged in public senior
secondary schools.

At the conference, education was reaffirmed as the responsibility of all levels
of government—local, state, and federal. Although primary education is statu-
torily the responsibility of local and state governments, there is a lot of involvement by the federal authority in the area of financing. Teachers' emoluments
come from the federation account to the states. Provision of infrastructure,
equipment, books, materials, and maintenance is handled at the state and local
levels. Even then, some states are unable to adequately meet the educational
needs of their citizens.

Although states and individual organizations can now own tertiary institutions, including universities, approval and accreditation requirements set by the
various supervising agencies of the central government must be met. Postprimary institution graduates must pass at least six subjects in national examinations organized by the West African Examination Council (WAEC) or the
National Examination Commission (NECO) to be issued a certificate acceptable to employers or university admissions.

CONTROL AND FUNDING OF EDUCATION

Through its statutory agencies, the government formulates policies that
guide the education system. The National Council on Education (NCE) constitutes the highest policy-making body in the country. The NCE is chaired by
the minister of education and has all state commissioners of education and representatives of all education parastatals and universities in attendance. Issues
handled by the NCE would generally have been discussed at the Joint Consultative Committee on Education (JCCE). The overriding policy of government
on education is in the National Policy on Education (NPE), a document that
came out of the 1969 conference discussed earlier. This policy has been

reviewed to reflect some changes and reforms being implemented. The policy which has sustained successive national development plans has the following tenets:

That Nigeria is/has

1. a free and democratic society;
2. a just and egalitarian society;
3. a united, strong, and self-reliant nation;
4. a great and dynamic economy; and
5. a land of bright and full opportunities for all citizens.

Bearing in mind the tendency toward disunity, the policy has articulated the integration of the individual into a sound and effective citizenry through the educational process. It would also create and facilitate opportunity for all Nigerians at the primary, secondary, and tertiary levels within and outside the country. Education, as espoused by the policy, must inculcate in the individual respect for human dignity, and the promotion of emotional, physical, and psychological health of all children (Federal Republic of Nigeria 2004). As beautifully crafted as the policy is, its implementation has not been done with enough dedication and professionalism. Critics are of the opinion that so far civil service inefficiency and underfunding have undermined its effectiveness.

The issue of education funding has become politicized because of the over-whelming power the federal government has in terms of disbursing funds from the federal account. Although allocation of funds is supposedly based on an agreed formula, some states and institutions are sometimes more favored than others when it comes to extra budgetary allocations. The result is that the less economically viable states are shortchanged and unable to improve the quality of services available to their institutions.

A few states like Lagos and Delta have done reasonably well because of their buoyant economic conditions. They are more able to supplement whatever revenue is received from the central government in Abuja. The level of commitment of each state to the development of education is very critical to its success in this regard.

It must be pointed out that the federal government also bears a great deal of the burden of directly funding nearly two thirds of all tertiary institutions and secondary schools across the nation. These federal universities and unity secondary schools are intended to break the barriers of ethnicity and regionalism among Nigerian youth. Although some critics may view this as the central government's way of exerting more control, it is nevertheless a much-needed solution to the country's need for social and political integration. The National Youth Service Corps (NYSC) program, which all university and polytechnic graduates must participate in outside their home states, has also served as another instrument of social integration. In other words, some of these policy efforts are mostly well intentioned but somewhere along the line they may become politicized to the advantage of some individuals in public and civil service.

Observers of Nigeria's education systems have opined that the country has every reason to be more successful in its developmental aspirations. They argue that its resources—human and material—should place it among the league of such emerging nations as Japan, Singapore, South Korea, Malaysia, and India, to say the least. The near absence of visionary leadership has become a recurrent challenge. Similar to some less endowed countries around it, the political leadership in Nigeria must take the bull by the horns and allocate more funds to the education sector. For example, while Ghana and South Africa were allocating 18 percent and 22 percent, respectively, of their budgets to education, oil-rich Nigeria managed to spend 11.53 percent in 1997 and 10.94 percent in 1998. Between 1987 and 1990 when a sum of US$6.2 billion was spent on defense, education received US$3.7 billion (UNESCO Guardian April 1998). The reason why more money is spent on defense in Nigeria (that is not at war) is because the military rulers of yesteryear have, as politicians, exchanged their military titles and uniforms for civilian and native attires in the new democratic dispensation. We will now examine each level of schooling.

PRESCHOOL AND KINDERGARTEN

There are two types of preschool programs: formal and nonformal. Whereas the formal operates as part of the normal school system with government approval and supervision, the other is an informal gathering of children in the neighborhood under the tutelage of mothers and babysitters who engage in casual learning activities. In what has come to be known as "Akara school" in Nigeria, children are generally taught under a tree or in the veranda of the teachers' homes. They verbalize the alphabet and numbers in songs and stories as in traditional education as discussed earlier (Omatseye 1982). Many Nigerian children in urban and rural areas attend these "schools" while parents are at work at the market or on farms.

The state ministry of education has the responsibility for preprimary education in schools where this level is provided. The private sector is mostly responsible for these kindergarten programs. Government approval is based on the suitability of the premises, location, quality of staff, and learning resources available in the school. Proprietors are expected to ensure that the children are safe and will be cared for and taught by efficient and qualified staff. For the three- to five-year-olds, the play method is applied. In recent times, the programs have acquired considerable sophistication with the introduction of some Montessori activities.

PRIMARY SCHOOL EDUCATION

In keeping with the national policy on education, primary education in Nigeria is considered basic and universal. Inasmuch as many states would like to make it free and compulsory, it is not exactly so for many families in Nigeria.

Hence, the law making it compulsory is hardly enforced. Although the government gives the impression that primary education should be available to all school-age children, it lacks the will to match its utterances with action. The state of deterioration in some school facilities is nothing to be proud of in spite of some sporadic but usually uncoordinated efforts to provide some support to schools. What is no longer a problem is payment of teachers' salaries. There was a time when teachers' salaries were unpaid for months and strikes were incessant. As a result, learning was often disrupted. With the federal government's direct payment of salaries through local education authorities, the situation has improved.

As for who comes and is retained for six years, the background of the child matters a great deal. Children entering the first grade from a good kindergarten program tend to adjust well and quite quickly to their learning. Their command of the English language is usually an advantage even though many children, especially from middle-class homes, are not always able to communicate in their mother tongue. On the other hand, children from poor or working-class families in urban and rural areas tend to speak pidgin English (an adulterated form of English) more often their mother tongue (that is, the language of the home). At school, these children are hardly good at communicating well in oral and written English—a situation that tends to hinder their academic progress in school. Some children from Muslim homes who attended Quranic schools prior to the regular primary school have generally fared quite successfully.

In the late 1970s, there was a debate about whether or not children should first be taught in their mother tongue before their exposure to the English language. Babs Fafunwa, a veteran educator and strong advocate of the mother tongue, was able to implement the use of mother tongue when he later became Nigeria's minister of education. This policy has also encouraged the use of Nigeria's other three main languages—Yoruba, Igbo, and Hausa—in schools, along with over 200 languages and dialects spoken in the country.

The development of an appropriate curriculum for primary education has, over the years, been the responsibility of the Nigerian Educational Research and Development Council, a federal agency. From time to time, the council has promoted research, organized workshops and seminars for stakeholders in education, and advised the government on issues pertaining to education. In a recent policy initiative, extending basic education to include junior secondary school was proposed. The average child is now expected to spend a minimum of nine years in school. How this is going to play out in terms of cost has yet to be known. Nevertheless, this is a welcome development because six years of schooling can no longer be considered sufficient to acquire enough literacy and numeracy in the present technology-driven world.

UNIVERSAL BASIC EDUCATION

The need to improve the quality of basic education at the primary school level has been a matter of concern to Nigerians. Twenty years after the

Universal Primary Education (UPE) was introduced in old western and eastern Nigeria, it was reintroduced in 1975 by the military government. Poor planning and inadequate funding caused the program to collapse. Because of the lack of sufficient teachers and inadequate facilities and funding, the large number of pupils who were attracted could not be provided for. Again, in 2003, a civilian administration reintroduced the program and renamed it the Universal Basic Education (UBE) and is currently supervised by another commission. The aim this time is to achieve the World Bank's recommended goal of promoting a literate and numerate population in pursuit of the development of human capital (World Bank 1990). The expectation is that errors of the past will not be repeated. So far, the activities of the new commission seem impressive although it may be too early to judge the success of their drive to attract and retain pupils in schools across the land.

In the nonformal sector, adult literacy programs have been organized by state ministries and nongovernmental agencies. Some religious bodies are also part of this drive to reduce the high adult illiteracy level in the country. A federal agency has also started organizing mobile schools for the children of nomads—herdsmen and fishermen. The success of this scheme has yet to be determined. Critics are of the view that money spent on these schemes would be better used getting children selling their wares off the streets instead of being in school. Again, this is another example of the government's lack of will to act. Of course, some political undertone underlies this seeming weakness to act. If Nigeria must exceed the current enrollment of school-age children in their primary schools, more can be done to achieve this goal.

SECONDARY SCHOOL

Secondary education is still not readily available to many primary schools graduates because only 20 percent can afford to attend. Indeed, it is a key determinant of how far the Nigerian child can ascend the professional or economic ladder and pull himself out of the vicious cycle of poverty and illiteracy. This make-or-break phenomenon has accounted for the serious sacrifice some poor parents have had to make to ensure that their children obtain a high school certificate. For some parents and their wards, this drive for a diploma has become an obsession that has accounted for examination malpractice—a scourge now being tackled by concerned citizens.

Although only less than 10 percent of postsecondary schools graduates make it to tertiary institutions, it is the dream of nearly all to find their way to the "the promised land": the university. Selection of subjects at the junior level leading to senior secondary schools is mostly geared towards meeting the admission requirements of an anticipated degree from a university. Except for the few federal government-owned Unity Schools, most good but expensive secondary schools are privately owned by religious organizations and individuals. The high failure rate in the national organized certificate examinations has made extramural classes one of the most thriving businesses in Nigeria in recent times.

The sciences have attracted a lot of students because of their desire to share in the petroleum wealth of the nation. Computer science has become one of the most sought after subjects in secondary schools. Business studies, including economics, accounting, banking, and commerce, constitute another area of interest while technical education subjects that lead to university-level engineering follows the social sciences closely. Except for some art subjects leading to law and other lucrative professions, there is less interest in the arts these days. When an area of study is not seen as leading to a lucrative job, young Nigerians tend to shy away from it. This focus has raised questions about the very essence of education in the country.

Although some comprehensive commercial and technical schools have recently attracted more students in view of the government's liberalization policy on admission to tertiary institutions, grammar school has remained preferred to others. Grammar school gives more flexibility in terms of career choice pursued in a university. Until recently, admission into certain professions, such as medicine, law, and engineering, was not possible for many except those who were products of a grammar type of secondary school because of the candidate's choice of subject combinations. Since the inception of the National Examination Council (NECO) operating side by side with the West African Examination Council (WAEC), there has been some flexibility in choice of final year examination bodies in the secondary school leading to university admission or jobs. Some universities are grudgingly accepting certificates issued to technical school graduates by the National Board for Technical Education (NABTE) for the purpose of admission. Standards in many technical schools are not usually high compared to grammar schools.

For nearly fifty years, the main objectives of secondary education have not changed much. Much of the goals still reflect the outcome of a 1962 conference of African ministers of education under the aegis of UNESCO. Consequently, secondary school graduates must be able to

1. think effectively;
2. communicate thoughts clearly;
3. make relevant judgments;
4. play his part as a useful member of his home and family;
5. understand basic facts about health and sanitation;
6. understand and appreciate his role as a citizen of a sovereign country;
7. understand and appreciate his cultural heritage;
8. develop economic efficiency, as a consumer and producer of goods;
9. acquire some vocational skills;
10. recognize the dignity of labor;
11. develop an ethical character;
12. appreciate the value of leisure;
13. understand the world outside his environment;

14. develop a scientific attitude; and
15. live and act as a well-integrated individual. (UNESCO 1962)

If Nigeria must achieve the above-stated objectives, some deliberate effort must be made to overcome the current utilitarian perspective that tends to overlook other aspects of the life of a truly educated person. Its political and economic development must be achieved; it takes more than a narrow focus on utility to succeed. The near absence of visionary leadership in Nigeria would seem to be a key factor to national development. That may not be unconnected with the level of authentic education, exclusive of mere vocational training, attained by some leaders in some sphere of human endeavor. Secondary education is that level where the foundation of such leadership dispositions is cultivated.

Since the introduction of the two-tier, six-year secondary school structure, the junior secondary curriculum has exposed students to a wider range of subjects from which they must pick at the senior level. With the guidance of counselors today, they are more able to decide which professions they would like to be prepared for. This is a far cry from what it was three decades ago. Some critics of the present system have argued that the government should reintroduce the two-year higher school program as a prelude to admission to the university in order to avert a perceived falling standard in secondary school education. Deans of faculties of education in Nigerian universities have, over the years, facilitated an increase from two to three years as the period spent by graduates of colleges of education working to attain a bachelor's degree in universities. There is even a demand that the number of years be increased because of a perceived falling standard in the colleges of education (Omatseye 2005).

TERTIARY EDUCATION

The Nigerian university has become one the most influential institutions because of its role and contribution to the economic and political development of the country. As a product of this institution, the country's elite have dominated directly and peripherally every aspect of national life because of the appreciation most people now have for tertiary education as a way of attaining the good life. Because only about 6 percent of the population has access to tertiary education, it is the aspiration of many to obtain a degree or diploma from one of them.

In nearly fifty years the number of universities has increased from one in 1948 to seventy-five in 2006. Additionally, there are also about forty colleges of education, twenty-five polytechnics, and numerous colleges of agriculture and technology. The number grows every year. Religious bodies also have numerous secondary and related institutions turning out graduates in large numbers. It is estimated that over one million Nigerian students and professionals live in the United States, Europe, and around the world. For a population of nearly 150 million, the number of applicants that can be admitted to existing Nigerian universities is so small that many are compelled to look outward.

University education is under the control and supervision of the federal government through its agency, the National Universities Commission (NUC), which zealously prevents the proliferation and bastardization of Nigerian degrees. It was only five years ago that organizations and individuals were first licensed to operate universities after meeting many stringent requirements. The adequate provision of infrastructure, facilities, and a proven ability to fund, maintain, and administer a university have to be met before approval is obtained. Degree programs are accredited every five years or else such degrees would be considered worthless.

Higher education curriculum in addition to a list of disciplines and orientation include a variety of modes of programs including full time, part time, block release, day release, sandwich[,] etc[.]; a maintenance of minimum educational standard[s] through appropriate agencies such as the National Universities Commission (NUC), National Board for Technical Education (NABTE), and the National Commission for Colleges of Education (NCCE); technically based professional courses in the Universities shall have as components, exposure to relevant future working environment; All non-professional teachers are being required to undergo training in methods and techniques of teaching for effective delivery of content requirement to continuously match their admissions conditions with practices directed by the National policy on Education. (Ivowi 2005)

CONTROL AND STANDARDS IN NIGERIAN UNIVERSITIES

Successive administrations in the country have tried to maintain the integrity of degrees awarded in their tertiary institutions. When for the first time the federal government allowed private organizations, mostly religious bodies, to establish universities, the National Universities Commission recently demanded and received assurance that would-be proprietors would meet the rigid conditions required of them.

The existing federal and state universities have also come under critical scrutiny to meet the minimum standards set by the NUC. The National Commission for Colleges of Education and the National Board for Technical Education are also doing the same to ensure quality in their programs. Although these intermediate tertiary institutions were intended to produce midlevel manpower for schools and other industries, their students tend to be more concerned about how to obtain a degree from a university. Students in Nigerian universities euphemistically refer to their degree as a meal ticket.

Accreditation has become a veritable tool for determining the strength and weakness of academic programs in institutions. If left unremedied, evidence of weakness in a program could lead to withdrawal of recognition from such a department. Usually, such factors as staff strength, facilities, infrastructure, library, resources, and admission criteria are closely monitored to ensure that quality is ensured in the execution of all degree programs. According to the NUC:

[O]f the 72,704 staff in the (31) federal university system in 2005, more than three-quarters (55,848) are non-academic staff. Only 16,856 are academic staff. From the NUC calculations on teacher/student ratio based on approved minimum Academic standards, the system requires about 21,912 teachers. This leaves a deficit of 5,056 of the 16,856 serving academic staff, about 60 percent are junior academic (10,046). Whereas, the minimum academic standards require that 25 percent should be professors, only 12 percent are full professors. (2006)

In view of this obvious threat to the quality of their programs, the government agency has taken some steps to deal with institutions where these shortages were more critical. The measures taken included

1. encouraging the first generation of universities (six) to increase their production of PhDs without lowering requirements and standards;
2. retaining retired professors who are still strong and willing to work;
3. promoting intrasystem academic staff resource sharing; and
4. providing special overseas doctoral training programs for young academics.

The NUC's drive for quality is borne out of the need to meet the labor market's expectation of university graduates. On every occasion when deficiencies are experienced, appropriate measures are taken to correct them.

Concern about unemployment among university graduates had led to the introduction of entrepreneurial studies in many tertiary institutions. The idea is to encourage young graduates to initiate their own businesses instead of seeking jobs that soon may not be available. With training and financial assistance, it is expected that the enterprising graduate would generate work for himself and others. Gradually, the idea is gaining considerable acceptance.

In an era of globalization, Nigeria expects its tertiary institutions to take the lead in facilitating the giant leap into the world market by tapping its huge mineral and agricultural resources in order to overcome the scourge of poverty, ignorance, and disease. Somehow, Nigeria's academic community is very skeptical about the commitment of the government and other stakeholders to the priority that must be given to education. In the last twenty years, the academic staff union of Nigerian universities has had a running battle with successive administrations over the issue of underfunded education. As a result of strikes and other industrial actions, academic calendars in Nigerian universities were not steady for some time.

On a happier note, some improvement in salaries and other remunerations have restored normalcy to the system as fewer academics are attracted to overseas jobs. This has reduced the phenomenal brain drain that has been the plague on Nigerian manpower for some time now. If and when the time comes when the large number of Nigerian professionals, including doctors, professors, engineers, and computer technology experts, will return home to rebuild the country's economy, the sleeping giant of Africa can rise again to take its rightful place in the comity of emerging nations.

ANIRE'S TYPICAL SCHOOL DAY

Anire is twelve years old and a final-year pupil at Uwangue Primary School in a village ten kilometers from a major city in Nigeria. Her typical school day begins at 6:00 AM when she wakes up to assist her mum with household chores in the kitchen and around the house before heading to school. Like most children from a lower-class family, she attends a modestly equipped and staffed government school from Monday through Friday.

Anire must leave home at 7:00 AM to arrive at school by 8:00 AM. On arrival, she must join other pupils in sweeping her classroom and cleaning around the school yard. Failure to arrive at school on time can result in severe sanctions from the head teacher who usually metes out such punishments during the early morning assembly. During the assembly, Anire joins other pupils in praise-worship, because Christian training is encouraged to promote children's moral and spiritual development. Schools in Muslim areas also allow their students to pray and express their religious devotion. Before the end of the assembly, the principal makes his announcements and afterwards, the children march to their classes singing choruses.

Although it is not usual to have kindergarten classes attached to a typical government primary school, this school has one to which Anire must escort her four-year-old younger brother. A secondary school with a boarding facility in which Anire's older brother is a student is not too far from her school. Indeed, she is lucky to have two brothers as siblings in the family because a typical girl in an African family cherishes her brother's "protection" in society. Anire has the rare opportunity of experiencing what her brothers at the upper and lower levels are experiencing as students.

The first of five lessons before break time begins immediately after roll call and lasts for thirty-five minutes. Subjects like mathematics, English language, health, and physical education are taught almost daily along with introduction to science. These are emphasized in anticipation of an entrance examination to a good secondary school whose selective processes could be very demanding for a twelve-year-old. Because entry to good schools is competitive, Anire's teacher must prepare her for the task ahead.

During her thirty-minute break period, Anire has a chance to join other girls in groups who have fun gossiping about the boys, playing games of hide-and-seek, and using the swings while the boys play soccer matches and other sports. Anire's younger brother is with the kindergarten children sitting and running around the premises under their teacher's supervision. Break time for the nursery kids is usually not at the same time as it is for the older primary school pupils.

When the break period is over, Anire resumes her classes in required subjects. On this day, Anire got into a fight with a boy who borrowed her pencil and would not return it. Considered a "trouble maker," John denied taking Anire's pencil but was quickly challenged by another bully who is Anire's friend. It took the teacher time to calm everyone before she resumed teaching social studies on that day.

School ends at 12:30 PM for the nursery pupils and 1:30 PM for the primary pupils. Anire will usually ask for her teacher's permission to make sure that her younger brother is settled in a safe place in the nursery section. Even though she will be dismissed one hour later, her older brother in the nearby secondary school occasionally comes by to make sure that their baby brother is fine.

As part of her parents' efforts to ensure that Anire excels in her final examinations, including her preparation for secondary school, she takes part in an after-school lesson organized by teachers in the school. For an additional two hours, Anire and others who are interested and can afford the extra costs are coached in key subjects like mathematics, English language, and science. It is usual for Anire and her younger brother to return home at 5:30 PM. Anire's after-school activities include playing with her friends and other siblings. She must also complete her homework from her regular and preparatory lessons before dinner.

Anire usually visits her brother at the boarding school on some weekdays and weekends. In anticipation of joining the brother's routine a year later, Anire prepares her mind for life in the dormitory, which is more regulated than at home. For these boarding school students, classes are over at 2:00 PM during which time they proceed over to the dinning hall. The junior students in the hostels more or less serve the senior students. Anire has seen her brother ordered to carry a bucket of water on his head to the bathroom for a senior student many times.

At the end of the senior prefect's announcement in the dining hall, everyone heads to the dormitory for a siesta and quiet hour. Anire has also noticed that her brother must participate in games and sports between 5:00 PM and 7:00 PM. Afterwards, they must clean up and head over to the dining hall again for supper and the last round of their private studies before 11:00 PM, when everyone must be in bed. Anire's brother does not have the freedom that she has to stay up at night watching her favorite television programs. He can only have that opportunity on weekends. Like any African child who must strive to overcome poverty and the ignorance that illiteracy brings to anyone, Anire's struggle for a good life is inevitably linked to schooling.

BIBLIOGRAPHY

Anya, Anya O. *Leadership, Education and the Challenge of Development in the 21st Century.* Lecture at the 29th Convocation of the University of Benin, Nigeria, 2003.

Education: Focus on Primary Education. Benin City: Institute of Education, University of Benin, Nigeria.

El-Garh, M. S. "Philosophical Basis of Islamic Education in Africa." *West African Journal of Education* 9 (1971): 8–20.

Fafunwa, A. Babs. 1974. *History of Education in Nigeria.* London: Allen & Unwin Ltd.

Federal Republic of Nigeria. 2004. *National Policy on Education (NPE)* (new ed.). Abuja, Nigeria.

Ivowi, U. M. O. 2006. *"Nurturing and Sustaining Catholic Tertiary Education: A Corporate Challenge."* Paper presented at the Catholic Bishops' Conference in Abuja.

Iyoha, M. A. *When Will Africa's Sleeping Giant Awake?* Inaugural Lecture series 75, University of Benin, Nigeria, 2005.

Leach, A. F. 1969. *The Schools of Medical England.* London: Methuen.

Les Editions, J. A. 2002. *Africa Atlases: At Last of Nigeria.* Paris.

Lyons, Charles H. 1970. "The Educable African: British Thought and Action (1835–1865)." In *Essays in the History of African Education.* Edited by V. M. Battle and C. H. Lyons. New York: Teachers College, Columbia University Press.

National Universities Commission. 2006a. Monday memorandum, Feb.

National Universities Commission. 2006b. Monday memorandum 5, no. 8.

Omatseye, J. Nesin. 1978. "African Philosophic Thought and Nigeria's Educational." PhD dissertation, University of Kentucky.

Omatseye, J. Nesin. "The Essence of Liberal Arts Education in Nigeria." *Journal of General Education* 33, no. 4 (Winter 1982): 263–272.

Omatseye, J. Nesin. *Philosophizing on the Enigma Called Man: Does Education Really Matter?* Inaugural lecture series 67, University of Benin, Nigeria, 2003.

Omatseye, J. Nesin. "Quality Control of Teacher Education in Nigeria." Presidential address at the annual Conference of Deans of Education of Nigerian Universities, Ilovia, June 15, 2005.

Onokherhoraye, A. G. 2006. *On the Hot Seat: The Memoirs of a Vice Chancellor*, Ibadan: Spectrum Books.

Raun, O. E. 1940. *Chaga Childhood.* Oxford, UK: Oxford University Press.

Smyth, H. H., and Mabel M. Smyth. 1960. *The New Nigerian Elite.* Stanford, CA: Stanford University Press.

UNESCO. 1962. "Conference Report on the Adaptation."

University. Presidential address at the annual conference of Deans of Education of Nigerian Universities, Ilorin, Nigeria, June 15, 2005.

World Bank. 1990. *Policy Paper on Primary Education in Nigeria.* Washington, D.C. June 15, 2005.

Chapter 8

SCHOOLING IN SOUTH AFRICA

INTRODUCTION

South Africa as a nation has had a checkered history, much of which is appropriately reflected in its national slogan, "South Africa: Alive with Possibility". For nearly four decades, its name was synonymous with apartheid—an obnoxious racist policy that served as an instrument of repressive governance. The country is endowed with an abundance of natural resources including fertile farmland and rich minerals, such as gold, diamonds, coal, uranium, and platinum. Its pleasant climate has been described as similar to that of the San Francisco bay area in the United States and the forest resources have for over a century attracted European and other settlers—a situation that has brought mixed blessings to the native Africans whose destiny has been greatly affected.

South Africa's population of about 44,334,136 comprises blacks (79 percent), whites (10 percent), colored (8 percent), and Asians (3 percent) (2001 Census). South Africa is more racially diverse than most African countries. Although eleven languages are officially recognized, English is the most common. Isizulu, Isixhesa, Afrikaan, Setswana, Sesotha, and others are a few of the other languages spoken.

South Africa has a land area of about 1.2 million square kilometers (that is, 472,000 square miles). It is bordered by the Atlantic Ocean on the west and the Indian Ocean on the southeast. Stretching from the northeast to the northwest are Namibia, Botswana, Zimbabwe, Mozambique, and Swaziland. The small independent Kingdom of Lesotho is totally enclosed within South Africa and is located in its east central plains.

South Africa has three regions: a wide central plateau; and a continuous escarpment of mountain ranges encircling the plateau on the west, south, and east; while a strip of low-lying terrain stretches across to the coast. Most of the plateau consists of high-rolling grasslands known as the *highveld*. The world famous Gemsbok National Park, one of Africa's largest game reserves, lies northwest of the Kalahari Desert, another well-known African landmark. From the northwest, the *highveld* plateau joins the Bushveld and the Limpopo River basin where another safari haven and resort, the Kruger National Park, is situated. It is not surprising that tourism has become a major booster of South Africa's economy.

With a literacy rate of about 86.4 percent, South Africa probably has one of the highest literacy rates in Sub-Saharan Africa. However, a closer look at the black population reveals nothing better than other African nations in terms of literacy. Educational opportunities for blacks in South Africa are still a far cry for them because the legacy of apartheid has remained a major constraint nearly two decades after its abolition. Only one quarter of the cost of educating a white child is currently available to a black child in South Africa (Mafisa 1994).

EARLY VICTORIAN SCIENCE OF MAN

Long before the Dutch immigrants landed in South Africa to evolve apartheid, some precedents had been set by the activities of Victorian scientists on whose work early British educational policy in the colonies was based. Before the publication of *The Educated African* by Ruth Sloan Associates in the 1960s, there was a century-long debate in Europe about the intellectual capacity of blacks. The question was whether or not Africans were educable or just trainable. According to Lyons (1970), the doubt raised about the educability of the black man was an outgrowth of the simplistic empiricism of the Enlightenment. Preoccupied with the study of cranial capacity, phrenology, and comparative head shape, some Victorian scientists concluded that Africans were less intelligent than whites. Although other studies contradicted the conclusion and pointed out inaccuracies, those studies were somehow ignored.

The controversy indeed started in the 1780s when S.T. Soemmering, a German scientist, reported that the skeleton of the European was bigger than that of the African. This claim was supported by Charles White, a polygenist (one who denies the single origin of man). The findings of the two scientists were later disputed by Thomas Winterbottom, a physician, and other monogenists (those who accept a single origin of man). In the heat of an argument, James Hunt, the president of the British Anthropological Society at that time, in answer to a question raised by another colleague retorted, "Black men can be trained, not educated" (Hunt 1863). The view that the brain of a black was unlike that of a white was so prevalent that even when other scientists came up with contradictory evidence, some physical anthropologists of the 1860s felt obliged to qualify their findings in such a way as to conform with accepted theories—often with puzzling results (Lyons 1970).

As the debate raged on, the opinions of some European missionaries who had worked in Africa were dismissed whenever they differed from the one held by the influential anthropologists of that era. Indeed, one of them said, "The missionaries are on the whole not trustworthy, as they are not dependent agents ... the report of the missionaries ... after their receipts in this country are very much altered and modified" (Seeman 1863).

The debate over the various studies and their conflicting reports arose against the background of what type of education would be provided to suit the "native capabilities" of Africans. A warning was also issued against literary education because the authorities believed it would be of "no use to the natives in the colonies." At the same time, there was admonition for creating model farms to promote "native industriousness" (Lyons 1970). This debate was a prelude to the formulation of European educational policies in their colonies in Africa.

APARTHEID POLICY

Given that trade and the eventual colonization of South Africa were the aims of the Europeans in the seventeenth century, the education of Africans was not the primary concern of the British and Dutch settlers who occupied different parts of present-day South Africa at that time. The mind-set created by the Victorian scientists certainly did not favor any meaningful attempt to relate to Africans as equals who should necessarily be accorded due respect. Similarly, the Dutch, too, felt dominated by the British in South Africa—a situation that led the Dutch, now called Afrikaners (or Boers), to move to the new colonies of Orange Free State and Transvaal. However, the discovery of diamonds in 1900 in the new colonies later attracted a British invasion, which eventually triggered the Boer war. At the end of the conflict, a precarious relationship existed between the Afrikaners and the British until 1940 when the former outwitted the latter and took control of the economic and political system. Eight years later, Afrikaners enacted laws establishing apartheid as a state policy. With racial discrimination at the core of this policy, the repercussion on education was devastating.

Even though racial discrimination has existed in immigrant nations like the United States and Australia, none ever made it a state policy as was the case of Apartheid South Africa where it was more or less a civil religion for the Afrikaners. Civil religion denotes the dimensions of the state where it is invariably associated with the exercise of power with constant regeneration of a social order. A civil religion provides a transcendent reference for sovereignty of the state within a given territory. The ultimate nature and destiny of political power is thus connoted in the symbols of the civil faith and reenacted by civil rituals (Moodie 1975). In other words, apartheid for the Afrikaners was nothing short of a religious faith disguised as Christianity.

The social implication of this civil faith was that the leadership of the apartheid regime suggested to the whites that if the status quo must be maintained the policy itself must be viewed as a reflection of a historically legitimized "state of nature" (Cohen 1986). Indeed, as unacceptable as this religious experience was to the outside world, apartheid had to give meaning to the ruling

Afrikaans—more still when they could look back into history to justify their actions as may have been initiated by the Victorian scientists a century earlier.

If the protagonists of apartheid as a religious experience cared to justify its expediency, it would have been futile to discover in any other religious experience the veracity of their claim to authenticity. Not even the British National Movement, the Ku Klux Klan of the United States, or the French Ordre Nouveau would justify the tenet inherent in apartheid as a universal principle. If the desire of the proponents of apartheid was to centralize labor and urban social control, it was anything but democratic and, as such, the oppressed majority would naturally resist its implementation. Inevitably, Africans in their resistance received support from the international community to overturn the policy (Cohen 1986). The negative consequences of this political saga was manifested in education in more than any other institution in South Africa.

BANTU EDUCATION

At the height of their powerful grip on the governance of South Africa, the Afrikaans had always feared the possibility of a revolt by the African majority. Education was one way the regime thought it could control South African citizens, especially the blacks. Therefore, Bantu (African) education was intended to maintain white supremacy, provide a permanent source of semiskilled but cheap labor, and arrest the detribalization of blacks, especially among the urban population. To achieve this goal, blacks would be brainwashed to accept they were inferior and this concept subsequently would reduce whites' fear of resistance and of the eventual collapse of apartheid. On the other hand, the European population was encouraged to assert their superiority in a way that alienated the majority African population. These actions only served to infuriate blacks and increase their resentment and resistance of this oppressive policy.

The apartheid government viewed education as key to creating a "proper" relationship between Europeans and non-Europeans because education in their view had to be based on the culture and background of "the native himself in his tribal setting." According to de Wet Net, the policy must be viewed as an attempt to overcome any danger "to western civilization." He further asserted that white youth would be filled with ideas of race superiority and power to enable them to "worship Boerenasie" and be obedient to "the leadership." The deification of the Afrikaan leadership is obviously more evidence of apartheid as a religious experience. A former minister of Bantu education once asserted that the non-European must be trained for serfdom to the satisfaction of the leadership and the white community (Tabita 1964).

With self-protection and regime survival as their ultimate goal, the Bantu Ministry of Education created special schools for the children of black chiefs and councillors to ensure that their people were kept under control. This gesture of appeasement was unacceptable to many black leaders although some succumbed—a situation that often led to violence among Africans (Okonkwo 1988).

The regime expected that some private proprietors of schools, most of whom were Christian missionaries, would assist in promoting apartheid was not always met. Refusal to cooperate led to government's threat to withdraw subsidies or possible closure of their schools. Some missionaries' insistence on transmitting appropriate skills and learning experiences to all students regardless of race and ethnicity was viewed by the government as an affront and dangerous to their goal.

To further water down Bantu education, the government enacted Bantu Education Act 29 of 1949, legislation that brought about the establishment of a commission to determine "the independence of natives, their distinctive characteristics, aptitudes and needs in view of their changing circumstances." The Act would further determine the syllabi and content of education to conform to the future occupations of non-Europeans (UNESCO 1967). The all-white commission, which excluded even Christian missionaries, surprisingly reached the following conclusion:

The Bantu child comes to school with a basic physical and psychological endowment which differs so ... slightly if at all from that of the European child that no special provision has to be made in educational theory. (Bunting 1964)

Although the report acknowledges the commonality of humanity shared by all races, one would have thought that the state of poverty and deprivation that black children experienced would be grounds to make additional provisions for their education. It did not happen because it would have defeated the aims of apartheid.

In pursuance of the goal of producing a semiskilled workforce, a leading politician, H. F. Verwoed argued in a parliamentary debate that it was unnecessary to teach the African child mathematics because he would not be able to use the knowledge in his community. Education, he further stated, must train and teach people in accordance with their opportunities in life. Furthermore, Verwoed stated he would seek to control native education and reform it so that the African child would be taught from childhood that equality with the European was not for him. Indeed, "People who believe in equality are not desirable teacher formatives" (Bunting 1964). The parliament passed the Bantu Education Bill in 1953 and it took effect in 1955.

The legislation was characterized by Reverend Father Trevor Huddlestone as the most deadly in eight years because it set the stage for the effective reduction of access to education for blacks in South Africa. Gradually, subsidies to private mission schools were initially reduced and later eliminated. Most private schools that could not survive without their grants-in-aid were either closed or handed over to the government. Only the Catholic mission held on to their schools. Consequently, the number of unaided schools fell from 720 to 438 with the Catholic mission maintaining 417 (UNESCO 1967). When other proprietors handed over about forty teacher training colleges, the Catholic mission retained 15 percent of theirs. The Catholic Church's liberal attitude towards the education of blacks angered the apartheid regime to a point where the missionaries were prohibited from admitting non-Catholics to their institutions. Unlike the Catholic mission, the Dutch Reformed Church cooperated fully with the government in their implementation of the Bantu education policy. It is interesting to note that the Portuguese Catholic in Angola cooperated with the colonial government there the same way the Dutch Reformed Church did in Apartheid South Africa.

The legislation also introduced a new arrangement in the way education was financed. The new arrangement involved having a separate account for each community into which a fixed payment by the government was made. Eighty percent of taxes collected in each community was paid into the account for education funding. Because the tax base of these black communities was poor, less amount of money was available to their schools. Due to lack of essential services and resources, decline in educational standards was set in motion. As would be expected, concerned and willing parents were compelled to part with more money from their meager resources to support their children's education. This happened at a time when many South African blacks had begun to appreciate the importance of schooling for their children. Even with such awareness, many could not afford the costs. Consequently, there was resentment in the face of their helplessness.

With fewer funds coming from the regime, each community levied its members large sums of money to provide more classrooms, employ more teachers, and provide learning materials for their schools. In spite of the efforts made by these generally poor communities, the infrastructural facilities and quality of staff attracted did very little to improve standards. In 1972 when the Bantu Education Act was finally abolished and funding was to come from the consolidated pool, it was expected that the school conditions would be better. It did not happen.

If the situation in primary schools was that bad in the 1970s, the condition of secondary education in the black communities of South Africa was worse. There were only seventy-four junior secondary schools in the entire country. The vast region of Transkei that was mostly populated by blacks only had one school to serve 80,000 pupils who applied for admission. In Seweto township, another black neighborhood, the overcrowding was so bad that only 1,307 classrooms were provided instead of the 2,016 needed in 1972. Things were so bad that even the government of South Africa for once acknowledged the constraints and offered to provide loans to some black communities to build more facilities for their children due to overcrowded schools.

Because of the overwhelming number of children in some schools, double sessions were introduced. A teacher taught two sets of children in one day. In view of the critical situations existing in black schools in the 1970s, the government in a rare public acknowledgment of the situation stated:

The Bantu teacher has to carry an abnormally heavy burden. Those that are teaching double sessions in the sub-standard classes of 55 or more in the high schools have a very difficult task. The department is conscious of the struggle they have to wage and has the greatest appreciation for the devotion and diligence that they show under extremely difficult, circumstances. (Bunting 1964)

Another interesting aspect of schooling in South Africa is that many schools attended by blacks in rural areas were located on large farmlands owned by white farmers. Therefore, it was necessary to obtain the farm owner's permission before a child was allowed to attend. Moreover, the school curriculum included children's participation in farm activities side by side with their parents who were also employees on the farms. Whenever a parent was laid off or fired from a farm where his child's school was located, chances were that the child would have to leave also.

If the agenda of Bantu education—open or hidden—was to reduce access to education for poor blacks, it worked. Over half of the 6.05 million African children in school had to leave schools to work and support their poor parents. Indeed, 95 percent of primary school pupils did not make it to secondary school (Okonkwo 1988).

THE CURRICULUM BATTLE

The apartheid regime's desire to use education as an instrument of destabilization of the African population was evident in the Bantu education curriculum. In 1961, F. H. Odendaal, the education administrator of Transvaal, stated, "We must strive to win the fight against the non-whites in the classroom instead of losing it on the field" (cited in Hunter 1966).

Consequently, school syllabi were made to focus on the rural and tribal aspects of life in South Africa with the ultimate goal of reinforcing tribal differences and links. The strong influence of urbanization was a great challenge to this aim of strengthening tribal units pitched against each other. The influence of city life was such that ethnic ties had become weakened.

The struggle against politically oppressive policies and for economic survival had become a source of uniting the Africans against the Boers in government. At every point in time, the South African government was not sure how successful their desire to use education as a silencer of black resentment would turn out. Such worries led to the idea of creating more separate "homelands" for blacks to reinforce barriers between the races.

The hope of successfully creating black homelands had become more doomed when the regime discovered that the strategy was unacceptable and indeed had to crumble. Not even an inferior education could stop the movement toward freedom for the African majority in Apartheid South Africa in view of the international community's support and with the Organization of African Unity (OAU) leading the fight. While some members of the international community openly opposed the regime, others vacillated between support and opposition. Although the African states were sure that the injustice of apartheid would not stand, at least not for a long time, some Western powers had no choice but to support a proposition whose time had come.

With only 12.47 percent of qualified teachers in the school system, the rest were those with a little more than primary school graduate certificate. Mathematics and science were hardly taught because of the teachers' low educational backgrounds and the fear that exposure to these subjects might raise children's ambitions to be more than servants in white homes.

For the few who ventured into the rare areas of mathematics, science, and technology, their teachers had very little to offer because of their weak backgrounds and low qualifications—sometimes no more than a matriculation pass. These teachers could not motivate or inspire children who merely repeated simple concepts with little or no depth of understanding of the basic principles. In view of the few practical experiments done in some classes, the pupils were hardly able to develop any reasoning skills for problem solving and drawing logical conclusions from their observations.

The role of women in the apartheid system was anything but subservient. This is because the authorities paid more attention to female teachers. Females were preferred in South African schools because they were paid lower than their male counterparts. As the minister of education, Verwoed expressed disapproval of 70 percent of teachers in Bantu schools being males. Within a few years, the ratio of males to females was reversed in order to save money for the system. The number of hours spent by pupils in school was also reduced, from four to three hours, especially in schools handling double sessions due to overcrowding. It was not unusual for first- and second-grade pupils to have their lesson hours cut drastically. As a result, a total of 600 hours of study per annum could be lost (Okonkwo 1988). Even then, with a reduced contact period with pupils, no meaningful teaching and learning took place as more time was spent on tree planting, soil conservation, needlework (for girls), woodwork (for boys), and metalwork, which took most of the time in the higher primary school. Additionally, religious instruction; health parade; Afrikaan, English, and vernacular languages; and arithmetic were also taught in the final year at the primary school. Use of vernacular (mother tongue) was part of the regime's attempt to stop detribalization, especially among urban Africans who were instead encouraged to speak Afrikaan or their ethnic dialect.

CHALLENGES, CHANGES, AND REFORM SINCE THE 1990s

After several decades of apartheid during which education was virtually instrumental to its entrenchment, the system of governance collapsed as a result of internal and external forces. When the Afrikaan-led government finally crumbled, with the African National Congress (ANC) picking up the pieces, little did they realize the damage done over four decades would take long to repair. Nearly two decades later, very little has changed in terms of an entrenched inequality in the social and political life of South Africans. The economic structure left behind by apartheid has hindered the political and social setup in a way that meaningful change has become difficult.

In the midst of the euphoria of the transfer of power from the minority European government to the majority ANC, it was initially expected that the economic and social status of South African blacks would experience a dramatic change for the better. That has not materialized. Indeed, before the final push to end apartheid, it was thought that the "people's education movement" supported by the "people's power" would cause the final collapse. It did not happen as expected. Instead, it was the "people's power," strongly supported by the rest of Africa and the international community, that did it.

The desire of the new South African government to quickly initiate training for skills acquisition and other educational opportunities for blacks has yet to be significantly achieved. The discourse on how to move education forward, in practice if not in rhetoric, has begun to revolve narrowly around human resource development abstracted from political formation. Badat argues:

Programs of human resource development are crucial in eroding the massive race, class and gender inequalities that exist in respect of the occupational structure, and especially within high-level person power categories with state departments, the public sector, and the economy. However, such human resource development programs could have precious little impact on overall social transformation. (Badat 1995)

The postapartheid government has been careful to critically balance "people's power" with the social and economic realities of the political transition and transformation taking place in South Africa (Harris 1992). At its inception, the ANC government gave considerable thought to a comprehensive development strategy to enable it to go beyond the notions of "growth through redistribution of resources." The move was toward a more concrete actualization of its goal in the overall interest of all South Africans. The slow pace of educational development is related to the concern for the continuous growth of the South African economy in relation to its technological development. In other words, political realities are counterbalanced with economic goals, which in turn have had repercussions for educational development.

Inasmuch as education for all is needed to produce skilled human resources for economic development and demands for equalization are being made, is it possible to achieve these at the same time? Which of these would have to wait? These were the issues that the new government of South Africa had to grapple with. For them, it has been like walking a tight rope, in view the expectations, especially from blacks who for decades have suffered under the yoke of apartheid. It is pertinent to observe at this juncture that South Africa is fortunate to have a political elite whose leadership has demonstrated considerable maturity and tolerance by not resorting to a vendetta against whites or engaged in civil war, as was the case in Angola or the Democratic Republic of the Congo.

If making development a priority inevitably delays equalization, the hope is that it might also, in the long run, be beneficial to all, including blacks. However, it is also an economic reality that a rising standard of living is oftentimes a source of inequality among the population. In order words, as desirable as an increase in the overall standard of living may be, it may have little or nothing to do with equality because there will always be winners and losers. Even when there are signs of growing equality, it is mostly among the middle to upper classes that benefit most. At that point, it is more or less a social class rather than racial issue.

In multiracial societies, it is not unusual that some middle-class whites will be more sympathetic with the plight of poor blacks than some middle- to upper-class blacks. That is the plight of the enigma called man (Omatseye 2003). The educational process in South Africa, as elsewhere, ought to be viewed as a leveler as well as a means of social mobility. How much individuals invest in education will usually determine who is pulled out of poverty and ignorance in any society. The attainment of a higher status as a result of educational advantages has generally been the case, as it was in emerging South Africa.

The question also arises as to whether economic development and social equity can be achieved simultaneously in the context of a democracy. When development is considered to occur in a democratic environment with growth and equity as its goals, then social equity becomes achievable only in a healthy and sustained economy within the context of political stability. This means that minimum requisites of equity must be met because the interdependence of growth and equity is necessary to advance toward the achievement of both simultaneously rather than sequentially—a state of affairs that presents a great challenge to any state (Badat 1995). The thorny issue of providing opportunity and also satisfying both equity and developmental demands has been the focus of the Coalition of South African Trade Union (COSATU) since the inception of the new political dispensation (Krael and Badat 1997).

In what has become known as the COSATU model, equity is problematized and disaggregated into different types (institutional, race, class, and gender) to facilitate a trade-off between different kinds of equity. Bearing in mind that in any kind of equity framework there will always be political tension between and within the races, classes, genders, or institutions, such would necessarily prompt hard choices that may be unpalatable or uncomfortable for anyone to make. As a result of these complexities, the process of change in South Africa continues slowly. An awareness that if change must be successful and meaningful to all in the long run indeed prompted the ANC government to be more gradual than rash and dramatic, as was the case with Zimbabwe where the economy has been in shambles because of Mugabe's mishandling of race relations.

Notwithstanding these difficulties, many South Africans are optimistic that the COSATU social change has a chance of achieving some measure of equity through established education goals. The expectation is that high-skill, high-participation, macro-institutional framework can dissolve the equity developmental tension through "disaggregation and problematization of obstacles to success" (Badat 1995).

PRIMARY EDUCATION REFORM

When the ANC assumed governmental power in the early 1990s, it was not in doubt about the need to use primary education as an instrument of social reconstruction. The zeal to do so was almost as enthusiastic as that of the apartheid regime's in using the same institution for its consolidation of power. However, the constraints on the ANC government were underestimated and there has not been as much progress as anticipated. As pointed out earlier, "people's power" has not been able to turn around the situation in the education sector as quickly as expected. Change had to begin at the primary school level. In comparison to the resources available to the government, the overwhelming number of pupils to provide for has not been easy to deal with. With the issue constantly staring at the government, it cannot be swept under the rug—this is how to deal with the existing inequality while pursuing development.

Even though it was generally expected that primary education would be largely funded by the ANC government as soon as it came to power, it would appear that people's expectations still have not been met. At the inception of the transition, the assumption was that educational policy would simply lead to identifying and choosing an alternative that is considered "best" or "relevant" or not "wasteful." However, the serious constraints of the economic and political realities of the time were not in focus. These constraints included a consideration of alternatives to be determined in the political crucible of competing interests (Sroufe 1985). Unlike the apartheid era, the new democratic dispensation demands that all interest groups must negotiate and secure the consent of their people—who eventually will live with the outcome of decisions reached. This implies that Afrikaans, Africans, the colored, and Asians would have to reach a compromise on issues before decisions were made and executed (Friedman 1992).

It was in light of such dispensation that the National Education Teachers Forum (NETF) (1993) brought together all stakeholders in education in South Africa to deliberate on the poor state of primary education in the 1990s. Stakeholders were informed that between 51 percent and 62 percent of African pupils in the first grade remained in school for twelve years whereas 96 percent of white pupils did so in eight years to obtain their certificates (Motala 1995). Although poor funding was identified as a problem, there was also the issue of inefficiency in the human and material resources management. It was observed that if there had been proper management of resources and an efficient administration, there would have been better results even with the limited funding available. There is no doubt these difficulties have had their negative effect on recruitment and retention of pupils in South African schools, especially in the black urban areas.

In view of these observed inadequacies, the school authorities then shifted focus to the attainment of quality in primary education in the country. Quality in this context was viewed as a descriptive and normative concept usually linked with efficiency optimized in terms of input and output—output being human resource development and acquisition of knowledge and skills (UNESCO 1989). Because the task of efficient school management lies squarely on teachers and school administrators, the need to train them for better performance became the cardinal focus of the South African government. Critics of the system believe that not enough has been done to train teachers and furnish classrooms adequately.

Although adequate classroom management is essential to learning effectiveness in a good school, the quality of content and dissemination of knowledge will always be a reflection of the teachers' educational background. The need to enhance the quality of teachers prompted the South African administration to upgrade teacher education colleges by affiliating them with universities. In-service training programs were also introduced to update teachers' knowledge and skills in pedagogy. The new scheme is a radical departure from the past when less qualified and untrained teachers populated the rural as well as urban slums. Although the number of schools benefiting from the present program is relatively small compared to the large number of schools crying for attention, the current effort appears to have brought some relief to many underprivileged schools, especially in the rural areas.

The task of teacher redistribution has been a daunting one for the education authorities. Many teachers who were in well-endowed schools with better facilities and remuneration were reluctant to be transferred to rural schools with fewer resources and opportunities for advancement. Any attempt to bring about greater equity to the education system through teacher redistribution would obviously have financial implications, resulting in a problem that the government has not always had the resources to address. Again, the implementation of policies, such as the redistribution of teachers, were slowly enforced. Consequently, more affluent families still have their children sent to good fee-based private schools for better educations. Some working-class families are also known to have denied themselves of basic needs to send their children to private schools for better educations.

The low survival rate among rural pupils can be traced to several economic factors: their inability to acquire basic materials for learning, the labor mobility of their parents, erratic school attendance patterns due to having to provide support for their parents, child labor, and a host of other situations too numerous to address. The intricate relationship between education and socioeconomic factors has always been a key determinant to the quality of education available to children everywhere including South Africa. In spite of the legacy of apartheid, the South African elite have managed to sustain fairly high standards of living that are hardly available in many African countries. Although the education system seems to have contributed to this, its critics argue that more could have been achieved if the level of commitment were higher.

A unitary system that is committed to redress access and quality in education through policies affecting macrolevel practices of the school system is pertinent. Therefore, stakeholders in South Africa's education have insisted that utmost consideration ought to be given to external factors in order to provide a level playing field for all children in matters pertaining to their education. This has hardly been the case since the postapartheid government introduced reform in the education sector.

When it was initially proposed that parents should bear part of the cost of financing primary education, it was supposed to be a temporary measure to enable the new administration to find its feet financially. Fifteen years later, people have wondered why primary education is still not free for all children in South Africa. The anticipated teacher-student ratio of 1:35 was still a far cry from what was experienced in overcrowded classrooms where a single teacher sweats it out among fifty or more pupils (Crouch and Perry 2003). With over 12 million pupils in South African schools, a staff of 350,000 teachers is woefully inadequate (Chisholm 2004). Because many of the best teachers were found in the private fee-based schools, only a few good ones were left in the less-equipped state schools.

Several years ago, when a pro-poor funding policy for schools was announced, many hoped that it would alleviate the pressure of fee payments from parents. The program was expected to fund school materials, maintenance, basic services, and reflect favorably in the poverty index of communities and the condition of their schools (Chisholm 2004). This did not materialize.

The South African School Act of 1996 enabled local school authorities to collect fees and employ additional teachers through their governing body—a local committee operating outside the control of the provincial department of education. To say the least, such local boards currently control between 1 percent and 8 percent of the teaching force in terms of employment and emoluments. Because poor parents in the country have continued to bear the costs of primary education, questions have been raised about the priority given to education. The amount charged to parents for primary education as stated in Table 8.1 has not changed significantly since 1992.

If reform in the South African school system must succeed a unitary nonracial approach to school management, the area of funding must be given special

Table 8.1
Annual Cost of South African Primary Education per Child

White	=	R3,600
Indian	=	R2,700
Colored	=	R2,100
African	=	R900

Source: Ayodele-Bamisaiye (2000).

priority. More would also have to be done to reduce waste and increase efficiency in order to curb the current high dropout and repetition rates in primary schools. Ultimately, primary education ought to be made free and compulsory to reach poor, rural dwellers (Motala 1995).

SECONDARY AND TERTIARY EDUCATION

Traditionally, the pursuit of education beyond the primary school level has remained fairly exclusive to the few who are fortunate to have access. Costs and admission requirements have generally constituted the greatest obstacles. Because there are only a few secondary schools available, an entrance examination followed by an interview is conducted to screen the usually large number who can afford to pay for the selection process. The number of those selected is further reduced when they are asked to pay the initial deposit towards school development, uniform, books, and other fees. When these charges are added up, many are unable to pay and subsequently withdraw. Some schools may allow their students to pay their fees over a period of two to three months during the school term. When they are unable to pay, they are sent home. At that point, 20 percent may not return. For example, in homes around the slums of Seweto and other urban areas where unemployment is about 40 percent, sending a child home for nonpayment of fees may be the end of his or her ambition to attend school and receive a graduation certificate.

The 6-3-3-4 structure in South Africa requires six years in primary, three in junior secondary, three in senior secondary, and four for a bachelor's degree in a university, except in such professional areas as medicine, engineering, pharmacy, and others requiring more time, depending on the degree requirements. A range of two to five years is required in the colleges of education and *technikon* to obtain certificates and diplomas. The midlevel tertiary institutions that were intended to provide midlevel manpower tend to serve as another stepping stone to a university degree. As part of the recent reform in South Africa, colleges of education and *technikon* (polytechnics equivalent) have become part of some universities with the aim of improving quality.

Education in any given society is intimately related to status mobility because it serves as a means of self-advancement in a hierarchy of social goods, particularly in the occupational ladder of modern industrial societies (Levine 1967).

More than any other level, secondary education is culturally organized to prepare youth for active participation in status mobility. Teaching and learning experiences at this stage enable the individual to formulate rules of behavior needed to adjust to the new heights he or she aspires to attain (Ogbu and Levine 1967). Without question, this realization has accounted for whites and the emerging black middle class in South Africa to provide secondary education for their children. Although such aspirations have eluded the poor masses, some would wish their children would also escape the crippling cycle of deprivation in which they are trapped.

Ideally, implementation of a policy to expand facilities and provide resources for access to more children of the lower class would be the solution to the problem. Needless to say, that investment in education as human development capital is vital to the country (Sobel 1982). That concept would be in line with what many developing countries did between 1960 and 1975 when enrollment in secondary schools rose from 14 percent to 26 percent while postsecondary school enrollment rose from 1.5 percent to 4.4 percent (Farrel 1982). Indeed, South Africa like several other Sub-Saharan nations multiplied their tertiary enrollments between 1970 and 1988 by eightfold—a feat that exceeded the sixfold increase in East Asia, and the increase by four and one-half in Latin America and the Caribbean. According to Bower (1994), almost half of the students enrolled in higher education worldwide were in developing countries. More than a decade later, how much enthusiasm for higher education has been translated into meaningful development has yet to be seen in many African countries. China's and India's rising fortunes in recent times is good news. Hopefully, Africa may yet have her place in the sun.

As a leading economic power in the African continent, South Africa tends to view education as a means of reproducing wage labor for the monopoly-capitalist economic systems. While its citizens expect education to serve as a primary agent for social change and upward mobility for the majority, economic constraints have yet to allow this to happen. The basic incompatibility between the production needs of capitalism and the aspiration for equal educational opportunities has continued to inspire the political agitation of the poor in South Africa for social and economic justice. On the whole, the expectation of the poor in South Africa is not different from others in the world that seek equality through the educational process (Levine 1967).

It has been argued that if the number of African pupils with access to primary education is as small as it is, the few who are successful in breaking through barriers of deprivation to make it into the secondary level should indeed be assisted more if the principle of fairness must be sustained. It is further contended that increasing inequality at the secondary level would be translated into further occupational disparity in the labor market where the capitalist workforce is again produced. In other words, inequality in the preparation and allocation of workers in the economic hierarchy will require compensating inequalities at some higher level along with the egalitarian reforms taking place at the lower level (Levine 1982). In one way or the other, some hard choices must be made in favor of the lower class of South Africa.

Although the South African government appears to appreciate the need for maximum access to secondary and tertiary education as desirable in the interest of justice and equity, especially for the African population, its efforts have fallen short of expectation. In 1985, the number of black students in universities was 39,700 compared to 141,000 whites. If those statistics are anything to go by, bridging the gap of the last two decades can be a tall order (Herman 1995). For one thing, there is still a great disparity between the number of blacks and whites in primary and secondary schools—a disparity that is also replicated in gender participation and choice of disciplines or professions.

CURRENT TREND IN TERTIARY ENROLLMENT

The desire of the ANC government of South Africa to remedy inequality in higher education is constrained by the cumulative effects of apartheid. Socio-economic factors still do not allow the state to bring about a quick fix to the disparity that is starkly reflected in the enrollment of students in universities across the country. While 51 of every 1,000 white students were in tertiary institutions, the number of Indians, colored, and blacks remained 35, 13, and 9, respectively (NEPI 1993). Although the overall picture for non-whites remains unattractive, their enrollment in historically black universities (HBU) has dramatically improved while only 1 percent of blacks are enrolled in histori-cally white universities (HWU) since the 1990s. Of the little percentage of blacks attracted to some predominantly white universities, more were taken in English-speaking ones than in those using Afrikaans (Bunting 1993). An expe-dient overhaul of higher education ought to take place in all of South Africa's current twenty-three universities and affiliated institutions. Those institutions ought to reassess their selection criteria while working to upgrade their faculties for greater effectiveness.

The three-university system—Afrikaan language, English language, and rural black universities—under the coordination of the National Commission of Higher Education (NCHE) has the onerous task of planning and integrating programs to facilitate greater access for all South Africans, regardless of race, ethnicity, class, or religious affiliation. The ANC framework of integration dis-cussed earlier can work if given a chance by all interest groups.

As part of its effort to boost industrialization in the 1960s, the country attempted to promote its human resource development by establishing several technical colleges, including *technikons*. Over the years, there has been some decline in the area of technology courses. There seems to have been a drift of students towards the areas of commerce and social sciences; fewer students are attracted to science and technology. The recent change from polytechnics to polytechnic universities in the United Kingdom and Australia would seem to have influenced the affiliation of South Africa's fifteen *technikons* to some uni-versities. Its 129 technical colleges are still viewed as sources to raise the sag-ging enrollment in *technikons*, whose staff must now be upgraded to the level of university lecturers in view of the recent affiliation.

The apartheid legacy on gender inequality is still a negative reflection on higher and secondary education. The fields of science and engineering have remained heavily biased towards males. Available data indicate the field of engi-neering had between 97 percent (white) and 94 percent (black) male students. Computer science courses had 65 percent male enrollment for all racial catego-ries. The only exception was in health sciences, which attracted more females than males. The low representation of females and non-whites in the areas of technology and engineering can be traced to their low exposure to science and mathematics at the primary and secondary levels.

There is also a general perception that the country is not measuring up to expectation in the area of engineering education. Compared to Japan, which has produced 500 per million and Australia with 220 per million, South Africa graduates only 35 per million (SECA 1989). Although South Africa looks beyond the African continent in the area of technology education, it has every reason to do so in view of its level of industrialization, especially in the area of manufacturing and large-scale farming.

One could blame past colonial powers and the perpetrators of apartheid in South Africa for the legacy of miseducation and an impoverished society, but that cannot be done forever. Although a few decades may not be sufficient to undo the damage of over a century, the current African leaders have not done enough to convince anyone that they are truly committed to the overall development of their continent using education as a viable tool. Most leaders neither have the political will nor the wherewithal to evolve an appropriate educational machinery to harness the huge natural resources available in their countries. The year 2007 has sent a clear signal to the politicians that the patience of the electorate is wearing thin, in view of the recent replacement of the ANC leadership of Mr. Mbeki with Mr. Zuma, a less conservative leader (CNN 2007).

Like all African countries, South Africa must adopt an iconoclastic but rational approach to educational expansion and development because that would sooner rather than later spill over into other sectors, such as health and industry. India's and China's experiences as economic emerging continents and the emerging Asian tigers are examples for South Africa to emulate. The effect of such bold steps taken now will in another decade or two facilitate an upward turn in South Africa's fortunes.

BIBLIOGRAPHY

Ayodele-Bamisaiye, Oluremi. 2000. "Education for Social Transformation in a New South Africa. The Context of Pedagogies of Literature." In *Philosophizing About African Education*. Edited by A. Adewole and O. Ayodele-Bamisaiye. Ibadan: Macmillan Nigeria.

Badat, Saleem. "Educational Politics in the Transition Period." *Comparative Education* 31, no. 2 (1995).

Bunting, Brian. 1964. *The Rise of South African Reich*. Harmondsworth, UK: Penguin.

Bunting, I. A. "An Unequal System: South Africa's Historically White and Black Universities." Discussion paper at UCT, August 1993.

Chisholm, Linda. 2004. "The Quality of Primary Education in South Africa." Department of Education, South Africa.

CNN Broadcast. Dec. 2007.

Cohen, Robin. 1986. *Endgame in South Africa*. Paris: UNESCO Press.

Coldough, C., and K. Levine. 1993. *Educating All the Children: Strategies for Primary Education in the South*. Oxford, UK: Clarendon Press.

Cooper, Donald. "Technikons and Higher Education Restructuring." *Comparative Education* 31, no. 2 (1995).

Curtin, Philip D. 1964. *The Image of Africa: British Ideas and Action: 1780–1850*. Madison: University of Wisconsin Press.

Donaldson A. 1992. "Financing Education." In *Education Alternative*. Edited by R. MacGregor and A. MacGregor. Johannesburg, South Africa: Juta.

Farrel, J. P. 1982. "Educational Expansion and the Drive for Social Equality." In *Comparative Education*. Edited by P. G. Altbach. New York: Macmillan.

Friedman, S. 1992. "Beyond Symbol: The Politics of Economics Compromise." In *Wealth or Poverty: Critical Choices for South Africa*. Edited by R. Shire. Cape Town, South Africa: Oxford University Press.

Herman, D. Harold. "Social Leaving Examinations and Equity in Higher Education in South Africa." *Comparative Education* 31, no. 2 (1995).

Horrelle, Muriel. 1970. *A Survey of Race Relations in South Africa*. Johannesburg, South Africa.

Hunt, James. "On the Physical and Mental Characters of the Negro." *Anthropological Review* 1 (1863): 388–91.

Joubert, D. A. *The Education and Training of Engineering and Technical Human Resources in Africa and Winning Industrial Nations*. South Africa '92 Conference, Swaziland, September 1992.

Kruger, M. M., and E. P. Whittle. 1990. *Fundamental Perspective in Education*. Johannesburg, South Africa: Juta.

Levine, H. M. 1982. "The Dilemma of Comprehensive Secondary School Reforms in Western Europe." In *Comparative Education*. Edited by P. G. Altbach. New York: Macmillan.

Levine, R. A. 1967. *Dreams and Deeds*. Chicago: University of Chicago Press.

Lyons, Charles H. 1970. "The Educable African: British Thought and Action (1835–1865)." In *Essays in the History of African Education*. Edited by V. M. Battle & Charles H. Lyons. New York: Teachers College, Columbia University Press.

Moodie, T. D. 1972. *The Rise of Afrikanerdom: Power, Apartheid and the Afrikaner Civil Religion*. Berkeley: University of California Press.

Motala, Shireen. "Surviving the System—A Critical Appraisal of Some Conventional Wisdoms in Primary Education in South Africa." *Comparative Education* 31, no. 2 (1995): 162–177.

National Education and Teachers Forum. 1993. *Stakeholders Forum's Document*.

Ogbu, J. U. 1982. "Equalization of Educational Opportunity." In *Comparative Education*. Edited by P. G. Altbach et al. New York: Macmillan.

Okonkwo, Chuka E. 1988. *Introduction to Comparative Education*. Owerri Totan Publishers.

Omatseye, J. Nesin. *Philosophizing on the Enigma Called Man: Does Education Really Matter?* Inaugural lecture series 67, University of Benin, Nigeria, 2003.

Power, C. *International Trends in Tertiary Education*. Keynote address, Conference on Tertiary Education, South Africa, 1994.

Seeman, Berthold. *Reports of Missionaries*. Paper presented at the Anthropological Society of London, June 22, 1863.

Sobel, I, 1982. "The Human Capital Revolution in Economic Development." In *Comparative Education*. Edited by P. G. Altbach et al. New York: Macmillan.

Sommering S. T. 1785. *Concerning the Physical Differences Between Negroes and Europeans.* Frankfurt am Main, Germany.

Sroufe, G. "The Assumptive World of Three State Policy." *Researcher: Peabody Journal of Education* 62, no. 4 (1985).

Tabita, I. B. 1964. *Education for Barbarism in South Africa.* New York: Praeger.

UNESCO. "House of Assembly Debates." *Hansard* 52 (1967): 30–31.

White, Charles. 1977. *An Account of Regular Gradation in Man.* London.

Winterbottom, Thomas. 1803. *An Account of the Native Africans in the Neighborhood of Sierra Leone, with an Account of the Present State of Medicine Among Them.* 2 vols. London: John Hatchard, Booksellers.

Wolpe, H. 1992. "Towards a Short Term Negotiating Policy on Education and Training." National Education Policy Investigation: Working Paper.

Wolpe, Hazold. "The Debate on University Transformation in South Africa: The Case for the University of West Cape Town." *Comparative Education* 31, no. 2 (1993): 276.

Chapter 9

SCHOOLING IN TANZANIA

INTRODUCTION

The United Republic of Tanzania is the largest country in East Africa. Although Dar es Salam is currently the capital and largest city, Dodoma, located in the center of Tanzania, has been designated the future capital and seat of parliament. Other major metropolises include Arusha, Mwanza, Mbeya, Mtwara, Stonetown, and Zanzibar. The 1990 population estimate of Tanzania was 24,500,000. The official languages are Swahili and English while 120 other local languages exist. The Swahili language seems to be quite dominant. The population in Tanzania is predominantly native Africans (about 99 percent). About 95 percent of them are Bantu, out of which 4 percent are Nilotic or a related origin, including the nomadic Masai and the Luo. Asian and Arab immigrants account for 1 percent of the total population. Religions in Tanzania comprise 45 percent Muslim, 45 percent Christians, and 10 percent of indigenous faith.

From history, what we have today as the United Republic of Tanzania is a formal political union between mainland Tanganyika and the offshore islands of Zanzibar and Pemba. This union officially gained independence on April 26, 1964. However, before then, the two parts of the union had attained their independence from Britain separately in 1961 and 1963, respectively. Thus, having become one country under the leadership of Julius Nyerere, on the platform of the Tanzanian African National Union (TANU), the United Republic of Tanzania in 1967 sought to revamp its economy and reconstruct the society using education as the tool. Nyerere evolved a social ideology, which he proclaimed in the Arusha Declaration, in February 1967. The declaration was in response to the neglect of education suffered by the country under colonialism. Influenced by the Chinese communist model, the ideology was intended to change the economic orientation from capitalism to a socialist type. The Tanzanian emphasis was on rural development through self-help.

To fully realize the implementation of the Arusha Declaration, Nyerere and his government thought it essential to first enlighten the people by giving them access to education. The new orientation soon led to a new philosophy for the Tanzanian education system: a philosophy of education that reflected socialism, democracy, and self-reliance. Thus, in March 1967, President Nyerere proclaimed his now-famous Education for Self-Reliance policy for Tanzania. This policy was only an expression of the way education could be designed to serve as an instrument for national development. In the context of a socialist philosophy in Tanzania, the policy of self-reliance significantly pervades all governmental efforts and courses of action. In effect, the new philosophy of education was quite critical of what existed before independence. To get a clearer picture of this, it is imperative to trace the evolution of the Tanzanian education system from the traditional to the present day, highlighting at every phase aims and objectives of education, methods of teaching, levels of education, curriculum content, etc.

TRADITIONAL EDUCATION

The traditional education system in Tanzania is quite typical of traditional Africa in general. The Tanzanian family as a unit was considered an extension of a holistic community characterized by a collectivistic tendency. In other words, the people were united for the common good of the society where individualism was considered selfish and discouraged. There was hardly any distinction between social, religious, economic, and political life. Whatever educational policy there was in traditional Tanzanian society was primarily based on the terms of equipping them with basic skills for living a productive life. It was the parents' duty to prepare children to cope with and fit into the social and economic life of the society. In other words, the traditional society had broad policy guidelines for childrearing and education. Unfortunately, these qualities were not incorporated into formal schooling during the colonial period.

Essentially, close family ties provided the foremost support needed as foundations in children's lives. Children were provided with adequate love, care, and security during the early stages of life. It was in the family that children's physical, social, emotional, and mental needs were met. Within the context of this childrearing system, the mother played a prominent role in establishing a warm and cordial relationship with her children. Generally, Tanzanian society has always attached much importance to children as assets to the family and the community at large. For them, the birth of a child had a stabilizing effect in the marriage and the home. As children grew, they became sources of assistance to their parents. Young boys helped their fathers on farms and in fields to graze the cattle. Girls were left at home to help their mothers with little household chores. Boys grew to become young men, marry, and carry on the family name and status, while girls got married to bring wealth to the family by way of bride price. Most learning in traditional Tanzania was quite informal. The oral tradition was employed in transmitting knowledge, skills, attitudes, and patterns of behavior to young learners. Through proverbs, riddles, stories, songs, myths, and legends, children were taught respect for elders, instilled with morals and positive attitudes, and imbibed with the cultural heritage and values of their people. In Tanzania, like most traditional African societies, education was more formal during initiation ceremonies, which marked the transition from adolescence to adulthood. For boys, it was circumcision and for girls, clitoridectomy.

COLONIAL EDUCATION

Education as an effective tool of social change in Tanzania can be traced to the colonial era when British authorities introduced formal schooling. Schools were used as institutions to transmit knowledge—so it seemed to the colonial authorities. However, critics of this education system, especially the Tanzanians, described the colonial schools and their educational aims and objectives as powerful weapons for weakening the stability of Tanzanian cultural values. Development of education during the colonial era introduced literacy and skills for acquiring knowledge in language, arithmetic, and other professional and vocational skills, but to a large extent weakened the cooperative spirit of the people.

For this reason, Tanzanians were prompted by Nyerere to condemn the colonial or pre-independence education system. According to Nyerere (1967), the "[e]ducation for self reliance policy is aimed at eliminating the shortcomings of the inherited colonial system of education."

The aims and objectives of colonial education in Tanzania can be summarized as follows:

1. It was aimed at inculcating in its recipients values of the colonial society. Essentially, it was aimed at training Tanzanians to provide service to the colonial administrators. In effect, it cannot be strictly said to prepare individuals for the service of their country.
2. Colonial education emphasized and encouraged the individualistic instinct of mankind, which was quite contrary to the traditional cooperative instinct. This resulted in the possession of individual material wealth as a criterion of social status, merit, and worth.
3. The result of the above induced attitudes of human inequality that ultimately led to the domination of the weak by the strong, especially in the economic sector.
4. The colonial system of education aimed at inculcating British values. This weakened Tanzanian cultural values and was thus seen as a deliberate. Even though the colonial system of education was said to be aimed at educating the people, not much of that was recorded. By December 1961, when the people were supposedly independent, not many educated men were available to take over

the mantle of administration of the country. The education provided did not seem appropriate and adequate. The leaders who took over at independence were too few to face the massive economic development and social reconstruction they had ahead of them.

5. Finally, the inherited cultural education was based on race. This was quite a negation of the moral cause and principles of the independence movements.

Even though the colonial education system laid the foundation for formal schooling, not much was done by way of transmitting knowledge to the people for meaningful development. The colonialists also had a major motive of educating the people to suit their own purposes.

EDUCATION IN POST INDEPENDENCE TANZANIA

Having attained independence under Nyerere's leadership and on the Tangayika African National Union (TANU) platform, Tanzanians began to promote their version of a localized, socialist ideology with self-reliance as its focus. They adopted the slogan *Ujamma*, a Swahili word meaning family or living and working cooperatively, as their Tanzanian brand of socialism. Their concept was based on the following principles:

1. equality and respect for human dignity
2. sharing resources produced by the efforts of all and
3. work by everyone and exploitation by none.

Using the above as a guide, Nyerere and his team made education the bedrock of self-reliance. In other words, with education as a basis, national planning and development would demand that people should actually determine the kind of society they desire to build. Based on this principle, they could then demand an educational outcome and service to meet their established goals in the society. More importantly, the Tanzanian government believed in both formal and nonformal education translated into massive efforts. In realization of this, Nyerere expanded children's access to primary education and encouraged literacy among adults. In his opinion, "The nation cannot wait until the children have become educated for development to begin." It was this zeal for mass literacy that earned him the UNESCO Literacy Award.

In 1967, Nyerere's government released the Arusha Declaration. The declaration defined socialism for Tanzania. The crux was based on true commitment to self-reliance for Tanzania's development; it stemmed from the central theme of the Arusha Declaration on "Socialism and Rural Development." It recognized the African tradition of the extended family system where all work together cooperatively for the common good. Based on this, the Tanzanian government evolved a new philosophy for education as education for self-reliance. Nyerere defined education as the development of the individual's consciousness to think, decide, and act. In effect, it should aim at improving the individual's physical and mental status. The recipient of such an education is free to have control over the self, his life, and the environment in which he lives. Essentially, the summation of the above definition is simply that ideas and skills acquired from education for self-reliance are quite liberating.

AIMS OF TANANZIAN EDUCATION FOR SELF-RELIANCE

1. Education must foster the social goals of living together and commitment to work by all for all;
2. Education should stress equality and a sense of responsibility to give service to the community by those who have acquired abilities, skills, and privileges through education and training;
3. Education is aimed at preparing youth for work in rural environments in agriculture and village development;
4. Because education is an expensive venture, all who gain from it must be willing and ready to serve the community in various capacities according to his training and skills acquired;
5. Education should go beyond book learning. It should be a combination of classroom work and productive practical work. Students should be encouraged to learn as they work and work as they learn. Students are also encouraged to engage in productive school projects where they can make some money to aid themselves while schooling;
6. Education provided at every level or stage should be "complete education in itself." The idea is that any learner who cannot go further already has the basic skills and abilities of any of the stages of learning. The implication is that each phase of education must satisfy the needs of the majority by equipping them to go into the working world;
7. Education should be geared towards the skills, attitudes, and values needed to live well and happily, as well as in a socialist ad predominantly rural society, and contribute to the improvement of life in that community; and
8. The community and the school should interact to serve each other. In this way, the school is seen as an agent of the community, and not an institution to educate people above communal living or take them away from farming and their rural way of life.

Using the above as new directions for education, the government of Tanzania evolved a new educational structure to replace the colonial ideas for education.

THE TANZANIAN STRUCTURE OF EDUCATION

The structure of formal education and training in Tanzania constitutes two years of preprimary education, seven years of primary education, four years of junior secondary (ordinary level), two years of senior secondary (advanced level), and three or more years of tertiary education depending on the courses of study. However, the Tanzanian education system can be summed up by three levels: basic, secondary, and tertiary or the 7-4-2-3 system. It is in the above order that each level will be discussed.

THE BASIC LEVEL

This stage of formal learning comprises both preprimary and primary education.

Day Care/Preprimary Education

Tanzanians have paid particular attention to the care of children before they are ready for formal schooling. However, preschool education is mostly private. In Tanzania, preschool is undertaken by women's organizations and religious institutions. Even then, the government also plays an essential role. For instance, the Tanzanian government has legislation in place that enables people who meet the stipulated criteria to establish nursery schools and kindergartens. Registration is usually done through the Ministry of Education while registration and supervision of day care centers is done by the Ministry of Health and Social Welfare. Essentially, preschool programs care for children aged between two and six years old.

The Tanzanian concept of day care centers has been quite appreciable and gaining recognition. These centers are mostly related to Ujamaa villages. The functions of the centers are specified as follows:

1. a place that provides custodial services and supervision for children while their mothers are engaged in Ujamaa activities
2. children are taught cleanliness and acceptable social norms
3. children are endowed with national ideals
4. children are prepared for formal education and
5. children are introduced to the Swahili language if they are from non-Swahili-speaking ethnic groups.

UNICEF has financially assisted Tanzania's government with the maintenance and building of these Ujamaa-related day care centers. Records show that as of 1972, there were more than 260 day care centers in Tanzania. To also maintain standards in these centers, between 1975 and 1976, UNICEF undertook an analysis of the existing day care center programs. UNICEF's main aim was to assess the techniques and methods of teaching and see how adaptable they were to meeting the needs of rural Africans. Regarding the improvement of standards of rural day care centers, UNICEF with the cooperation of the Tanzanian government organized a workshop in Iringa on the use of local materials in the development of teaching aids, equipment, and toys for day care centers. Representatives were invited from other African countries, such as Kenya, Mozambique, Lesotho, and Ethiopia. A major recommendation from the outcome of the workshop identified the need to establish a relationship between day care services and community programs and allow that relationship to be an integral part of the total community program. Significantly, there is emphasis on the need for closer cooperation between day care services and education, health, and nutrition programs. The role of parents as contributors of funds and materials and as important partners in day care services was also articulated. Finally, it was recommended that the teacher training for day care centers should include self-reliance, initiative, and the ability to work with parents as well as children.

Essentially, the aims and objectives of preprimary education in Tanzania are to develop the young learner physically, intellectually, socially, and emotionally. All of these are done through play. The goals of preprimary education in Tanzania include

1. creating opportunities for learning and living through play;
2. helping the young learner develop mental capabilities as well as grow physically;
3. teaching the child moral and health habits;
4. developing in the child an appreciation for his cultural background, customs, and values;
5. developing in the child the spirit of brotherhood and family life;
6. developing the child's imagination, thinking skills, and preparing him to appreciate self-reliance; and
7. enriching the child's experiences so as to enable him to cope with primary schooling.

Structure of Primary Education/Basic Level

Formal schooling in Tanzania beginning with the primary level is compulsory. This spans a period of seven years. Before the implementation of education for self-reliance policy, the entry age in primary school was as low as four years old. This oftentimes depended on the parents' social status, educational attainment, or level of awareness. This practice hardly favored poor and uneducated families. It was not quite favorable to the growth of the new Tanzanian concept of socialism, either. Thus, with the implementation, primary school entry age was raised to seven years old. This automatically raised the school graduating age to fourteen years old. An important argument for raising the school graduating age was that at fourteen years old, the individual is already an adolescent who is mature enough to move on to productive occupations, such as farming or an apprenticeship in a trade, especially if primary school happened to be the terminal point in his education. In fact, the Tanzanian child, after receiving primary education, is already considered old enough to be self-reliant and responsible to contribute to his society.

The leadership was also of the view that the primary school graduating age was quite an appropriate age for entry to the secondary level of learning. Their view was centered on the fact that the older the child, the more mature and better disposed he would be to acquire knowledge, skills, and attitudes.

Enforcement of the school entry or graduating age could vary occasionally. There are always exceptions, but the government has tried to regulate this fairly well and insists most times on birth registration and its certification to verify a child's age. The government considers these practicable steps in the plans and control of educational development.

Essentially, the medium of instruction in primary school is Kiswahili, which is also taught as a core subject. English language is taught like mathematics or any other subject. Perhaps one of the aims of Kiswahili as a medium of instruction in primary school is to help the children learn to communicate (from an early age) easily without having to depend on a foreign language. However, the major aim is to provide young learners with a channel of interaction, which was seen as a necessary condition for national integration and political socialization. Notwithstanding modern education, the Tanzanian children do not lose sight of the values, beliefs, ideas, and patterns of behavior of their people.

Among the former British dependencies in Africa, Tanzania is perhaps the only country that has adopted an African language (Swahili) as the medium of instruction in school. Furthermore, all primary school textbooks, except the ones for English language studies, are written in Swahili. Between August 1972 and June 1973, many in-service courses, workshops, conferences, and seminars were held in Tanzania. The aim was to review the primary school curriculum content and develop a new syllabus, textbooks, and teaching materials to suit Tanzanian goals for primary education. This was encouraged both financially and morally by the Ministry of National Education and the Institute of Adult Education at the University of Dar es Salaam.

Generally, the objectives of primary education can be summed up as educational opportunities that will enable pupils to

1. acquire literacy, numeracy, and manipulative skills;
2. develop a good sense of direction, self-expression, self-discipline, and full utilization of their senses;
3. develop a zeal to be self-reliant and aim towards being a productive member of society;
4. acquire the basic foundation for the working world, especially within the context of the economy and the manpower needs of the nation;
5. appreciate and respect the dignity of labor;
6. develop desirable social standards and positive attitudes;
7. appreciate and uphold his cultural heritage, values, and the beliefs of his people; and
8. grow toward maturity and self-fulfillment as a useful, responsible, and well-adjusted member of his immediate community and the nation as a whole.

Primary Education Curriculum

The primary education curriculum provides Tanzanian children with intellectual and practical skills that are useful for living in both rural and urban areas. Significantly, it also meets the needs of the majority of children who may not have the opportunity to go beyond primary education. Thus, the seven years of primary education equips the child in a variety of developmental tasks.

Subjects taught in primary school include Swahili, English language, English literature, French, mathematics, the sciences, politics, and agriculture. Every child who aspires to go on to secondary schools must pass Kiswahili at the end of the primary school examinations. Also, local history and geography dominate primary school work in all subjects taught. Finally, local handicraft is a basic subject that is taught with all seriousness. It is another way of emphasizing self-reliance even at an early stage of learning.

SECONDARY EDUCATION

Secondary education in Tanzania lasts four years and leads to Ordinary Level (O/L) examinations in nine subjects. This is followed by another two years of study, which leads to the Advanced Level examination in nine subjects, including general studies. In the second year of the first level of secondary education, a national assessment examination is given to all; those who pass it advance to complete another two years of study. At the end of this stage, students take the Certificate of Secondary Education Examination (CSEE); those who pass it move on to the advanced level classes for another two years. On completion of studies at that level, Advanced Level examinations are taken to earn the Advanced Certificate Education Examinations (ACSEE). The Certificate of Secondary Education Examination (CSEE), with passing scores in five approved subjects, and the Advanced Certificate of Secondary Education Examination (ACSEE), or its equivalent, are minimum entrance requirements for university and other tertiary institutions in Tanzania.

Subjects in the Secondary School Curriculum

Subjects taught in secondary school include civics, Kiswahili, English language, foreign language, social sciences, technology, mathematics, agriculture, natural sciences, commercial studies, and home economics. At the advanced level of secondary education, general studies and basic applied mathematics are also taught.

Generally, the objectives of secondary education in Tanzania can be summed up as follows:

1. establish continuity with the training in discipline begun in primary school;
2. meet the intellectual, social, and emotional needs of the adolescent;
3. instill in students national consciousness, leadership qualities, and develop in them, national character;
4. prepare them for a responsible and responsive adult life;
5. prepare them for a vocation and career in life so as to effectively play roles in the larger society; and
6. make them productive members of society with the skilled manpower necessary for the development of the country.

Most secondary schools in Tanzania are coeducational. Generally, the secondary schools specialize in the arts and sciences, and technical, commercial, or agricultural education. They also partake in the usual academic activities. In the pursuit of Ujamaa and self-reliance, most secondary schools engage in self-help projects, such as projects involving large agricultural farms and poultry keeping. They are often very productive. Some boarding schools feed the students from their farm products and sell extras for income. The yields come as financial support for the development of the school.

TERTIARY EDUCATION IN TANZANIA

Tanzania has five major universities and five other specialized higher institutions. The universities are

1. The University of Dar es Salaam
2. Sokoine University of Agriculture at Morogoro
3. St. Augustine University in Mwanza
4. Open University of Tanzania, which offers degrees through correspondence
5. Tumaini University (private university and Lutheran institution)—it has campuses in major towns like Iringa, Moshi, and Arusha

Other institutions of higher learning are:

1. The University College of Lands and Architectural Studies (UCLAS)
2. The Muhimbili University College of Health Sciences
3. The Institute of Finance Management in Dar es Salaam
4. The Institute of Development Management in Morogoro

The academic year for tertiary institutions begins in September or October. The minimum requirement for entry into tertiary institutions are the Certificate of Secondary Education Examination (CSEE) with passing scores in five approved subjects or its equivalent, or the Advanced Certificate of Secondary Education Examination (ACSEE) (or its equivalent with two major level passing scores in the appropriate subjects). The minimum number of years spent in Tanzanian universities to be awarded a degree is a total of three years. However, there are some diploma and certificate courses and programs.

Until recently, university enrollments suffered some setbacks. Indeed, the policy that favored the growth of primary schools at the expense of secondary education in the seventies ultimately meant a decline in the number of qualified candidates for tertiary learning. In the case of the foremost Tanzania (state-owned) university, the University of Dar es Salaam (UDSM), statistics reveal that between 1967 and 1976, enrollment was quite fair with 711 in 1967 rising to 2,145 students in 1976 (Ministry of Science, Technology and Higher Education 1990). Between 1976 until 1984, not much can be said about growth in most universities. There was more or less a lull in university

Table 9.1
University Undergraduate Enrollment in Tanzania, 1985–86 to 1998–99

University	1985–86	1995–96	1996–97	1997–98	1998–99
University of Dar es Salaam	2,987	3,544	3,770	4,131	4,172
Muhimbili University College of Health Sciences	0	357	379	443	548
University College of Lands and Architectural Studies	0	0	91	463	501
Sokoine University of Agriculture	480	1,100	1,040	1,253	1,300
TOTAL	3,467	5,001	5,280	6,290	6,521

Source: Ministry of Science, Technology and Higher Education, *Some Basic Statistics*.

enrollment. Between 1984 and 1993, UDSM enrollment had barely increased by less than 2 percent; that is, from 2,913 to 2,968 students. This decline in enrollment was also the case in the Sokoine University of Agriculture (SUA); its population fell from 465 in 1986 to 383 in 1990. As of 1990, some statistics show that Tanzania has a total population of 3,146 students in its two universities (see Table 9.1). This was put at less than one tenth of the number of tertiary enrollment in Kenya. Generally, this slow growth of education in Tanzania is not typical of the trend in all Sub-Saharan African countries where enrollments grew by over 60 percent in the eighties.

However, in more recent times, increased enrollment in Tanzania's universities has been recorded.

New universities have also sprung up. For instance, new private universities are registered with the newly established Higher Institution Accreditation Council. The Catholic Church owns Augustine University situated at Mwanza. Tumaini University is owned by the Lutheran Church; it maintains campuses in Arusha, Iringa, and Moshi. There are also two private medical universities, both located in Dar es Salaam. Three more universities are also proposed for establishment: one public and two privately owned, both to be located in Zanzibar. Bukoba University in Bukoba is often described as a semiprivate university. So far, one can say Tanzania has joined the league of Sub-Saharan Africa countries in the growth of universities and the advancement of tertiary learning.

ADULT EDUCATION, NONFORMAL STUDIES, AND CORRESPONDENCE LEARNING

Tanzania's premier president throughout his years ensured the incorporation of many adult education principles and methods in his development strategy for Tanzania. Thus, central to his philosophy of self-reliance for education was a constructive connection between learning and development, children and parents, and between community and teachers.

Nyerere was a firm advocate of literacy and adult learning and pioneered Tanzania in that direction, which has to the present day given education in Tanzania a meaningful status. His idea of formal and nonformal education expanded access to basic primary education and accounted for the rapid growth in literacy rates, even among adults. His ideal stemmed from his belief that "the nation cannot wait until the children have become educated for development to begin." The campaign for mass literacy won him the UNESCO literacy award. Nyerere not only was interested in education but also a key player in adult education. In his lifetime, he was a close associate with the International Council for Adult Education (ICAE). This led him to host the first ever ICAE world assembly in 1975 in the capital city, Dar es Salaam.

Today, the Institute of Adult Education of the University of Dar es Salaam is one of the main instruments for the training of adult educators in Tanzania. The institute also caters to the development and implementation of modern adult education programs and methods throughout Tanzania. The institute has the following departments:

1. Training Department
2. Publications Department
3. Planning and Research Department
4. National Correspondence Institute

Notably, the Department of Publications has worked very hard in publicizing government policies and more importantly mass education, literacy, and health campaigns. They are also involved in the training of producers and special broadcasters for adult education programs. Today, Tanzania is an African country that has gone beyond local broadcasting and television to launching its own satellite. Adult education programs are done via satellite as well.

The National Correspondence Institute that was put in place in the early 1970s as a department in the Institute of Adult Education is today enjoying its status as an autonomous institute. Its main objective is to extend adult education to individuals who cannot be reached by one-on-one instruction yet enjoy interactive learning. Since independence, Tanzania's government, under Nyerere's leadership, has strived very hard to attain mass literacy and adult and nonformal education. All of this was and is still in pursuit of the policy of self-reliance.

EDUCATION REFORM

In redefining its educational status for the benefit of the populace, Tanzania established an Educational Sector Development Program (ESDP). In this program, cognizance was taken of primary education as the basic foundation in education. In 2002, the five-year Primary Educational Development Plan (2002–06) was implemented. It had four major objectives:

1. expansion of enrollment
2. improvement of quality education
3. capacity building and
4. strengthening of institutional arrangements.

The government and local communities shared responsibility for the implementation of this plan. For example, in the construction of school buildings, the government made provisions for development grants while the communities gave their financial support (though limited) and self-help labor. To further ensure proper implementation of the Primary Education Development plan, the government undertook the following strategies:

1. School fees in primary school were abolished to afford all children of primary school age (seven years old) educational access to the first grade. This strategy was quite important because, before then, most children from poor families had no opportunity to send their children to school. Even when they did, children dropped out of school midstream due to being unable to pay school fees. This brought about a great decline in the net enrollment ratio (NER) to about 58 percent in the year 2000.
2. Enrollment in primary school was made compulsory by law for all Tanzanian children of primary school age, irrespective of sex and parental economic status. Even children with disabilities were encouraged to enroll. Essentially it was mandatory that Tanzanian children stay in school from age seven until completion of primary schooling at about age thirteen. So far, this strategy has boosted enrollment. In 2004, the gross enrollment ratio (GER) shot up to 106.3 percent and NER to 90.1 percent. However, the same cannot be said of increased enrollment in the secondary education sector. Enrollment in secondary schools has remained low and not quite encouraging. In 2004, statistics showed that secondary school GER was 12.9 percent with the NER at 8.4 percent. Notwithstanding this situation, the government is not relenting in its implementation of the Secondary Education Development Plan (SEDP) beginning from 2004–09. The plan was intended to improve the quality of secondary education as well as increase the NER to about 50 percent by 2010. The expectation is that by the year 2010, the population of students in secondary schools would have increased from 430,000 as recorded in 2004 to 2,000,000.
3. To effectively implement plans for the education sector (primary and secondary), new classrooms were built and old, dilapidated ones were renovated. Classrooms were adequately furnished with desks and chairs. Textbooks and other reading and writing materials were provided. All this was aimed at improving teaching and learning.
4. The Tanzanian government also provided a capital grant of US$10 per child per year for the purchase of essential school needs.
5. With the expected increase in pupil enrollment, more quality teachers were recruited. The old teacher training program for primary schoolteachers was

reviewed and the course duration was extended. In the new teacher education program, teachers in training spent one year of course work in school, followed by another year of in-service training. So far, the government has approved the new teacher education program as quite effective. This has drastically reduced the shortage of teachers.

6. To increase teachers' sense of duty, working conditions were also improved. By way of incentives, teachers' quarters were built in schools. For those who went into teachers colleges, school fees were abolished. Teachers' salaries were also upwardly reviewed. All of these changes were intended to attract qualified young men and women to the teaching profession. Ultimately, the increase in number of teachers to meet the increasingly enrollment of pupils has been enhanced. Over-aged children were not left out of this educational plan. The government created a special program called the Complementary Basic Education in Tanzania (COBET). This afforded the overaged primary education child to complete schooling within four years using special informal teaching methods and materials.

REFORMS IN THE LEGAL FRAMEWORK OF TERTIARY EDUCATION: THE CASE OF THE GOVERNMENT-OWNED UDSM

The instrument establishing the University of Dar es Salaam, Act Number 12 of 1970, was proposed for change and amendment. The concern was over Section 4(a) of the Act, which states:

[T]he objectives and functions of the university shall be to preserve, transmit and enhance knowledge for the benefit of the people of Tanzania, in accordance with the principles of learning as accepted by the people of Tanzania.

Section 4(a) was suggested to be outdated and needed to be amended to suit the challenges of the present and future. In a fast-changing socioeconomic society, the aims and functions of a citadel of learning like the University of Dar es Salaam ought to be more rational and possess a long-term plan. Therefore, the Ministry of Science, Technology and Higher Education, in collaboration with UDSM jointly proposed another bill, loosely referred to as the "University Umbrella Act." The proposals included

1. A revision and expansion of the objectives and functions of the university will serve to give it a broader outlook with new visions, policies, and strategies.
2. Enacting a more flexible act that would give the university increased external and internal autonomy, especially in such crucial matters like staff appointment, governance, financial management, admissions (to boost enrollment growth), structural reforms, and policy matters.
3. In recognizing the public nature of the university, the new act proposed alliances (without government interference) with various stakeholders, especially in such areas that are quite crucial to the development and self-sustenance in the delivery of the university programs as well as the funding and marketing of its products.
4. Creating relevant institutional mechanisms to enable UDSM to respond in a timely manner to rapid socioeconomic changes.

The University Umbrella Act also provides for the establishment of a commission of higher education. The commission is expected to function as follows:

1. help promote the objectives of higher education
2. audit the university academic programs on a regular basis to ensure the quality of higher education and
3. promote cooperation among higher educational institutions in Tanzania.

Finally, the act also provided for the establishment of a committee of vice chancellors and directors. The committee is expected to play vital roles in the affairs of the Higher Education Commission. Unlike the 1970 Act where the president, in his capacity as chancellor, appointed all key administrative officers (vice chancellor, chief administrative officer [CADO], deans and directors), the University Umbrella Act separated the function of the president from that of the chancellor. The act suggested that the president appoint a chancellor and chairman of university council for a definite period of tenure. The vice chancellor remains a presidential appointee but must be recommended to the president by the university council. All other key administrative officers would be appointed by the council for a period of tenure.

BIBLIOGRAPHY

Ministry of Information and Tourism (1970). *Who, What, Where in Tanzania*. Government Press: Dar es Salaam.

Cameron, J. (1970). The *Development of Education in East Africa*. Teachers' College Columbia University, New York.

Nyerere, J. K. (1967). *Education for Self-Reliance*. Ministry of Information and Tourism, Dar es Salaam.

Nyerere, J. K. (1967). *Socialism and Rural Development*. Government Press, Dar es Salaam.

Ministry of National Education, Tanzania (1973). *Educational Statistics Handbook*, 1969–1972, Dar es Salaam.

Mtenga, P. "Towards Motivation of students in Adult Education Programme," *Tanzania Education Journal*, 1, no. 2: 31–33.

Chege, W. (1999). "World Mourns death of Tanzania's Founder," *The Toronto Star*, October 15, A24.

Cooksey, B., Levey, L. and Mkude, D. (2003). "Higher Education in Tanzania: A Case Study". World Education News and Review (WENR). Jan./Feb. 2003, Vol. 16, Issue 1.

Dodd, W. A. (1969). *Education for Self-Reliance in Tanzania: A Study of Its Vocational Aspects*. New York.

Resnick, I. N. (ed.) (1968). Tanzania: Revolution by Education, Tanzania: Arusha.

Chapter 10

SCHOOLING IN UGANDA

INTRODUCTION

The Republic of Uganda can be described as a country of many contrasts. The contrasts among the various people of Uganda are reflected in the variety of surroundings and demonstrated in the multiplicity of cultures, traditions, and lifestyles. Uganda is a creation out of diverse ethnic people with different traditions, customs, and ways of life inherited from their ancestors.

The Republic of Uganda lies across the equator between latitude of 1° north to 4° north and longitude 30° east to 35° east. Uganda is a landlocked country in the heart of Africa covering a land surface of about 241,139 square kilometers. Uganda is bordered on the east by Kenya, on the west by the Democratic Republic of Congo (Zaire), on the north by the Sudan, on the southwest by Rwanda, and on the south by Tanzania. Uganda occupies most of the Lake Victoria Basin. Uganda's terrain is mostly plateaus interspersed with mountains and numerous rivers. The mountain regions lie between the east and west with Uganda's highest peak Margherita on Mount Stanley covering 5,110 square kilometers. Altogether, about 18 percent of Uganda is made up of water surface and about 7 percent comprises highlands. Generally, most parts of the country lies between 900–2000 meters above sea level. This altitude creates a generally mild tropical climate with temperatures ranging between 17°C–28°C. Uganda has an average rainfall of 1,500 millimeters per annum. Basically, it can be said that Uganda is one African country that is blessed with a good geographical location. From Uganda's earliest history, before 1900, historical documents tell us that Uganda's strategic position—along the central African Rift Valley had a favorable climate and reliable rainfall around the Lake Victoria basin and was a major attraction for African cultivators and herders as early as the fourth century BC.

Uganda is divided into four administrative regions, which are further subdivided into a total of thirty-three districts. Kampala is the capital and largest city in Uganda. As of the year 2000 estimate, the population of Uganda was put at 24.4 million with an annual growth rate of 3.3 percent and a density of 124 persons per square kilometer. The census data show that 49 percent of the population is under age fifteen and that females constitute 51.2 percent of the total population. Also, life expectancy for males is forty-seven years and fifty years for females. Infant mortality is eighty-three per one thousand, while the fertility rate stands at seven children per woman. On the whole, there were 11.9 million males and 12.5 million females in the total population (Uganda's National Policy and Housing Census 2002). The implication is that for every ninety-five males there are one hundred females. Uganda's overall literacy rate is 68 percent, out of which 76 percent accounts for males and 61 percent accounts for females. Other statistics show that at the primary school–leaving stage, less than 71.1 percent of children between ages six to fifteen are enrolled in schools. Of this, 83 percent accounted for females and 84 percent accounted for males. At the secondary level, 43 percent of children of fifteen years and older were enrolled in school.

About 90 percent of Ugandan inhabitants live in rural areas. However, a majority of Uganda's populace is concentrated in the southern and western regions of the country. The major ethnic groups include Baganda, 17 percent; Karamojong, 12 percent; Basogo, 8 percent; Iteso, 8 percent; Langi, 6 percent; Rwanda, 6 percent; Bagisu, 5 percent; Acholi, 4 percent; Lugbara, 4 percent; Bunyoro, 3 percent; Batobo, 3 percent; non-African (European, Asian, Arab), 1 percent; and others, 23 percent (Mukama 1991).

The official national language in Uganda is English. It is spoken by most educated Ugandans. It is also taught as a subject in schools and used as the language of instruction. It is also the language used in courts of law and by most newspapers and some radio broadcasts. Another language of importance is *Ganda* or *Luganda*, which is widely spoken and preferred for native language publication. It is sometimes used as the language of instruction and taught in schools. Other Niger-Congo languages and Sub-Saharan languages, such as Swahili and Arabic, are also spoken. In more recent times, Swahili, which is the East African lingua franca, has gained ground as a trade language. In September 2005, the Uganda government recognized it as an official national language. Luganda, which is widely spoken in central Uganda, remains the official vernacular language in education (Mukama 1991).

Most Ugandans are Christians. Uganda's official estimates report Christians represented 66 percent of the population in the 1980s. This figure comprised Roman Catholics and Protestants. About 15 percent of Ugandans are Muslim, while about 18 percent of the population practiced indigenous religions. It is worth mentioning that before the expulsion of Asians in 1972 by Idi Amin, religion in Uganda also recorded a small number of Sikhs and Hindus. However, in recent times, the current president of Uganda, Yoweri Museveni, is inviting Asians back into the country. Significantly, all through Uganda's history, especially from colonial until postcolonial times, religion or having a religious identity has had economic and political implications. In other words, church membership has in one way or another influenced opportunities in education, employment, and general social life.

SOCIAL AND HISTORICAL CONTEXT

From historical accounts, although Uganda had always been relatively peaceful, it was not due to isolation. Archaeological records and accounts of travelers show that Uganda has witnessed centuries of political migration, political changes that also culminated in cultural diversity.

The earliest occupants of Uganda were predominantly hunter-gatherers. These people who can be described as present-day ancestors of Uganda have their residual origin among the pygmies in contemporary western Uganda. The early inhabitants were later joined by Bantu-speaking Africans especially from the central and western part of Africa. They occupied the southern part of Uganda. These migrants brought with them agricultural and other skills in iron work as their major occupation. They also came with new ideas for social life and political organization. What eventually evolved was the development of centralized kingdoms of Buganda, Bunyoro-Kitara, and Ankole.

In about the tenth century, the original settlers of Uganda began to experience so much pressure of expansion from the growing influx of non-Bantu-speaking migrants (the Nilotic people) from the North of Africa. They were mostly cattle herders and subsistence farmers, who formally settled in the northern and eastern parts of Uganda. This influx of migrants resulted in rivalry among various regional groups that controlled and dominated other groups in varying degrees. It was more of a situation in which the larger society was dominated by several complex centralized ethnic groups marked by economic and social stratification. However, the Bunyoro and Buganda eventually emerged as the major group. By the nineteenth century, the latter gained control and dominated the region. This would later increase rivalry among them. By 1894, the British colonial administration would later bring them together as part of the kingdom of Buganda that was now part of the British protectorate.

In 1961, the first step toward internal self-government was granted Uganda by Britain. The first elections were held on March 1, 1961. Benedicto Kiwanuka on the platform of the Democratic Party emerged the first chief minister of Uganda. By October 1962, Uganda had gained full independence. Before then all existing ethnic and regional rivalries had crystallized in several political parties. The federal system had also granted a great degree of local autonomy to Uganda's traditional kingdoms. Milton Obote, a Lango School teacher had played an important role beginning from the 1950s in achieving this coalition. Indeed, it was this political compromise that brought about the smooth transition to independence. In October 1962, Kabaka, the king of Buganda was appointed the nation's president while Milton Obote was elected prime minister of Uganda which at this time adopted a parliamentary system of government, where much power was rested on the prime minister, with the president as the ceremonial head of state.

Uganda now an independent nation seemed to enjoy some peace and stability. It was indeed a truly independent nation that did not suffer continuous dominance of white settlers and monopoly of economy by aliens as was the fate of neighboring Kenya for a long time. At this time, Uganda's agricultural sector was getting its boost as the leading producer of coffee and cotton in Africa. This was of great benefit to their social life and living standards that also had a positive effect on their education system. Uganda had the endowment of rich, natural resources that strengthened her economy. The economy thus supported education in a way that Uganda could boast of a good number of educated and prosperous middle-class African professionals. Although Tanzania, its neighbor, could also boast of a stable government and political system under Julius Nyerere, it had to struggle to attain a good and stable economy like Uganda. In this same period, Zaire (now the Democratic Republic of Congo) experienced a first few years of blissful self-rule but quickly descended into chaos and misrule. In the midst of this, Uganda was enjoying a successful self-rule. This was evident in the development projects with marked achievements. Schools were built and transportation network was modernized and increased. The manufacturing sector gained grounds, and this boosted the country's national income. The prestigious national Makarere University was reorganized and a new teaching hospital was established at Mulango. Hydroelectricity was provided and sustained especially by the Owen-Falls. These prospects were hopeful signs for the nation. Just when this blissful period would have further helped continuous growth and development in Uganda internal political strife and maneuvers disrupted everything. The leadership style and political ambition of some leaders, which one may say is typical of many African rulers, thwarted a once-flourishing nation.

The climax of these political maneuvers started with Milton Obote, as prime minister, not feeling comfortable discussing national issues with the president, Edward Mutesa, the kabaka of Buganda. In February 1966, he changed the constitution and declared himself president. Obote would later abolish the traditional Bugandan monarchy and sent the president into exile. A year later, a new constitution was put in place. The constitution made Uganda a Republic and gave the president even greater powers to rule. This was however not to last long as Obote's government was later toppled by his own army Chief of Staff Idi Amin.

On January 25, 1971, having sacked the government of Milton Obote, Idi Amin Dada declared himself president. He dissolved the parliament and amended the constitution to give him absolute power. This began a reign of tyranny in Uganda. It made Uganda quite popular with the media and the world at large, unfortunately, the darker side of Uganda was portrayed. In Idi Amin's eight years of rule, Ugandan's knew untold pains and hardship. Their economy declined and social disintegration and great violation of human rights became the order of the day. Ugandans, particularly the Acholi and Langi ethnic groups who were great supporters of Obote were killed at will. Amin forcibly removed the entrepreneurial Asians and nationalized all British-owned companies. The consequences of the foregoing actions led the country to quick bankruptcy.

Worried by Idi Amin's continued reign of terror, the Tanzanian armed forces and Ugandan exiles used Tanzania as a base and waged war against Amin's troops and the Libyan soldiers he engaged to help him. On April 1979, the capital city Kampala was captured and Idi Amin Dada fled to Libya. He has since died in Saudi Arabia.

The end of Idi Amin's tyranny witnessed an interim government. This was instituted by the Uganda National Liberation Front with Yusuf Lule installed as interim president. The new government adopted a ministerial system of governance, while a quasi-parliamentary organ, the National Consultative Committee (NCC) was created, alongside. In June 1979, owing to a dispute on Lule's insistence on extending his presidential powers, the committee removed him and replaced him with Godfrey Binaisa. The government's instability continued with Binaisa's removal from office in less than a year, precisely in May 1980. Thereafter, a military commission, chaired by Pauto Muwenga ruled Uganda until December 1980.

An election was done in 1980 which returned Milton Obote back to power. He was elected under the platform of the Uganda's Peoples Congress (UPC). Obote's regime was later overthrown on July 27, 1985. The plot was carried out by an army brigade composed mostly of troops from the Acholi ethnic group, under the leadership of Lt. Gen. Bazilio Olara-Okello. A military government was later instituted with Gen. Tito Okello heading the new regime. The ousted Milton Obote was forced into exile in Zambia. He died in October 2005 in South Africa.

Okello's government, like that of Obote faced opposition from the guerrilla army, National Resistance Army (NRA). Under the leadership of Yoweri Museveni, the group resisted pressures from the government. This was further heightened by Okello's massive human rights violation; especially his brutal approach in countering the NRA. This destroyed his support. In 1985, President Daniel Arap Moi of Kenya called for a truce based on a sharing of power formula between Okello's government and the NRA. Even though the NRA agreed to a ceasefire, the opposition continued. In January 1986, the NRA seized Kampala, the state capital. What followed was a new civilian government in Uganda under the leadership of Yoweri Museveni.

Museveni, a military ruler who transformed himself into civilian ruler, initiated a new constitution that allowed for a two-year tenure of five years each. Even under the civilian governance, the NRA formed a formidable political force in Museveni's government. So far, Museveni's government is working to put an end to human rights violations that was typical of his predecessors. Even at that, he still has to battle with armed resistance group who have been opposing his government since 1986. These notably are such insurgent groups as the Acholi land rebels. Until recently there were the Uganda people's Democratic Army and the Holy Spirit Movement. The rebel group left today is the Lord's Resistance Army (LRA) under the leadership of Joseph Kony. The LRA is an Acholi based opposition group. They declared war on Museveni's government, and another faction of Acholi people. The picture of the political terrain in Uganda would be incomplete without the pathetic war zone area in northern Uganda. This civil war and violent conflicts have actually been fuelled by the LRA. Besides, it has left many people homeless and destroyed families and communities. As reported by the Women's Commission for Refugee Women and Children (2001), the war in northern Uganda may have displaced over 1.6 million people. They noted the abduction of children as slaves and soldiers by the LRA as one of the most heinous component of this war. It was noted that in the course of this conflict, over 28,000 children may have been abducted and currently, about 80 percent of fighters in the Lord's Resistance army are children. In another report by same commission (2004), in order to avoid the daily abduction by the LRA, the children have learned to "night commute." In other words, in the evenings children walk together from their homes to centers where they sleep en mass. This has forced them to sleep on cold floors in places with insufficient and inadequate toilets. They lacked water and light. In the mornings, the children would walk home, perhaps to eat before walking to school. This daily routine has had an untold psychological effect in the lives of the children. Certainly the experiences of children in war-torn northern Uganda has been most devastating to their education.

On Museveni's positive drive toward democracy in Uganda, he was generally tolerant on press freedom. Politically, his relationship with neighboring African countries has brought some stability to the region. Museveni's government played a major role in ousting the former Zairean President Mobutu Sese Seko in favor of the rebel leader Laurent Desire Kabila. Kabila's son, who replaced his father after he was killed by his bodyguard would later emerge as the president of the Democratic Republic of Congo through elections. Museveni would also be elected as president of Uganda after a constitutional amendment in February 2006.

ECONOMY

Uganda is a country well endowed with ample natural resources. These include fertile land, mineral resources, and regular rainfall. This ecological and cultural richness has generally earned her the appellation, "the true pearl of Africa." Uganda has great potential for economic growth, but her persistent political instability coupled with poor management of the economy has placed her as one of the world's poorest countries and least developed nation. Notably, the despotic rule of Idi Amin moreover started the serious economic decline. His reign of terror witnessed the exit of skilled manpower and other professionals while private and other foreign investors such as the Asians and Europeans were sent packing. The Ugandan shilling suffered an immense devaluation. Industries were ruined and most of the infrastructure for industries, the health and education sectors, transportation and other social and commercial services suffered lack of repairs and maintenance. Even after Amin's government was toppled in 1979, the political instability continued until 1986. This brought about further massive decline on the nation's economy.

However, with the coming to power of Yoweri Museveni in 1986, Uganda's economy began to experience positive change. Museveni's regime began a period of economic reforms. He sought the assistance of the International Monetary Fund (IMF) and the World Bank that enabled his government to embark on an Economy Recovery Program (ERP). The aim was to restore financial stability, and rehabilitate the country's productive and social infrastructure. This was also with a view to setting up a social foundation for an integrated and self-sustaining economy for Uganda. In implementing his economic policy, Museveni worked towards restoring price stability, sustaining balance of payment, improving capacity utilization, rehabilitated infrastructures, improving resources, and mobilization and allocation of such in the public and private sector. The result of these proved positive. By 2003, inflation had fallen from 240 percent in 1987 to 7.3 percent. In the 2004/2005 financial year, Uganda's GDP had recorded a 5.8 percent growth, with 35 percent of the population below poverty line. Before then, in the year 2000, with an improved economic status, Uganda had qualified for enhanced Highly Indebted Poor Countries (HIPC) debt relief worth $1.3 billion, and Paris Club debt relief worth $145 million (CIA World Fact Book 2001). This was a boost in terms of an increase in GDP as recorded in the 2004/2005 financial year.

Generally, agriculture has dominated the economic sector, employing about 82 percent of the workforce. Essentially, their foreign exchange earnings have come mostly from agriculture. The country ranks high as Africa's leading producer of coffee. Coffee accounts for 95 percent of Uganda's total value of export, alongside others like cotton, tea, tobacco, sugarcane, and copper. Uganda also boasts of large-scale animal farm products in poultry, cattle, goats, and sheep. There is also a sizeable fishing industry for small-scale export and local consumption. Major food crops include cassava, sweet potatoes, plantains, millet, sorghum, and maize. Besides agricultural products, other natural resources includes include copper, cobalt, limestone, phosphate, and tin.

Uganda's industrial sector is mainly agro-based. However, the country also produces plastic, soap, alcoholic beverages, and soft drinks. This sector is presently being rehabilitated to produce construction materials like cement, iron rods, roofing sheets, and house paints. Tourism that used to be the country's third largest source of foreign exchange was destroyed by the civil war and frequent political unrest, especially in the 1970s. As part of Museveni's economic recovery program, tourism was gradually revived.

In 2004, Uganda recorded an export earning of about $1.3 billion in products like coffee, tea, fish and fish products, electricity, and horticultural products. The country's approximated import in that same year was put at $1.306 billion. Imports are mainly capital equipment like vehicles, petroleum, medical supplies, chemicals, machinery, military equipment and supplies, construction materials, and cereals. Uganda's major business partners include the European Union (EU) countries, Kenya, South Africa, the United Kingdom, United States, India OPEC countries, Switzerland, and the Netherlands. Kampala is the largest city and economic center in Uganda; other important commercial cities include Entebbe, Gulu, Jinja, Masaka, and Mbale.

EDUCATION IN UGANDA

Traditional and Indigenous Education

According to Baker (1963), if one is to make a critical study of the typical traditional African education, and in this case, education in East Africa, cognizance must be taken of the natural environment of the child. In essence, an understanding of the natural habitat of the people will to a large extent explain the type of knowledge, skills and norms transmitted to succeeding generations. East Africa is viewed geographically as having a harsh environment because of its climatic features that sustain heat and seasonal rainfall. But western Uganda, unlike most parts of East Africa, can be said to be quite favored. The inhabitants enjoy comparatively fair climate, moderate rainfall, sloping hills, and rich pastures. This helps to support human and animal life. It is this beautiful vegetation that is the envy of other East African states that have suffered droughts, famine and pestilence over the years.

Consequently, Furley and Watson (1978) have asserted that under such conditions, survival has often depended upon the ability of one generation to pass on appropriate skills and knowledge to the next. It is against this background that the traditional African society has given considerable time and thought to what educational skills and practices are relevant to their lives. Most times they have insisted on educating their young in the most conservative tradition for meaningful living.

In the indigenous education system, the child was taught that the home was an integral part of the entire community. He must be taught by older siblings at home, and also by members of the larger society. Economic consideration is a crucial component of education, and as such training in relevant productive activities forms a good part of the activities at home. Parents and older siblings ensure that such were incorporated in the child-rearing process. The young boys are taught by the fathers and other male relatives. They are taught how to herd cattle, graze cattle in faraway fields, build houses, and farm. On the other hand, the girls are trained at home by their mothers. The Ugandan girl learns to cook, clean, and to prepare for marriage and motherhood. Significantly, women of traditional Western Uganda were known for beadwork used in the decoration of gourds for domestic and ceremonial occasions. This was one economic skill they imparted in their girls.

Generally, the performance of the adolescent girl in traditional Uganda was carefully monitored. The lazy girl had no chance of marrying the son of an influential man, or an affluent husband. The community was always quick to admonish such girls. Even at that, mothers have greater blame for their daughters' laziness. Typical of such admonishing are songs cited in Apoka (1967). Below is one of such songs used by the Acholi of northern Uganda in admonishing girls who refuse to help in the daily household chores:

The mother of the girl suffers all the way going to the well, grinding and so on as if she had no daughter to help her. The girl is hopeless.

Essentially, indigenous education in Uganda was quite typical of other East African countries like Kenya and Tanzania. Besides imparting knowledge in economic skills, sometimes through the apprenticeship system, the Uganda child, just like the young Tanzanian or Kenyan, was exposed to education for social living and the need to appreciate family life and his roots as a typical Ugandan. Just as the Tanzanians would emphasize the concept of *Ujaama* and the Kenyans, *Harambee*, the young Ugandan was taught respect for past heroes. The feats of such heroes were recalled in stories and songs. Also, respect for departed members of the family and also for the living was stressed. This for them was a way of strengthening kinship within the family and the community at large.

Generally, East Africans place a lot of importance on the dignity of persons, as well as their homestead. Also the customs and patterns of behavior of the child were always assessed within the context of his family background. This is crucial because the attitude displayed by the individual is a reflection of his family name and pride. These have meaning and significance in one's daily life.

Importantly too, a very common feature of traditional education among East Africans is initiation ceremonies. This was done by way of circumcision and the age group system. In his description of the importance of initiation ceremonies through circumcision amongst the Kikuyu people of Kenya, Furley and Watson (1978) have observed that it is a crucial stage in the traditional education of the Kikuyu boy who must pass through it. The outward sign of circumcision signified the boy's status. The initiation was compulsory for full admission into manhood in the traditional society. Kenyatta (1961) has also said that such initiations do not only provide moral instructions in right and wrong but also reinforce a host of other beliefs and customs of their people. To further prove their manliness and worth as "full or complete" men, who could defend their society, the initiates must bear the pains of circumcision without showing distress.

Still on the importance of age-set system in traditional African education Holis (1978) has said that the age-set system marked an important stage of education in the life of every young African. It also provided his society with a fighting force of warriors in the manner of the Spartans of ancient time. Citing the case of the Masai people as an example, the age-set system was brought to a state of perfect territorial control, so much so that they were able to control vast stretches of their territories. In practice, the age-set system was one of a recurring system where youngsters entered from boyhood, during which circumcision improves their manhood. Those qualified move on to the warrior class or military units. They remain there for about fifteen years before being moved to another fighting unit. This was the pattern adopted by the traditional Iteso people of eastern Uganda.

In traditional Uganda, stories, songs, riddles, and proverbs were some means of transmitting knowledge to the young; such stories and songs have underlying morals meant to teach the children. For instance, "Iculi, the clever Weasel who found water during a time of drought" is a familiar story among the Iteso people of Uganda. The underlying message was impartation of wisdom in ingenuity to children. The Bunyoro children were also told the story of how wrath, famine, disease, and death came into the world during the reign of a man called Baba. This story has a religious undertone. Still among the Iteso people, it was familiar to hear parents tell their children proverbs like, "You do not prepare the baby's sling before the baby is born." This is an equivalent of the moral truth in the English proverb "You don't count your chicks before they hatch."

Songs and lullabies also serve as a good vehicle for transmitting knowledge in traditional Uganda. According to Apoka (1967), such traditional songs and lullabies, besides the soothing feeling, give infants a good start in teaching them the learning and acquisition of their ethnic language and its correct pronunciation.

Finally, recitation of poetry was another traditional way of teaching. According to Furley and Watson (1978), teachers of the young pages at the court of Mugabe in Ankole in Western Uganda, would teach poems that speak of the bravery and pride of great Ugandans and great battles fought. On the whole, the child growing up in tradition Ugandan society would generally acquire knowledge from stories, myths, legends, songs, lullabies, riddles, proverbs, dances, and religion embedded in their early education at home. These instilled in him spiritual values, respect for elders, family, institution, and the social hierarchy. Also, he learned wisdom, morals, and all such norms that are appropriate for displaying positive behavior. All of these form the basis of indigenous education in the traditional Ugandan society. Such traditional education, not limited to Uganda alone, also cuts across most of East and Southern Africa in view of their ancestral origin in the region.

Missionary and Colonial Education at Independence

The first signs of formal education in Uganda occurred about the early eighteenth century during the interethnic war period. Formal education was first introduced in Uganda by volunteer missionary organizations who were mostly Protestants. They came to Uganda in 1877 and would be followed two years later by the Catholic Mission. The aim of education for the groups was basically evangelism. But even at that they made their impact as the first to introduce formal education to Uganda. Basically, the mission groups had tailored the content of education primarily to their primary goal of evangelism with the curriculum as a way of achieving this. The uniqueness of education in Uganda is aptly characterized by the Phelps-Stokes committee that stated that "only Nyasaland can equal Uganda in the extent to which Mission works have been responsible for schools" (Furley and Watson 1978).

Indeed, education in Uganda just after the World War I was mostly a mission concern. The government merely subsidized through bursaries to intelligent scholars. However, by 1921, the government increased grants-in-aids to these missionaries, to assist their work of expansion of schools and promotion of education. On the part of the African, the zeal for education at this period was first, literacy; thereafter, some general education would earn some "white-collar" job in the civil service and local administration. But on the part of the British officials, as was typical in the East African territories, they were not quite comfortable. As expressed in Ingham (1958), a committee appointed by the governor to report on Native Civil Service in 1929 stated, "We are opposed to any extensive literacy education for the native population. ... Unless literacy education is complete, or is accompanied by technical training, the native is apt to regard himself as a superior being for whom the ordinary duties and responsibilities of life have no significance."

The above was basically an indictment of missionary organizations, which were blamed and criticized for giving their students and pupils only literary education. It was also in response to this that Uganda Development Committee redirected its focus to technical training and education. The idea was to promote the technical education along with literacy, so as to impart technical skills in pupils. The expectation was that such skills would prepare them for work in the medical discipline, transportation, agriculture, survey, and the public works departments. Furthermore, the design was that trained Africans in these areas of skills would gradually replace the more highly paid Asian artisans. This drive for technical skills acquisition led to the establishment of the Government National Technical School located in Makarere. It was later discovered that this foremost "higher education" in Uganda could not be described as one with a foremost aim of producing intellectuals or educated recipients for the sake of education. Instead, the focus was more on churning out "human supplies" to meet the needs of government departments. This would later change to achieve a more positive educational goal, and also the renaming of the institution to become the Makarere College.

In 1922, the educational scene in Uganda witnessed another change under the leadership of Sir Geoffrey Archer who saw the need for reforms in education for Africans. The idea was a broad-based general education curriculum to meet the yearnings of the colonies. To support and fully implement these plans, he increased government grants to missionary efforts and brought in experts to review the general education needs of the people. About the same period, the Phelps-Stokes Committee visited Uganda to make further suggestions about putting education in Uganda on a better pedestal. While commending the enthusiasm of the missionary organizations to advance education in Uganda, the Committee criticized them for uneven spread in the location of schools. The Committee noted particularly the concentration of education in Buganda, especially in the Kampala area, at the expense of the northern province which was hit worse by the lack of mission presence. The missionary organizations were also accused of not injecting adequate technical training in their programs especially in agriculture. Noting too, that practical skills in agriculture would no doubt have thrived in view of their fertile soil in Uganda. In other words, the missions were faulted for not tailoring their educational schemes to suit the needs of the people. It was a lopsided education that favored literacy education at the expense of practical skills.

Another criticism was that the religious influence of the organizations was overwhelming. The greatest mistake in the whole Ugandan system was that the control of all schools was vested in the same people who controlled the churches. Inevitably, the whole education system was subordinated to the ecclesiastical system.

Generally, the recommendations of the Phelps-Stokes Committee, and government's decision, started another round of reforms for the advancement of education in Uganda. The syllabi were revised, school programs and school types revisited, and the administration and control of schools were reconsidered and legalized in Uganda's Education Ordinance of 1927. All of these were executed under the leadership of E. R. J. Hussey, the first director of education in Uganda. This was the beginning of a new age in education.

Consequently, the control of teachers and schools were in the hands of a local district education board with good African representation. The missions, in return for increased grants, embarked on a policy of close cooperation with the government. In line with the new policy, mission schools could not work with government schools using the official syllabi. This, in turn, enabled them to strive towards the same standard of education. For the first time in the history of education in Uganda, a secular training was established. Even then, in some quarters, some missions frowned at the cooperation between government and mission because such, they believed, could hamper their aim of evangelizing the people through teaching.

In terms of school types and their control, there were five main grades of schools, namely

1. Subgrade village schools
2. Elementary vernacular schools

3. Intermediate and central schools
4. Makarere College (now Makerere University)
5. Normal and technical schools.

The missions had total responsibility for the first two grades of school, while the others were mostly government controlled. Notably, the subgrade village schools afforded the villagers some training in the 3Rs (of reading, writing, and arithmetic) and instruction. It was more or less like exposing them to the premier steps in learning, though with great emphasis on religious knowledge.

In 1927, Makarere College had developed and attained the status of a leading vocational center. It specialized in the training of a good number of technicians and artisans. Students in the new Makarere College were exposed to a one year prevocational general course. They were taught subjects like English language, history, mathematics, and science. This was aimed at preparing the students for specialized vocational training in their chosen courses. The Makarere vocational center had specialist teachers who provided the necessary practical training in a variety of courses. Between 1923 and 1930, Makarere College had developed steadily in providing a variety of technical and vocational courses, with increased growth in the population of students (see Table 10.1).

It is of some significance that Makarere College took interest in medical training. This was re-echoed in 1929 by Professor Julian Huxley, in his visit to the college. In his words:

the medical programme is the most ambitious. Some of the lads are being trained for senior medical assistants...a grade now filled exclusively by Indians. If this works satisfactorily, the college will aim higher at the production of fully qualified medical men; but

Table 10.1
Makerere College between 1923 and 1938

Courses	1923	1924	1925	1926	1927	1928	1929	1930
Medical	10	4	9	7	4	5	8	9
Agriculture	–	1	1	1	–	7	6	6
Survey	4	4	5	2	2	6	5	7
Teacher training	–	–	2	4	3	16	30	30
Telegraphy	–	–	–	10	10	–	–	–
General vocational	–	–	–	–	29	27	31	33
Intermediate	–	–	–	25	21	–	–	–
Mechanics	14	14	14	11	13	12	–	–
Carpentry	17	31	52	38	26	7	–	–
Engineering	–	–	–	–	–	12	9	7
Clerical	–	–	–	–	–	–	33	34
Tertiary	–	–	–	–	–	–	5	6
Totals	**45**	**54**	**83**	**98**	**108**	**92**	**127**	**142**

Source: Furley and Watson (1978).

that will be in a matter of decades. Makarere will become a true University, the University of East Africa. It is difficult to prophesy, but I would put this time about forty or fifty years; after two more generations of education. (as cited in Furley and Watson 1978)

Huxley's prediction was quite apt, but the estimated period should have been cut by half. In other words, Makarere College in a rather shorter time had attained the status of a full-fledged citadel of learning. It had become a university that catered to the whole of the East African bloc and beyond. The first set of non-Ugandans students came from Tanganyika, and then Zanzibar. Indeed, Makarere University College as an institution of high repute in East Africa has come to stay. Even though the government had begun to realize the importance of participation in the education of her populace, they tended to have limited their involvement with the Makarere College and a few other government institutions, especially those intended for Muslim pupils. However, government interest took a new turn in 1940. The government set up an education committee. The objectives were mostly centered on coming up with principles of grants-in-aids and proposals for education for the period between 1941 and 1945. The committee was purely government sponsored, thus its findings were applicable only to African schools. However, the committee worked closely with the Advisory Council on African education. It is imperative to mention here that there was also the Advisory Councils on education that took care of the European and Asian races, especially as it concerned the education of their children. This kind of racial segregation was also evident in Kenya. But unlike the tense situation in Kenya, the case in Uganda was quite fair and almost not noticeable. This may not be far from the measure of freedom enjoyed by the Ugandans, even with the British presence. In essence, the kind of racial strife as that of the Mau-Mau in Kenya was carefully avoided in Uganda. This was even made more evident when in 1946 John Hall, the then governor of Uganda, declared publicly in an address to the Ugandan society, especially as it concerned their education, that the development and advancement of Uganda was the sole responsibility of the Africans themselves (*The Uganda Herald* August 7, 1946). This declaration without question caused some enthusiasm among the Africans. By 1951, the Ugandans had realized the need for education and fully embraced it. Table 10.2 shows the figures of Uganda's population in school in 1951.

The zeal for reforms in education in Uganda continued, especially one to prepare the people for self-government. Thus, in 1952, and with the arrival of Sir Andrew Cohen as Uganda's governor, the philosophy and policy for education was revisited. Cohen, in recognizing the nation as an agriculturally buoyant and viable one, made it a focal aspect of the economy, using educational policy as its hob. His major goal was to bring a closer link between economic development and education skills. To achieve this, he began by setting up a local education committee with Mr. Bernard de Bunsen as chairman. The committee worked with much zeal and urgency using the Kenya's Beecher Report

Table 10.2
Uganda's School Population in 1951

S/N	Primary Schools	Boys	Girls	Total
1.	The Buganda Kingdom	36,931	21,115	58,046
2.	The Western Province			
a.	The Toro Kingdom	7,172	1,503	8,675
b.	The Bunyoro Kingdom	5,026	895	5,921
c.	The Ankole Kingdom	8,900	1,519	10,419
d.	Kigezi	8,863	1,844	10,707
3.	The Eastern Province			
a.	Bugishu	8,000	3,300	11,300
b.	Busoga	10,950	3,700	14,650
c.	Bukedi	12,550	1,950	14,500
d.	Teso	12,350	2,600	14,950
4.	The Northern Province			
a.	Madi	1,452	240	1,692
b.	West Nile	7,511	819	8,330
c.	Karamoja	643	80	723
d.	Lango	5,654	605	6,259
e.	Acholi	6,732	696	7,428
	Total	132,734	40,866	173,600

S/N	Junior Secondary Schools	Boys	Girls	Total
1.	Buganda	1,554	117	1,671
2.	Western Province	587	155	742
3.	Eastern Province	628	63	691
4.	Northern Province	442	59	501
	Total	3,211	394	3,605

S/N	Senior Secondary Schools	Boys	Girls	Total
1.	Buganda	783	303	1,036
2.	Western Province	246	–	246
3.	Eastern Province	462	17	479
4.	Northern Province	151	–	131
	Total	1,592	320	1,912

Source: African Education in Uganda (Kampala: The Bunsen Report, 1953).

(1949) as reference point. Essentially, the Beecher Report had noted the need for educational development as crucial to the preparation of self-rule, in the African territories. Following this as a model, the Bunsen's committee recommended the following for education in Uganda:

1. The need for quality teacher training colleges for the production of qualified teachers. Based on this, the committee proposed higher entrance qualifications

with proficiency in English language as prerequisite for the candidates. The training duration was put at four years with two years for academic coursework and the rest on professional training or practicum. Other suggestions for the teaching profession included better conditions of service with good incentives, and pension schemes.

2. The Committee proposed an eight-year primary school education, to afford the average Ugandan child educational competence especially those whose primary education is terminal. However, noting the near impossibility of an eight-year duration, mostly because of shortage of qualified teachers, the committee settled for six-year duration. Generally, a 6-3-3 structure for education was recommended. This had six years of basic primary education, three years of junior secondary education, and another three years of senior secondary education.

3. In terms of control of schools, the recommendation was for continuance of denominational schools, but with emphases on secularization of education. Government desire was to extend educational access to children who were not within the radius of mission schools. This call for emphasis on secular education would be stressed by Obote as president.

4. The Bunsen committee was also concerned about improvement in the quality of secondary education, as well as the establishment of more secondary schools to match an increased population. It also encouraged the girl-child education.

5. Finally, what was proposed as curricula was one with a broad outlook, accommodating theory and practical aspects of education. There was also a desire to balance religion with moral training. Essentially, the committee focus for the curriculum included the most valuable features of the Ugandan and European culture.

Having implemented the Bunsen's report in the 1950s, visible changes and reforms were noticed. Recommended innovations brought about the following:

1. Teacher-education programs were improved in quality and the number of colleges of education also increased. This was also reflected in the status of teachers, especially with the revised teachers' salary structure.

2. Although the quality and number of primary schools improved, the same cannot be said about the high attrition rate in primary schooling—a situation that remained an urgent problem. Table 10.3 shows the number of recognized primary schools and the marked increase in enrollment between 1952 and 1957.

Table 10.3
Primary School Enrollment: 1952–1957

	Primary Schools	Boys	Girls	Total
1952	1,371	130,142	40,009	170,151
1957	2,010	215,915	81,854	297,769

Source: Furley and Watson (1978).

3. Even though the number of secondary school increased, as did the enrollment, there was the difficulty of providing adequate teaching equipment to meet the teeming population. This inevitably had its reactive effect on the standard of teaching. Another challenge experienced was the imbalance between theory and practice in education especially in such professions as agriculture, medicine, etc. This made the secondary education quite lopsided in favor of the arts.

4. On the control of schools, even though the missions still retained some marked dominance, the number of government schools (especially secondary schools) increased. Important too, this afforded African Muslims, who had hitherto suffered some educational exclusion, access to education.

5. Girl-child education was a serious challenge for the de Bunsen committee, and because they too believed in it, it was successful after all. Their recommendation for the expansion of existing girls' schools and improvement of girls' education yielded positive results, citing the number of girls from Gayanza who obtained secondary school certificates between 1952 and 1962. Hunter (1963) asserts that the list may have been a very small minority but was quite impressive. The success of the girls for him was a living example of successful Western educated elite. Girls' education had always been a special feature of Uganda's education system. It is remarkably ahead of other East African territories. As in the case of Tanzania with Julius Nyerere pioneering education, three things appeared paramount to the native Ugandans:
    •   education for all or mass literacy
    •   education for leadership and
    •   injecting technical reduction into the curriculum content.

The following had been listed in an earlier government publication:

1. To raise the standard of living of all classes of the community and to provide for as many children as possible the benefits of reasonable standard of education;

2. To produce, as quickly as possible, a sufficiency of well qualified men and women who are able and ready to hold posts of responsibility. In effect, numerous professional classes was an essential preliminary of self-government;

3. To train a large sub-professional class of qualified technicians, teachers, clerks etc. and to train an even larger number of craftsmen and artisans;

4. To attain in time universal literacy. Importantly, that a literate electorate is of prime importance in a state aspiring to self-governance. (session paper N2, 1958/54)

Using the above as working strategy, Uganda went into massive expansion of education at the primary and secondary levels. The expansion was so much that in October 1962 when she had gained independence, enrollment had increased drastically, yet deficient in the number of qualified persons for responsible positions in the then independent nation. One observer stated, "The decade 1953–63 saw the biggest secondary school expansion in Uganda's history, but out of a population of about seven million, there were only about 7,500 school certificates" (Furley and Watson 1978).

Contrasting educational developments with other East African nations, Furley further noted that in spite of Uganda's advantage over Kenya or Tanzania since independence, Uganda was still short of skilled manpower. In his comparison, he stated:

Uganda exhibits to some extent, a midway pattern between the Tanzanian system of expansion exactly according to manpower needs, giving a rural-based primary education, and Kenyans' response to the much wider technical, commercial and industrial aspect of her economy. Uganda had neither the special fervor of Tanzanian socialism nor the mixed economy of Kenya. She tended to concentrate on secondary education of a fairly general type, without specific relation to manpower planning, while expanding a primary system based on the virtues of a general education. (Furley and Watson 1978)

To improve her education and correct all such anomalies, the Ugandan government put another commission in place. Castle's Commission was to reassess Uganda's policy on education. The Report of 1963 diagnosed and recommended that:

1. the general policy on education in Uganda should stress character training, for citizenship and general education;
2. the eight-year duration of primary schooling was to be reduced to seven years. The Commission noted that the attrition rate in primary school was still too high. It blamed it on family problems, lack of value for education, hardship in domestic life leading to withdrawal of children from school, lack of interest on the part of parents in their children's education, and excessive work load for teachers. Other reasons included withdrawal of children to work in "shambas" (family property) and parents' preference of early marriage for their daughters instead of education; and
3. the Commission also described primary education as preparation for life. But while it appreciated the practical aspect of the primary curriculum, it also faulted the overemphasis on agricultural training. It therefore suggested that agricultural training should be redefined within the context of rural science. In this way, the child would acquire skills in simple, but scientific order, and the aesthetic aspect of his school surroundings and his entire environment would be appreciated. To this end, the report recommended that the pupils should keep school gardens for experimental purposes. Also a subject like geography should stimulate interest in farming at the primary level.
4. Castle's Commission redefined secondary school education and proposed four types of secondary education as follows:
    - A senior secondary school to offer liberal and technical-based curriculum.
    - A secondary school with a three to four years course duration. This would offer general and vocational education. This type would also replace the old secondary modern school, the rural trade school, and farm school most of that were in vogue at the time.
    - A technical school with a four-year course duration which would lead its recipients to the London City and Guilds examination or its equivalent.

- A new farm school with a four-year course duration to produce enlightened farmers. Important, students who performed well in any of the above secondary schools were recommended for further studies or training.
5. So as not to increase the number of the "educated unemployed" class, as was the outcome of the massive expansion of secondary schools, the Commission suggested that all education should be considered within the context of the nation's total economy;
6. For tertiary institutions, especially in the professions an upgrading to a higher standard in theoretical and practical courses was recommended by way of content improvement. For instance, a course in agriculture would have its practical done by way of experimental farm work, field extensions, and close contacts with well-known progressive farmers and undergraduates would serve as apprentices for a prescribed number of years.
7. Girls' education was once again articulated and encouraged by the Commission. The report recommended that government should give special "catch-up" grants to local authorities to support girls' education, and support the establishment of coeducational schools. The Commission also suggested that girls could also be encouraged by giving them attendance bursaries, free lunch, and free uniforms. This was needed especially for girls from poor homes. Also, female teachers would be attracted to work with special allowances in rural areas.

Generally, the Castle Commission commended Uganda's government for its budgetary allocation to the education sector in spite of her small GNP. But the Commission wished that the government's grants-in-aid were evenly spread, especially to educationally backward districts. This, they hoped, would afford many more Ugandan children access to education. The government, on its part, accepted to a large extent the Castle report and even went ahead to implement some of its recommendations between 1964–65. For instance, the seven-year primary education was begun, while the junior secondary school was absorbed into the whole secondary school system. On the whole, secondary education continued to enjoy expansion with the students fitting into the four secondary school types, as prescribed by the Commission.

In 1964, an education bill that came into being in Uganda focused on ownership, management, and control of schools. The underlying aim was to "nationalize" schools and to a large extent de-emphasize mission or denominational schools. This bill met with stiff opposition from all quarters. The different denominations kicked against it and argued that the outcome would affect their evangelistic activities. Parents' associations rejected it vehemently. For instance, the Catholic Parent Association declared that the intended introduction of interdenominational schools would lower the moral behavior of their children and wards. They rejected government's claim of being solely responsible for all education, more especially when the children were theirs.

The debate, protests, and struggle notwithstanding, the government settled for interdenominational schools. Catholic Parent Association, the church, and the local authorities were assured of fair representations on the government education board. The government saw the idea of interdenominational schools as a welcomed idea that would put an end to the unhealthy rivalry among missionary organizations. Also, it was anticipated that interdenominational schools would reduce the distances children had to walk to get to school.

Tracing the educational development so far, there was no gainsaying that by 1965, and having attained independence, too, the Ugandans seemed to have carved a path for their education system. Working with Uganda's Development Plan for Education (1964–65), all through to 1970, it was noted that secondary education had increased steadily. Not quite the same can be said for primary education. The increase in primary education was not quite noticeable, with the attrition rate only slightly reduced. This meant that Uganda still had to work on its attrition rate as well as the problem of overaged children in primary school. The Universal Primary Education Scheme that was more or less a declared aim in December 1964 was put on hold because of the adverse outcome predicted. In other words, the government had fears that a declaration of compulsory basic education would have its effect on the country's financial resources, as well as flood the labor market with unemployed youngsters.

In the government's development plan for education, attention was also paid to teacher education programs. This was quite crucial in meeting the needs of the large population of students that were graduated yearly at the primary and secondary levels. While the mission organizations still maintained their teacher training colleges, the government also took serious steps to establish secular teacher training colleges. The major aim was to cater to the interest barrier of mission-trained teachers, whose particular religious inclination may affect the secularization process.

The training of teachers for secondary schools was also a big task for the government. Their aim was to train indigenous teachers for their secondary schools. It was expected that such teachers would replace expatriates, whose continued stay was not only culturally unsatisfactory, but also quite an expensive venture. Even with some foreign aid, the employment of expatriates meant huge financial involvements, especially with passages paid by the government.

Between 1963 and 1964, the Ugandan government ran various teacher education programs for its indigenes. They began with a postgraduate diploma in education for nongraduates of education and about the same time, the Grade Five teacher training scheme was introduced. The latter was a three-year education program that was run at the National Teachers' College in Kyambogo. With time, Makarere University College would later run postgraduate diploma in education and also award bachelor's degree in education. By the early 1970s, most primary and secondary schools in Uganda were headed by indigenes.

Finally, technical education was also in the five-year education development plan. The Uganda Technical College enjoyed some expansion. Technical sandwich training schemes were introduced, while some technical courses were upgraded to a full degree level. In that same period, Uganda's Technical

College was elevated to the status of a Faculty of Technology of the Makarere University. These and many more positive changes were carefully planned and implemented in Uganda, until the military coup of January 1971. The new government in its educational plan began by calling on its own curriculum development center to revise the then-existing curriculum for a new one.

EDUCATION STRUCTURE

There are four levels in the structure of formal education in Uganda; it is often referred to as the 7-4-2-3 system. The Ministry of Education and Sports is responsible for all levels of education. The first level which is the primary school with an entry age of six years consists of seven grades starting from standard one to seven. At the secondary level four years is spent at the lower secondary level leading to the Uganda Certificate in Education (UCE). Another two years of upper secondary level leads the recipient to the Uganda Advanced Certificate in Education (UACE). Besides the regular upper secondary school education, the Ugandan student has other options of an advanced two years secondary training in teachers' colleges, technical institutes, or any other specialized training program provided by government.

On completion of any of the above, certificates earned served as entry or prerequisite for a three to five years plus (depending on course of study) of postsecondary or tertiary education in any of such higher institutions as the Makerere University in Kampala, Uganda Technical College, Institutes of Teacher Education, or National College of Business Studies. Some others who complete higher secondary school certificate travel abroad for further study.

Table 10.4 shows the structure of the education system in Uganda.

PREPRIMARY SCHOOL

Preschool education in Uganda, though not emphasized, is encouraged at this stage as basically a private enterprise. Most nursery and kindergarten schools in Uganda are located in urban areas. Children in the rural areas tend to wait for primary education and may end up entering primary school with little or no preparation for the intellectual task it requires. Others just come from homes where parents have no formal exposure to formal education nor does the home environment provide exposure to reading materials to prepare them for elementary reading and writing.

However, in recent times, since 2005, the Ugandan government has come out with a draft proposal on creating public awareness in early childhood education as well as strengthening the demand for it. The focus is on an education program that would articulate proper nutrition, health care, and intellectual stimulation during the early years of the child's life. This ultimately would

Table 10.4
Educational Structure in Uganda

Isced Level	Name	Ministry Responsible
Preschool (0)	Preschool	Ministry of Education
Primary (1)	Primary Education	and Culture (MOES)
Lower Secondary (2A)	1st Cycle of secondary Education (General)	
Upper Secondary (3A)	2nd Cycle of Secondary Education (General)	
Lower Secondary Vocational (2C)	1st Cycle of Secondary Education (Technical or Vocation)	
Upper Secondary Vocational (3C)	2nd Cycle Secondary Education (Technical or Vocational)	
Postsecondary nontertiary (4)	Technical College	
Tertiary, 1st stage (5)	Universities	
Tertiary, 2nd stage (6)	Universities	
NFE	Nonformal institutions	Ministry of Gender Labour Youth and Social Development (MGLSG) and MOES

Source: UNESCO, Institute for Statistics (2003–05).

improve learning and other abilities. In recognizing early childhood development as an integral part of basic education, the working group on early childhood development (UGED) was created in 1997 with UNICEF as the lead agency. The group that has been quite critical of lack of support and commitment in Africa held its first conference on early childhood in 1999 in Kampala in Uganda. This forum provided opportunity for Ugandans to participate. Indeed, the first forum helped them appreciate early childhood development and education as crucial to unfolding the cognitive, social, and physical potentials of the Ugandan child.

The early childhood development program in Uganda emphasized the training of local women in health and child development strategies that enhance early development in the child. Ultimately, this would reduce the burden of girls from being saddled with caring for their younger siblings instead of being in school.

Essentially, the early childhood education program would be a follow-up of the country's Education for All (EFA) at its commencement in the year 2000.

One outcome of the EFA in Uganda was the recognition of the need for early childhood education, an expansion of its program, and the development of its activities in nursery education. Thus, with regards to this, Uganda's government was concerned with enrollment in early childhood education. Before then statistics showed that the percentage of Uganda's children who attend organized nursery education before primary school was quite low and needed improvement.

Basically, the aims of early childhood education programs in Uganda were as follows:

1. to develop mental capabilities, health, and the physical growth of the child through play activities;
2. to inculcate moral values in the young learner;
3. to help the child appreciate his or her cultural background and customs;
4. to enrich the child's experience, by developing imagination, a sense of self- reliance, thinking power; and
5. to develop language and communication skills, including in his mother tongue.

Against this background, the EFA strategies and plans for the expansion of Early Childhood Care and Development (ECCD) activities were drawn as follows:

1. In the 1992–93 school year, Primary Teachers' College (PTC) would begin the training of early childhood education teachers, hoping the number would gradually increase according to improvements in the economy and manpower needs of the nation;
2. All PTC students would get basic training in early childhood methods and specialization and a comprehensive program for this scheme should be worked out so as to ensure standards and control.
3. Implementation of these strategies would involve the Ministry of Education and Sports (Inspectorate Division), the commissioner of preprimary and primary education, and every district and local council in the nation.
4. Learning needs for the expansion of early childhood care and development would incorporate a holistic development of the child's life skills, health and physical growth, good social habits, values, and imaginative skills. Others include an appreciation of self-reliance, thinking power, language and communication skills.

It is important to note that the above strategies were reviewed in 1995 by UNESCO and again 1997 by the task force on EFA. Still on the development of early childhood education programs. Uganda's minister of education reported that as a way of streamlining the country's preschool program, his ministry had developed a policy on Early Childhood Development (ECD). The government had also licensed private preschool owners and would continually monitor their activities. They would also take cognizance of the curriculum content of preschool teachers-in-training with emphasis on instructional methods. As of the time of his report, the minister put the enrollment of pupils in preschools of the age group two to five years old (in lower baby class to top class) at 41,775 (Ministry of Education and Sports 2005).

PRIMARY EDUCATION

Primary education in Uganda is officially the first stage of formal schooling. The entry age is six years, and its duration is seven years. In the seventh year of primary schooling, the child sits for an entrance examination that prepares him for entry into the first level of secondary education.

Tracing the growth and development of primary education in Uganda from pre-independence until now, there has been considerable improvement and great changes. Important, the high attrition rate that haunted primary education in the colonial and missionary era and even before independence seems to have abated. The government has paid considerable attention to primary education, through the introduction of the Universal Primary Education (UPE) in 1997, thereby making basic education accessible to all Ugandan children. This has had an impact on the economic and educational development of Uganda.

Clare Short aptly stated, "Uganda has already proved that it is committed to the intentional development target of Universal Primary Education by the year 2015" (BBC News October 1995). She further added that, giving a country like Uganda the capacity to set up an education system that would last forever would help it go forward, pull itself out of poverty and become independent of aid (BBC News October 1995).

The government's zeal to provide primary education to Uganda's children has been quite evident since 1989. As of that year, the government estimate of pupils who had enrolled for primary education was put at 2.4 million, of which 45 percent were females. This figure represented a fourfold increase from the enrollment of the late 1960s. This figure nearly doubles the 1.3 million pupils who enrolled in 1980. In the same year, just over half of the figure recorded of six to twelve year olds, was attending government-aided primary schools, while an additional 80,000 were enrolled in private primary schools. Official figures also revealed that in 1980, 61 percent of the total completed their education (that is, the official seventh grade), and of that figure, 25 percent proceeded for further education in secondary school (Uganda Information Resource 1990).

Following this upward trend, in 1999, the Uganda government had recorded 6 million pupils receiving primary education. This indeed is quite an achievement, especially when compared to only 2 million recorded in 1986. It may also be said that the increase in enrollment was boosted by the introduction of the UPE launched in 1997. Under that program free primary education was made available for four children per family at any public school at the government's expense (Source of statistics: http://www/myuganda.co.ug/edu/).

Similar to the preschool program of the EFA, government had set a goal for primary education in Uganda. The target was the provision of universal access to and completion of primary education for all Ugandan children of primary school age, by the year 2000. After the launch of the UPE, which recorded 6.591 million children in primary school, as of the turn of the year 2000, over 7.7 million Ugandan children of primary school age were in school (Ministry of Education and Sports 2004).

Besides the efforts to increase enrollment, the government has also tried to match enrollment with financial commitment. The government financial report revealed that public expenditure on primary education as a percentage of total public expenditure increased from 49 percent of the GNP in 1995/1996 to 62 percent in 1999/2000. This increase in funding also shows how committed the government was to ensure the success of the Universal Primary Education (UPE) program.

Although there was far more qualitative teaching in primary school, teacher education program for primary education was restructured to meet the demand of the UPE scheme. In like manner, the percentage of qualified teachers increased steadily from 52 percent in 1990 to 75 percent in 1998 of which 34 percent were females (1990 Uganda Information Resource). The increase in the number of teachers invariably improved the pupil–teacher ratio. On the whole, a comparative estimate of the teaching work force increased from 81,600 in 1996 just before the launch of the UPE scheme to 145,000 in 2000.

Essentially, primary school in Uganda has a seven-year duration, at the end of which the pupil sits for a primary school leaving examination (PLE). Subjects examined are basically core including English language, mathematics, science, and social science. A pass in these subjects earns the pupil a PLE certificate.

Primary schooling in Uganda falls into two categories. There are private primary schools run and managed by nongovernment-aided schools, primarily the business of the Ministry of Education and Sports. This ministry also takes care of teacher education, registration of teachers, and their posting. It is also the responsibility of the Ministry to prescribe the national curriculum and text-books. In more recent times, with the UPE scheme in progress, the government has been playing a major role in the supply of instructional materials, textbooks for core subjects, purchase of supplementary books for readers, provision of teachers' reference books, charts, and blackboards. The administrative and inspectorate divisions are also the responsibility of the government. Additionally, the Ministry of Education has constructed school buildings and staff quarters, sanitary facilities, as well as provided furniture in schools. To support the Ministry in the provision of physical structures, nongovernmental organizations, the local communities, and parents through the PTA provide land, blocks, labor, and at other times give financial support and instructional materials to schools.

Presently, with the steady increase in enrollment, the government is more committed in the provision of quality primary education in a conducive setting with adequate teaching materials. In the construction of classrooms, sanitary facilities, and teachers' houses, there is a grant for special school facilities. The program is intended to assist less privileged schools and communities. The government's aim is to house an increased number of teachers and provide more classrooms to meet the increasing enrollment. Their target includes a teacher–pupil ratio of 1:55, desk-to-pupil ratio of 1:3, toilets-to-pupil ratio of 1:40, and at least four teachers' houses per school. From present government figures, the number of classrooms has increased to 78,403, compared to only 25,676 classrooms in 1996. But as previously stated, the pupil-to-classroom ratio is yet high (Ministry of Education Annual Performance Report).

The primary school curriculum like that of other level of education is the responsibility of the National Curriculum Development Centre (NCDC). The Centre was set up in 1973 with a major aim of reviewing the curriculum content of Uganda's education to ensure it suited the educational goals of the country. It was also intended that the reviewed curriculum would produce employable school leavers, and productive members of society.

In order to have an adequate and effective primary school curriculum the government appointed a curriculum task force. The task force was made up of the National Curriculum Development Centre (NCDC), Uganda National Examinations Board (UNEB), the Education Planning Department, and the preprimary education department of the Ministry of Education. The task force reviewed and came up with a new national curriculum for primary education as well as other levels of education. However, current reform in primary education in Uganda, especially with the introduction of the UPE scheme, is centered on increasing retention and completion rate and attaches greater importance to reading and writing. Others include regular inspection of schools, the need to retrain teachers, and management training for head teachers. All of this it is believed would put in place quality primary education. Important too, the education sector is ensuring that primary school learners have access to books and other learning materials. Also, the use of the local language in teaching learners in the first grade through the seventh has been given serious thought.

SECONDARY EDUCATION

The education system in Uganda allows for continuity in education from primary to secondary education. In the seventh year of primary education, the child sits for a national examination that earns him a certificate (PLE), as well as prepares him for the secondary level of learning.

Secondary education in Uganda is made up of two levels: first is the four years of lower secondary education otherwise called the ordinary level that leads to the Ugandan Certificate of Education (UCE). To qualify for this certificate the students are tested in between nine and fourteen subjects. Having qualified, students are again accepted for two more years of upper secondary education or the Advanced (A) level. At this level of learning the student is expected to specialize in his best four subjects. He is made to sit for another National Examination to earn him the Uganda Advanced Certificate of Education (UACE). This certificate gives the recipient the option of going into the world of work or proceeding into the tertiary level of learning.

Secondary schools in Uganda are private and government-aided. In 2005, there were 1,651 government-aided schools, and about 1,898 private secondary schools. Most of the government-aided schools are built by parents on self-help basis, and some others by community effort. The private ones are owned by voluntary agencies and individuals. The high number of private secondary schools may be as a result of government's inability to meet the overwhelming demand of primary school leavers; especially with the introduction of the Universal Primary Education Scheme. As Kirungi (2000) rightly noted, "with the introduction of the UPE scheme, the problem of transition from primary to secondary level may pose a problem for the government judging from his figures recorded, out of the 211,749 candidates who sat for the primary school leaving examination in 1997, only 87,231 or 41.3 percent moved on to secondary schools the following year; even when about 70 percent actually passed the PLE." This simply shows a low transition rate. Making the same argument, a one-time commissioner for secondary education in Uganda, Yusuf Nsubuga has warned that failure to absorb the growing number of primary school leavers in Uganda may undermine the Universal Primary Education Scheme, and even broader national goals like the elimination of poverty (Kirungi 2000).

However, in more recent times the government is working hard on some strategies, especially at the secondary level. The idea is to create vacancies at the secondary stage for the primary school leavers, whose enrollment by 2003 was projected to increase to 262,074 from 149,840 in 1999. In this plan, the idea was to build more schools, rehabilitate and expand existing ones, as well as utilize more effectively the schools on ground. In an interview with the then Minister for Education, Mr. Kiddu Makubuya, in 2003 (*Education Today* September 2003), he cited postprimary or secondary education as the most pressing educational challenge facing his country. He was quite bothered about educational provision for Uganda's children who had completed the primary school cycle. He noted that so much attention in terms of funding has gone into primary education. His fear is that it may have negative financial implication for secondary education. Makubuya also had his worry about the lopsided nature of Uganda's secondary school curriculum. His opinion being that the curriculum was too academic and not comprehensive enough. He expressed an urgent need for inclusion of the vocational and technical aspects of education. Above all, with much emphasis placed on primary education, almost at the expense of secondary education, the minister wondered if there could be an onward linkage from the primary to the secondary by way of continuity. Where this is not the case, people may no longer see the need for primary education.

This may discourage the emphasis on the compulsory basic education currently in place.

Uganda has some other secondary types that are parallel to the mainstream secondary schools. The duration usually ranges from two to three years, and such schools are mostly technical or vocational in nature. The country has about 29 grant-aided such technical schools that absorb primary school leavers and offer courses in crafts and other vocational skills. There are also 33 technical institutes for postvocational level and posttechnical school leavers. These offer vocational and technical courses for a minimum of two years. Uganda also has about 16 community polytechnics, 45 Primary Teachers' Training Colleges, Schools of Business Studies, 5 colleges of commerce, and 5 Technical Colleges. All of these are also postsecondary level institutions. The government also encourages private ownership of technical and commercial institutes. This is another way of promoting vocational and technical education.

TERTIARY EDUCATION

Higher education in Uganda caters to secondary school leavers. The universities and related institutions run various courses and programs in the sciences, social sciences, the arts and humanities, and other professional courses like medicine, law, etc. The course duration varies from three to five years or more depending on the course of study. The qualifications earned at the end of course include certificates, diplomas, and degrees (bachelors, masters, and PhDs).

Uganda has a number of universities and higher institutions of learning—the major being Makarere University in Kampala. This has catered to higher education for the East African countries (notably Tanzania, Kenya, and Uganda) right from the colonial era. This has indeed made Makarere University a popular choice among universities in Uganda. An official government source stated that "although 9,000–12,000 students per year leave school qualified to enter higher education only some 25 percent of them find places at the limited number of institutions. Makaerere University in Kampala (MUK) accepts some 95 percent of the total population in Uganda's Universities."

Ministry of Education report of 2005 indicates that Uganda can boast of about four public universities and twenty-seven licensed private universities. The increase in the number of universities and other tertiary institutions was a result of the university and other Tertiary Institutions Act of 2001 Act that gave a legal framework for the management and administration of higher education in the country. This law in pursuance of quality in higher education created the National Council for Higher Education (NCHE) as the government agency responsible for the licensing of private universities. It also sets academic and management standards for all universities in Uganda (Uganda Government 2001). The Universities and other Tertiary Act. The expansion of Universities

Table 10.5
Growth of Enrollment in Tertiary Learning from 1969–2004

Year	Population Estimates in Millions	Enrollment	Growth	Percentage	Enrollment Per 100,000 of Population
1969	9.5	5,341	NA	NA	56
1980	12.6	10,352	5,011	48.41	80
1990	16.5	17,000	6,648	39.11	104
1995	19.2	30,268	13,268	43.84	157
2000	22.3	59,716	29,448	49.31	268
2001	22.8	68,408	8,692	12.71	300
2002	23.3	78,367	9,959	12.71	336
2003	23.9	89,775	11,408	12.71	375
2004	25.0	108,295	18,520	17.10	440

Source: Kasozi (2005).

has also resulted from the ever-increasing demand for higher education in recent years. Table 10.5 shows the growth of enrollment in tertiary learning in Uganda in recent times.

The development of a strategic plan for higher education in Uganda 2001–05 is a changing landscape.

According to Kasozi (2005), "There has been an unprecedented emergence of many new institutions of higher learning, including university and non-university ones. From one university institution in 1987, the country now has twenty-eight private and public universities, some of which are less than glorified high school ... from two universities in 1970 to 127 in 2004." There is service concern about falling standards and the lowering of the quality of higher education. This was highlighted in a report from the survey of the National Council for Higher Education (NCHE survey 2004). Findings revealed that educational facilities in higher institutions have not been expanding fast enough to match the increase in students' enrollment. This fear is heightened in view of current poor allocation of funds to higher education. Funds allocated to higher education have almost stagnated between 9 percent to 12 percent of the Ministry of Education budget (see Table 10.6).

In view of Kasozi's suggestion and judging from the financial allocation to tertiary institutions, there is urgent need to do more. More areas needing attention include the followings:

1. The introduction of a credit system
2. Rise in the number of students studying science and technology from 15 percent in 2004 to 30 percent by 2015
3. Increased access

Table 10.6
Recurrent Budget Allocation in Billions of Uganda Shillings, 2001/2002 to 2005/2006

Total Education Sector Recurrent (In Billions)	2001/2002 Estimate 350.53	2002/2003 Planned 403.07	2003/2004 Planned 65%	2004/2005 Planned 66%	2005/2006 Planned 66%
Primary Education	66%	63%	65%	66%	66%
Secondary Education (including NTCs)	16%	18%	18%	18%	17%
BTVET	4%	4%	4%	3%	3%
Tertiary (without tertiary BTVET/NTC)	12%	12%	11%	11%	11%
Others	3%t	3%	2%	2%	2%
Total	**100%**	**100%**	**100%**	**100%**	**100%**

Source: World Bank (2004).

- to the poor through loans
- to regions by establishing a university in the east
- by rehabilitating existing infrastructures
- encouraging private sector participation

4. Financing by the
   - government to fund tuition and not welfare
   - government to sponsor 75 percent science students and 25 percent arts and humanities
   - government to establish universities grants committee in the long-term
   - government to fund only students who are studying subjects that are key to economic development.

5. Governance
   - to empower the National Council for Higher Education by more funding and appropriate legislation.

6. Control and Prevention of HIV/AIDS
   - All institutions would be required to have programs for HIV/AIDS prevention. (Hayward 2004)

In his assessment of the above, Kasozi (2005) is of the view that when implemented the above reforms would make higher education as a subsector quite appreciable. However, he is yet insistent that for benefits to be achieved from lofty reforms like those above, the country must seek the financial means to overhaul the curriculum, and integrate ICT in the delivery of higher education. Significantly, he has also argued that for too long too much attention in terms of funding has been paid to other levels of education, almost at the expense of

tertiary education. While critics are not against funding of other levels of learning, they are worried about how little attention is given higher education in
Uganda. More so in an era when higher education must be so structured to
not only be relevant to a people, but also address global changes. In his final
argument, Kasozi states that:

As higher education becomes increasingly key to economic development, and as UPE
graduates move on to tertiary sub-sector, the eyes of internal and external actors must
refocus on higher education. Unless higher education is urgently reformed to address
internal and global forces, the reforms of the primary and secondary levels will not have
the best social impact. Students who are well trained at the lower levels need good tertiary institutions in a good tertiary sector (2005).

In the same vein, Mayanja (2005) has opined that the government of
Uganda cannot reverse the UPE policy and the political commitment to it, but
if it wants to transform the Ugandan economy, it must realize that the manpower bottleneck is not at the provision of UPE graduates, but of degree holders at the highest level as well as the Advanced and Ordinary levels.

Again, the curriculum imbalance that is not quite appropriate to development in Uganda needs some reforms. This will go a long way to giving the
nation a status in the midst of other technologically growing nations. The
expectation is that like most developing African nations, Uganda, too, is continuously striving to bring some reforms to all levels of education. This must
be an ongoing process in the development and growth in relation to the education of any nation.

GIRL-CHILD EDUCATION IN UGANDA

In Uganda, the population tends to have more females than males. The
school enrollment figure at the primary school level indicates that 49 percent
are girls and 51 percent boys. While the total percentage of girls in Uganda's
secondary schools can be put at 32 percent, the percentage in universities and
polytechnics is 32 percent and 13 percent, respectively. However, the disparity
in enrollment (between girls and boys) is mostly obvious between the first and
seventh grades of primary education. In the first grade, the disparity between
boys and girls is 1.1 percent. By the seventh grade it hits about 15.7 percent.
This disparity indeed led to the launching of a national strategy for the girl-
child education in Uganda. The main aim of this strategy was to educate the
Ugandan populace on the need for female education, and increase their access
to education and learning, many reasons for lack of access to education were
given. Notable among these factors are, first, the cultural barrier. For instance,
the traditional Ugandan society does not see the value in girl-child education
because it is expected that they will be given out in marriage and hence it
would be the husband's responsibility to educate her. It is seen as a valueless
venture. There is also the home-based barrier. In this case, there is often this

tendency by parents to retain their female child at home to do the household chores, instead of going to school.

Makubuya (2003) has also noted that Ugandan schools sometimes do not encourage female education. He stressed the need for schools to change their orientation in order to become more girl-friendly. He suggested that things like separate toilets in schools for girls, and the employment of more female teacher could make girls comfortable enough to remain in school. Significantly, Ugandan's constitution guarantees equal rights to men and women. But unless parents and the community, especially at the grassroots level, are educated on this, they may not appreciate the need for their girls to be kept in school to complete their education. It is on this score that most schools in Uganda today design programs to attract girls as well as keep them in school to complete their education. As explained by Mariam Luyombo, a director of education in Uganda, "At Taibah Primary and Secondary School, we have a personal development curriculum which teachers self-awareness and communication skills, and covers matters of sex, AIDS, infatuation and the use of contraceptives. As a result, we hardly have any girl who does not complete school" (Kirungi 2000).

On the other hand, the government on its part has recognized the effect of educational disparity and has thus come up with several gender-responsive projects being presently implemented under the Education Sector Strategic Plan (ESSP). The aim is to improve and expand females' education, and educate Ugandans on the role of all, including the female as an important contributor to the development of the nation. The projects for girl-child education in Uganda are

1. Girls Education Movement (GEM). This is a grassroots movement that aims to empower Ugandan girls on the need to be educated. Presently in Uganda, GEM clubs are formed in schools throughout all districts. Leaders of the clubs are expected to attend GEM facilitator training.
2. National Strategy for Girls' Education. This plans and maps out strategies for improving and expanding girl-child education. In launching this program in June, 2000, the Vice President Specioza Wandira Kazibwe noted that the percentage of females enrolled in primary school is yet lower than that of their male counterparts.
3. The Early Childhood Development Program. This program is geared towards the training of local women in health and child development. In emphasizing the importance of girl-child education, the programs stress the need for early childhood education and imparting in young girls correct health habits.
4. Child Friendly Basic Education and Learning Program. This one deals with the most comprehensive matters concerning quality education, equitable participation attainments, retention of girls in school, and other such challenges that could affect female education.
5. Breakthrough to Literacy (BTL). This is basically a child-centered and gender responsive support program for the retention of girls in school. It also promotes teaching children life skills, as well as reading and writing.

6. The SARA Initiative Centers on Building in the female folks Self-esteem and Raising life Aspirations (SARA). This is another way of bringing to the fore an awareness and support for girl education.
7. Finally, the Basic Education Child Care and Adolescent Development (BECCAD). This focuses on the rights of the child, promotes awareness of girls' education especially at the basic level, and stresses not just the retention of girls in primary school, but also an increase in female enrollment.

ADULT AND NONFORMAL EDUCATION

The Ugandan government is quite concerned about education for her populace at whatever age or level in life. During the colonial and missionary era, the missions in their zeal to spread Christianity to the people provided mainly adults some opportunity to read and write. If nothing else, the idea was to prepare them to appreciate the religious messages and scripture.

When they attained independence, the Ugandan government, through various programs continued their adult literacy activities that included helping the citizenry develop social and health habits. Even at that, not enough was accomplished to help the adult achieve the goal of true literacy more especially, when the females hardly had access. This meant that there was need for more focus on females in this regard.

Uganda has recently initiated a more Functional Adult Literacy (FAL) program. It is quite a comprehensive national program run by the Ministry of Gender, Labour and Social Development (MOGLSD). The main aim of the program is to assist adults acquire skills in reading, writing, and arithmetic. This would empower them to employ these skills in their everyday life activities. For instance, it is expected that women who have acquired numeracy skills can control their businesses and manage their accounts and income. An effective adult education scheme would also empower women economically and socially.

The Ministry of Gender, Labour and Social Development in conjunction with some nongovernmental organizations (NGOs) have helped to promote adult literacy through the provision of literacy materials like charts books, teaching aids, etc. Also, books have been written in local languages to help the rural learners read, write, and understand. Other educational programs run by the Adult Education Unit include vocational training, extramural studies, community development, and club activities. There are also mass mobilization programs for general and specific adult groups. Generally, the progress and success of the Functional Adult Literacy (FAL) program in Uganda has been through the assistance of notable NGOs like the Action-Aid, National Adult Education Association, Uganda's Community Association for Child Welfare, Uganda Joint Action for Adult Education, religious bodies, and some agencies. The prison departments also carries out some literacy programs in prisons to occupy, teach, and assist their inmates.

NONFORMAL EDUCATION

The Ugandan government also takes cognizance of her citizens especially children who do not have access to education. Such children usually reside in fishing villages, pastoral areas, overaged children, etc. The government with the support of NGOs has put in place several initiatives to bring to the doorsteps of these disadvantaged children alternatives to formal schooling. Some of such initiatives are

1. Alternative Basic Education for Karamoja (ABEK)
2. Complimentary Opportunities for Primary Education (COPE)
3. Basic Education for Urban Poverty Areas (BEUPA)
4. Child-Centered Alternative Nonformal Community Based Education (CHANCE)
5. Empowering Lifelong Skills in Masindi (ELSE).

EDUCATION IN A WAR ZONE: THE CASE OF TWO DISTRICTS (GULU AND KITGUM) IN NORTHERN UGANDA

As previously noted at the introduction of this work, Uganda has had its sour-times of internal strife and civil war. This has also had its devastating effect on the educational growth and development of the people. Yoweri Museveni who assumed power at the end of the civil war, as president of Uganda, indeed tried to rebuild the ruins of the education system. At the primary school level, Museveni performed well, especially with the introduction of the UPE scheme in 1996. Uganda was recorded as the first African country to successfully execute the UPE scheme. In his regime, the number of secondary schools increased tremendously, and standard and quality of learning improved. The teaching cadre has had its fair share of improvements, with the status of teachers made more appreciable through incentives. At the tertiary level, Uganda could boast of more than the well known Makarere University. Just like the number of higher institution has increased, so also has enrollment. So much so that the financial and human resources have almost become inadequate as they can no longer match their employments. The girl-child education, adult and nonformal education have also been given attention. On the whole, Uganda's funding of the education system is quite appreciable.

The above picture of a thriving education system may be said of the other parts of Uganda, but not quite so for northern Uganda. The latter is more of a war-torn zone with Ugandan citizens suffering. As aptly described by the Women's Commission for Refugee Women and Children (2001), the war in Uganda has displaced over 1.6 million people in northern Uganda. Perhaps the most heinous component of the war is the kidnapping and use of boys and girls as soldiers and slaves by the Lord's Resistance Army (LRA). On the average, more than 28,000 children have been abducted and about 80 percent of the fighters in the LRA are children. Important, not only have people been displaced, children dehumanized, but their education has been drastically altered. While their kith and kin in other parts of Uganda may be enjoying the benefits of the UPE scheme, the same cannot be said of them.

Citing the case of two districts, Gulu and Kitgum in northern Uganda, the Women's Commission for Refugee and Children through interviews have painted a very pathetic picture of the war zone. The Commission had interviews with NGOs, youth groups, teachers, heads of schools, local government officials, multinational actors, parents and the children, as victims. From their findings, one thing that cuts across was that in spite of the pains of war, the victims still believed in education as the one sure hope that could redeem them. The young people in the war zone stated that education was perhaps the most important way to prevent their being recruited into the armed groups. Some others interviewed called for the establishment of schools around refugee camps. Adults interviewed stressed the need for the Ministry of Education to attend to their plight in terms of education. (Excerpts from interviews carried out by the Women's Commission in the Districts of Gulu and Ketgum with education officers.)

PRIMARY EDUCATION IN THE WAR ZONE

The children of primary school age and in primary schools in northern Uganda may not be as fortunate as others in southern Uganda who benefit from the UPE scheme. In the interview with the District Education Officer (DEO) of Gulu (September 24, 2004) and that of Kitgum (September, 20, 2004), it was expressed to the Commission that in both districts, tuition may be free, but other essentials like reading and writing materials, uniforms, PTA fees (usually negotiated by parents at PTA meetings) lunch, and building fees come to a total of 5,000 and 15,000 Ugandan shillings per term at three terms in an academic session. In other words, paying that much, and paying no tuition cannot be truly said to be free. Thus, parents, who in a war-torn zone may not be fortunate enough to get good jobs and pay so much to get education for their children. The Commission also noted that such fees charged may be quite a hindrance to school attendance. In addition to this, the commission also named insecurity; lack of school buildings, classrooms, and desks; lack of toilet and water; shortage of qualified teachers; and illness as barriers to effective learning and regular school attendance.

In terms of regular physical school and class structures, both districts may not boast of too many. Such is expected of an area ravaged by war, insecurity, and regular abduction and killings. Such destructions have led to displaced schools. However, there are makeshift classroom structures and learning centers in camps and under trees. But as the DEO of Kitgun said, if these were not

Table 10.7
Some Recorded Number of Schools in Kitgum and Gulu Districts

Schools	Kitgum	Gulu
Primary	174	
Secondary	22	35
Tertiary	2	
Vocational/Technical	5	
Early Childhood Education centers	5	

Source: Women Commission for Refugee Women and Children (2005).

created to replace displaced schools, then education would come to an end in these districts. Table 10.7 shows the total number of schools in both districts.

SECONDARY EDUCATION IN THE WAR ZONE

In spite of its present status as a war-devastated area northern Uganda still has some form of secondary education activities. Most secondary schools in Gulu and Kitgum are located inside the towns, far from attacks. Secondary schools in these districts are private and public. Unlike private schools, public schools suffer lack of teachers and in most cases settle for untrained teachers. These untrained teachers are those who have not fulfilled the mandatory two years training.

Generally, one major problem with the teaching profession is lack of incentives for teachers. As a result so many young people are not attracted to it as a profession. On the average, teachers earn 59,000 Ugandan shillings a month (an equivalent of US$34). Even at that, they work for eight to ten hours daily for six days a week. This unattractive situation has led to a shortage of teachers. Tables 10.8 and 10.9 show this.

In the same way that they suffer shortage of teachers, these districts also have lacked accommodation—classrooms, physical learning environment, and toilet facilities. Other facilities as furniture, blackboards, and other teaching aids have been in short supply.

Table 10.8
Ratio of Children to Teachers in Kitgum and Gulu Districts

	Kitgum	Gulu
Government standard ratio of children per teacher	50:1	50:1
Actual ratio children per teacher	150–300:1	Was 150:1 Now 80:1

Source: Women's Commission for Refugee Women and Children (2005).

Table 10.9
Ratio of Children to Schools and Learning Environment

Ratios of Children and the Physical Learning Environment	Kitgum	Gulu
Students to classroom ratio	400:1	No information
Government standard children per toilet	40:1	No information
Actual children per toilet	150:1	No information

According to the Commission, even though children in northern Uganda may seem to be schooling, what is on ground by way of education is woefully inadequate. They have thus recommended as follows:

1. There is need for Uganda's Ministry of Education together with the districts and subdistricts in the north, as well as the community to work for the improvement of education in the areas.
2. The Ministry should provide adequate funds to meet some educational needs such as uniform, books, reading and writing materials of the schools.
3. The number of schools as well as teachers is presently inadequate and should therefore be given urgent attention.
4. Existing technical and vocational education opportunity is quite limited in scope; this needs expansion. Graduates of these programs could be encouraged through apprenticeships and the provision of working tools on completion.
5. Early childhood education programs should be refocused to include early learning and development of children.
6. The disarmament, demobilization, and reintegration (DDR) program should be reworked to include more educational elements. The idea is to accelerate their return to their various levels of education.

BIBLIOGRAPHY

Apoka, A. 1967. "At Home in the Village: Growing up in Acholi." In *East African Childhood*. Edited by L. K. Fox. Nairobi, Uganda: Nairobi Press.

Baker, S. J. K. 1963. "The East African Environment." In *A History of East Africa*. Edited by Harlow and Smith. London: Oxford University Press.

CIA. 2001. *World Fact Book*. Washington, D.C.

Furley, O. W., and T. Watson. 1978. *A History of Education in East Africa*. New York: NOK Publishers.

Hayward, F. M. "The Uganda Strategic Plan for Higher Education, 2003–2015: Strengths Challenges and Prospects for implementation." *The Uganda Education Review, The Journal of the National Council for Higher Education* 1, no. 21 (2004): 28–31.

Ingham, K. 1958. *The Making of Modern Uganda*. London: Allen & Unwin.

Kasozi, A. B. K. 2003. *University Education in Uganda: Challenges and Opportunities for Reform*. Oxford, UK: African Books.

Kasozi, A. B. K. *The Development of a Strategic Plan for Higher Education in Uganda 2001–5: The Interplay of Internal and External Forces in Higher Education Policy Formation in a Southern Country.* Paper presented at the Nuffic Conference, The Hague, May 23–25, 2005.

Kirungi, F. "Uganda Tackling School Bottlenecks." *Africa Recovery* 14, no. 2 (2000): 20.

Martin, P., and P. O 'Meara. 1995. *Africa.* Bloomington: Indiana University Press.

Mayanja, A. K. "The Way Forward on Varsity Fees." *New Vision* (2005): 12.

Mukama, R. G. 1991. "Recent Development in the Language Situation and Prospects for the Future." In *Changing Uganda.* Edited by H. B. Hansen and M. Twaddle. Kampala, Uganda: Fountain Publishers.

Ministry of Education and Sports. 1998. *Education Strategic Investment Plan 1998–2003.* Kampala, Uganda.

Ministry of Education and Sports. 1999. *Interim Report of Education for All (EFA) 2000 Assessment.* Kampala, Uganda.

Ministry of Education and Sports. 2004. *Uganda's 2003/04 Education Annual Performance Report.* Kampala Uganda.

Ministry of Education and Sports. 2005. "Education for Rural People in Africa: Policy, Lessons, Options and Priorities." Report on Uganda in the Ministerial Seminar, Addis Ababa, Ethiopia, Sept. 7–9.

Trowell, M., and K. Wachsmann. 1953. *Tribal Crafts of Uganda.* London: Oxford University Press.

Uganda Government. 1992. "Education for National Integration and Development." Government white paper on Implementation of the Recommendation of the Report of the Education Policy Review Commission. Kampala, Uganda.

Women's Commission for Refugee Women and Children. 2004. *No Safe Place to Call Home: Children and Adolescent Night Commuters in Northern Uganda.* New York.

Women's Commission for Refugee Women and Children. 2005. *Learning in a War Zone: Education in Northern Uganda.* New York.

WEB SITE

Uganda country information: http://www.myuganda.co.ug/edu.

BIBLIOGRAPHY

Adelman, Kenneth L. "The Zairian Political Party as Religious Surrogate." *Africa Today* 23–24 (Oct.–Dec. 1976).

Adibe, Clement. "Accepting External Authority in Peace-Maintenance." *Global Governance* 4, no. 1 (1998): 107–172.

Akeredolu-Ale, E. O. "Some Thoughts on the Indigenization Process and the Quality of Nigerian Capitalism." *Nigerian Indigenization Policy: Proceedings of the Nigerian Economic Society Symposium, 1975.*

Amin, Martin. 1997. *Report on the Demand for Primary Education in Cameroon, 1980–1995.* Washington, D.C.: World Bank.

Anderson, J. E. 1970. *The Struggle for the School: The Interaction of Missionary Colonial Government and Nationalist Enterprises in the Development of Formal Education in Kenya.* London: Longman.

Anya, Anya O. *Leadership, Education and the Challenge of Development in the 21st Century.* Lecture at the 29th Convocation of the University of Benin, Nigeria, 2003.

Apoka, A. 1967. "At Home in the Village: Growing up in Acholi." In *East African Childhood.* Edited by L. K. Fox. Nairobi, Uganda: Nairobi Press.

Ayodele-Bamisaiye, Oluremi. 2000. "Education for Social Transformation in a New South Africa. The Context of Pedagogies of Literature." In *Philosophizing About African Education.* Edited by A. Adewole and O. Ayodele-Bamisaiye. Ibadan: Macmillan Nigeria.

Badat, Saleem. "Educational Politics in the Transition Period." *Comparative Education* 31, no. 2 (1995).

Baker, S. J. K. 1963. "The East African Environment." In *A History of East Africa.* Edited by Harlow and Smith. London: Oxford University Press.

Berg, Elliot J. "The Economic Basis of Political Choice in French West Africa." *American Political Science Review* 54, no. 2 (1960).

Berthelemy, J. C., and F. Bouguignon. 1996. *Growth and Crisis in the Ivory Coast.* Washington, D.C.: World Bank.

Biloa, E. 1999. "Bilingual Education in the University of Yaounde I: The Teaching of French to English Speaking Students." In *Bilinguisme officiel et communication linguistique au Cameroun*. Edited by G. Echu and A. W. Grundstrom. New York: Peter Lang.

Blakemore, K., and Brian Cooksey. 1981. *A Sociology of Education for Africa*. London: Allen & Unwin.

Bolibough, J. 1964. French Educational Strategies for Sub-Sahara Africa: Their Intent, Derivation, and Development. PhD diss., Stanford University, 1964.

Bot Ba Njok, H. "Le probleme linguistic au Cameroon." *L'Afrique et l' Asie* 73 (1966).

Bull, Nancy. 1999. *Power, Alternative Theory of Encyclopedia of Violence, Peace and Conflict*. London: Academic Press.

Bunting, Brian. 1964. *The Rise of South African Reich*. Harmondsworth, UK: Penguin.

Bunting, I. A. "An Unequal System: South Africa's Historically White and Black Universities." Discussion paper at UCT, August 1993.

Callaghy, Thomas M. 1984. "External Actors and the Relative Autonomy of the Political Aristocracy in Zaire." In *State and Class in Africa*. Edited by Nelson Kasfir. London: Frank Cass & Co. Ltd.

Cameroon Tribune. April 17, 1998. Law No. 98/004 of April 14, 1998, Guidelines for Education in Cameroon.

CIA. 2001. *World Fact Book*. Washington, D.C.

CIA. 2006. *World Fact Book*. Washington, D.C.

Chabal, Patrick. 1997. *Apocalypse Now? A Post-Colonial Journey into Africa*. Inaugural lecture, King's College, London, March 12, 1997.

Chinery, Hollis. 1978. *Ivory Coast: The Challenge of Success* (a World Bank country economic report). Washington, D.C.: Johns Hopkins University Press.

Chingono, Mark. "Reflections in War Time Social Research: Lessons from Mozambique Civil War." N.p.: n.d.

Chisholm, Linda. 2004. "The Quality of Primary Education in South Africa." Department of Education, South Africa.

Clignet, R., and P. Foster. 1966. *The Fortunate Few*. Evanston, Ill.: Northwestern University Press.

Cohen, Robin. 1986. *Endgame in South Africa*. Paris: UNESCO Press.

Coldough, C., and K. Levine. 1993. *Educating All the Children: Strategies for Primary Education in the South*. Oxford, UK: Clarendon Press.

Coleman, J. S. "The Academic Freedom and Responsibilities of Foreign Scholars in African Universities." *Issue: A Journal of Opinion* 7, no. 2 (1977): 14–33.

Coleman, James, and N. Ngokwey. 1983. "Zaire: The State and University." In *Politics and Education*. Edited by E. M. Thomas. New York: Pergamon Press.

Cooper, Donald. "Technikons and Higher Education Restructuring." *Comparative Education* 31, no. 2 (1995).

Cox, Robert. 1981. "Social Forces, States, and World Orders: Beyond International Relations Theory." *Millennium: Journal of International Studies* 10, no. 2 (1981): 126–155.

Curtin, Philip D. 1964. *The Image of Africa: British Ideas and Action: 1780–1850*. Madison: University of Wisconsin Press.

Datta, A. 1984. *Education and Society: A Sociology of African Education*. New York: St. Martin's Press.

Delancey, Mark, W., and Mark Dike Delancey. 2000. *Historical Dictionary of the Republic of Cameroon*. Lanham, Md: The Scarecrow Press.

De Lusignan, Guy. 1969. *French Speaking Africa Since Independence*. New York: Frederick A. Praeger.

Donaldson, A. 1992. "Financing Education." In *Education Alternative*. Edited by R. MacGregor and A. MacGregor. Johannesburg, South Africa: Juta.

Dore, R. 1976. *The Diploma Disease: Education Qualification and Development*. London: Allen & Unwin.

Duffield, Mark. 2001. *Global Governance and the New Wars*. London: Zed Books.

Echu, G. "The Language Question in Cameroon." *Linguistik Online* 18 (2004). http://www.linguistik-online.de/.

Education: Focus on Primary Education. Benin City: Institute of Education, University of Benin, Nigeria.

El-Garh, M. S. "Philosophical Basis of Islamic Education in Africa." *West African Journal of Education* 9 (1971): 8–20.

Fafunwa, A. Babs. 1974. *History of Education in Nigeria*. London: Allen & Unwin.

Fafunwa, A. Babs. 1980. *New Perspective in African Education*. London: Macmillan Education Ltd.

Farrel, J. P. 1982. "Educational Expansion and the Drive for Social Equality." In *Comparative Education*. Edited by P. G. Altbach. New York: Macmillan.

Farine, Avigore. "Society and Education: The Content of Education in the French African School." *Comparative Education* 5, no. 1 (1969).

Federal Republic of Nigeria. 2004. *National Policy on Education (NPE)* (new ed.). Abuja, Nigeria.

Felgas, Helio Esteves. 1958. *História do Congo Português*. Uige, Angola: Carmona.

Fonlon, B. "A Case for Early Bilingualism." *ABBIA* 4 (1963): 56–94.

Foucault, Michel. 1997. *Ethics, Subjectivity and Truth*. Edited by Paul Rabinow. New York: New Press.

Friedman, S. 1992. "Beyond Symbol: The Politics of Economics Compromise." In *Wealth or Poverty: Critical Choices for South Africa*. Edited by R. Shire. Cape Town, South Africa: Oxford University Press.

Furley, O. W., and T. Watson. 1978. *A History of Education in East Africa*. New York: NOK Publishers.

Glinne, Earnest. "The Congo Crisis and the Katanga Affair." *Presence Africaine* 4–5, no. 32–33 (1976).

Godfrey, E. M. "The Economics of an African University." *Journal of Modern African Studies* 4 (1966): 436.

Gould, D. 1980. *Bureaucratic Corruption and Underdevelopment in the Third World: The Case Study of Zaire*. Oxford, UK: Pergamon Press.

Graham, C. K. 1971. *The History of Education in Ghana: From the Earliest Times to the Declaration of Independence*. London: Frank Cass Publishers.

Gran, Guy. "Zaire 1978: The Ethical and Intellectual Bankruptcy of the World System." *Africa Today* 25, no. 4 (1978): 5–24.

Gwanfogbe, M., A. Meligui, J. Moukam, and J. Nyuoghia. 1983. *Geography of Cameroon*. Hong Kong: Macmillan Education Ltd.

Hailey, Lord. 1957. *An African Survey*. London: Oxford University Press.

Harman, H. A. 1975. "Education in the Gold Coast, 1910–1935." In *The Development of Education in Ghana*. Edited by H.O.A. McWilliam and N.A. Kwamena-Pon. London: Longman.

Hayward, F. M. "The Uganda Strategic Plan for Higher Education, 2003–2015: Strengths Challenges and Prospects for Implementation." *The Uganda Education Review, The Journal of the National Council for Higher Education* l, no. 21 (2004): 28–31.

Henderson, Lawrence W. 1979. *Angola: Five Centuries of Conflict*. Ithaca, NY: Cornell University Press.

Herman, D. Harold. "Social Leaving Examinations and Equity in Higher Education in South Africa." *Comparative Education* 31, no. 2 (1995).

Horrelle, Muriel. 1970. *A Survey of Race Relations in South Africa*. Johannesburg, South Africa.

Houenou, Pascal V. 2003. *In African Higher Education: An International Reference Book Handbook*. Edited by D. Teferra and Philip G. Altbach. Bloomington: University of Indiana Press.

Hull, G. 1973. "Government Nationalization of the University: A Case Study of the Republic of Zaire." Presented at the 16th Annual Meeting of the African Studies Assn, Syracuse, NY, Oct. 31–Nov. 3.

Hunt, James. "On the Physical and Mental Characters of the Negro." *Anthropological Review* 1 (1863): 388–91.

Ilunga, K. 1978. "Some Thoughts on the National University of Zaire and the Zairian Political Dynamics."

Ingham, K. 1958. *The Making of Modern Uganda*. London: Allen & Unwin.

Ivor, Morrish. 1978. *The Sociology of Education: An Introduction to Society, Identity & Continuity*. London: Allen & Unwin.

Ivowi, U. M. O. 2006. "Nurturing and Sustaining Catholic Tertiary Education."

Iyoha, M. A. *When Will Africa's Sleeping Giant Awake?* Inaugural Lecture series 75, University of Benin, Nigeria, 2005.

Jalloh, A. A. 1973. *Political Integration in French-speaking Africa*. Berkeley, CA: Institute of International Studies.

Joseph, Richard A. 1984. "Class, State, and Prebendal Politics in Nigeria." In *State Class in Africa*. Edited by N. Kasfir. London: Frank Cass & Co. Ltd.

Joubert, D. A. *The Education and Training of Engineering and Technical Human Resources in Africa and Winning Industrial Nations*. South Africa '92 Conference, Swaziland, September 1992.

Kabeya, Luabeya. "Foreign Financial Assistance and Economic Growth in Zaire." *Africa Development Quarterly* 2, no. 3 (1977).

Kagia, J. *Integration of Education, Health and Care for the Total Development of the Child*. Paper presented at a seminar on Early Childhood Education in Kenya: Implications on Policy and Practice, Mombasa, Aug. 31–Sept. 4, 1987.

Kanda, Ciamaki. "Elements of Blockages in the Development of Rural Zaire." *Cas Labadu, Kasai: Cashier Economiques et Sociales* 15, no. 3 (Sept. 1978): 334–71.

Kasozi, A. B. K. 2003. *University Education in Uganda: Challenges and Opportunities for Reform*. Oxford, UK: African Books.

Kasozi, A. B. K. *The Development of a Strategic Plan for Higher Education in Uganda 2001–5: The Interplay of Internal and External Forces in Higher*

Education Policy Formation in a Southern Country. Paper presented at the Nuffic Conference, The Hague, May 23–25, 2005.

Kenyatta, Jomo. 1965. *Facing Mount Kenya: The Tribal Life of the Kikuyu.* London: Secker and Warburg.

Kipkorir, L. I. *Innovations in Early Childhood Education and Care—The Kenyan Experience.* Paper presented at a Seminar on Early Childhood Education in Kenya: Implications on Policy and Practice, Mombasa, Aug. 31–Sept. 4, 1987.

Kirngui, F. "Uganda Tackling School Bottlenecks." *Africa Recovery* 14, no. 2 (2000): 20.

Ki-Zerbo, J. *The Content of Education in Africa.* Final Report, United Nations Economic Commission for Africa/UNESCO, conference of African States on the Development of Education in Africa, Addis Ababa, May 15–25, 1961.

Kouega, J. "Promoting French-English Individual Bilingualism through Education in Cameroon." *Journal of Third World Studies* 22 (2005): 189–196.

Kruger, M. M., and E. P. Whittle. 1990. *Fundamental Perspective in Education.* Johannesburg, South Africa: Juta.

La Croix, B. "Pouvoirs et structures de l'Universite Lovanium." *Cahiers de CEDAF* 2–3, series 2 (1972).

Leach, A. F. 1969. *The Schools of Medical England.* London: Methuen.

Les Editions, J. A. 2002. *Africa Atlases: At Last of Nigeria.* Paris.

Levine, H. M. 1982. "The Dilemma of Comprehensive Secondary School Reforms in Western Europe." In *Comparative Education.* Edited by P. G. Altbach. New York: Macmillan.

Levine, R. A. 1967. *Dreams and Deeds.* Chicago: University of Chicago Press.

LeVine, R. A., and B. B. LeVine. 1963. "Nyansongo: A Gusii Community in Kenya." In *Six Cultures; Studies of Child Rearing.* Edited by B. B. Whiting. New York: John Wiley and Sons.

Libois, Jules G. 1966. *Katanga Secession.* Madison: University of Wisconsin Press.

Lyons, Charles H. 1970. "The Educable African: British Thought and Action (1835–1865)." In *Essays in the History of African Education.* Edited by V. M. Battle & Charles H. Lyons. New York: Teachers College, Columbia, University Press.

Marcum, John A. 1978. *The Angolan Revolution!* Vol. 2. Cambridge, MA: M.I.T. Press.

Markowitz, M. D. 1973. *Cross and Sword: The Political Role of Christian Missions in the Belgium Congo, 1908–1960.* Stanford, CA: Hoover Institution Publications.

Marks, Susan. 2000. *The Riddle of All Constitutions.* New York: Oxford University Press.

Martin, P., and P. O 'Meara. 1995. *Africa.* Bloomington: Indiana University Press.

Mayanja, A. K. "The Way Forward on Varsity Fees." *New Vision* (2005): 2.

Mbaku, J. M. 2005. *Culture and Customs of Cameroon.* Westport, CT: Greenwood Press.

McWilliam, H. O. A., and M. A. Kwamena-Poh. 1975. *The Development of Education in Ghana.* London: Longman.

Merriam, Alan P. 1961. *Congo: Background of Conflict.* Evanston, Ill: Northwestern University Press.

Ministry of Information. 1967a. *Report of the Commission on the Structure and Remuneration of the Public Service in Ghana.* Accra, Ghana.

Ministry of Education. 1967b. *Report of the Educational Review Committee.* Accra, Ghana.

Ministry of Education. 1971a. *Digest of Educational Statistics 1971–72.* Accra, Ghana.

Ministry of Education. 1971b. *Educational Statistics, 1968–69.* Accra, Ghana.

Ministry of Education. 1972. *Pre-University Education in Ghana.* Accra, Ghana.

Ministry of Education. 1974. *The New Structure and Content of Education for Ghana.* Accra, Ghana.

Ministry of Education. 1996. "The Development of Education 1994–1996," National Report from Ghana presented to the 45th Session of the International Conference on Education, Geneva, September 30–October 5, 1996.

Ministry of Education, Science and Technology. 1984a. *Republic of Kenya: Early Childhood Education Programme. The DICECE component, 1985–1989.* Nairobi, Kenya: Ministry of Education.

Ministry of Education, Science and Technology. 1984a. *Under Lines for Preschool Education in Kenya.* Nairobi, Kenya: Jomo Kenyatta Foundation.

Ministry of Education, Science and Technology. 1987. *Education in Kenya, Information Handbook.* Nairobi, Kenya: Jomo Kenyatta Foundation.

Ministry of Education and Sports. 1998. Education *Strategic Investment Plan 1998–2003.* Kampala, Uganda.

Ministry of Education and Sports. 1999. *Interim Report of Education for All (EFA) 2000 Assessment.* Kampala, Uganda.

Ministry of Education and Sports. 2004. *Uganda's 2003/04 Education Annual Performance Report.* Kampala Uganda.

Ministry of Education and Sports. 2005. "Education for Rural People in Africa: Policy, Lessons, Options and Priorities." Report on Uganda in the Ministerial Seminar, Addis Ababa, Ethiopia, Sept. 7–9.

Ministry of Information. 1969. *Ghana Official Handbook.* Accra, Ghana.

Ministry of National Education. 1995. *National Forum Report on Education.*

Ministry of Plan and Regional Development. 1986. *Sixth Five-Year Economic Social and Cultural Development Plan, 1986–1991.*

Moodie, T. D. 1972. *The Rise of Afrikanerdom: Power, Apartheid and the Afrikaner Civil Religion.* Berkeley: University of California Press.

Morgenthau, R. S. 1964. *Political Parities in French-Speaking West Africa.* Oxford, UK: Oxford University Press.

Mortimer, Edward. 1969. *France and the Africans (1944–1960).* New York: Walker and Co.

Motala, Shireen. "Surviving the System—A Critical Appraisal of Some Conventional Wisdoms in Primary Education in South Africa." *Comparative Education* 31, no. 2 (1995): 162–77.

Moumouni, A. 1968. *Education in Africa.* London: Andre Deutsch.

Mukama, R. G. 1991. "Recent Development in the Language Situation and Prospects for the Future." In *Changing Uganda.* Edited by H. B. Hansen and M. Twaddle. Kampala, Uganda: Fountain Publishers.

Ngijol, P. "Necessite d' une langue nationale." *ABBIA* 7 (1964): 83–99.

Ngoh, V. J. 1988. *Cameroon 1884–1985: A Hundred Years of History.* Limbe, Cameroon: Navi-group Publications.

Ngome, C. 2003. "Higher Education in Kenya." In *African Higher Education: An International Reference Handbook*. Edited by D. Teferra and P. C. Altbach. Bloomington: Indiana University Press.

Njeck, Alice Forsab. "Official Bilingualism in the University of Yaounde: Some Educational and Social Issues." Mémoire de Maîtrise, Université de Yaoundé, 1992.

Njeuma, D. L. 2003. "Cameroon Higher Education Profile." In *African Higher Education: An International Reference Handbook*. Edited by D. Teferra and P. G. Altbach. Bloomington: Indiana University Press.

Ogbu, J. U. 1982. "Equalization of Educational Opportunity." In *Comparative Education*. Edited by P. G. Altbach et al. New York: Macmillan.

Ogot, B. A. "British Administration in the Central Nyanza District of Kenya." *Journal of African History* 4, no. 3 (1963).

Okonkwo, Chuka E. 1988. *Introduction to Comparative Education*. Owerri Totan Publishers.

Okuma, Thomas. 1962. *Angola in Ferment*. Foreword by Rupert Emerson. Boston: Beacon Press.

Omatseye, J. Nesin. "African Philosophic Thought and Nigeria's Educational." (1978).

Omatseye, J. Nesin. "The Essence of Liberal Arts Education in Nigeria." *Journal of General Education* 33, no. 4 (Winter 1982): 263–72.

Omatseye, J. Nesin. *Philosophizing on the Enigma Called Man: Does Education Really Matter?* Inaugural lecture series 67, University of Benin, Nigeria, 2003.

Omatseye, J. Nesin. "Quality Control of Teacher Education in Nigerian." (2005).

Onokherhoraye, A. G. 2006. *On the Hot Seat: The Memoirs of a Vice*.

Oppong, C. "The Context of Socialization in Dagbon." *Institute of African Studies Research Review* 4, no. 1 (1967): 13.

Peaslee, Alexander L. 1971. "Primary School Enrollments and Economic Growth." In *Education in Comparative and International Perspectives*. Edited by K. I. Gezi. New York: Holt, Rinehart.

Phelps-Stoke Commission Report.

Power, C. *International Trends in Tertiary Education*. Keynote address, Conference on Tertiary Education, South Africa, 1994.

Prewitt, K. 1971. *Education and Political Values: An East African Case Study*. Nairobi, Kenya: East African Publishing House.

Radmann, Wolf. "The Nationalization of Zaire's Copper: From Union Miniere to Gecamines." *Africa Today* 25, no. 4 (Oct.–Dec. 1978).

Raun, O. E. 1940. *Chaga Childhood*. Oxford, UK: Oxford University Press.

Salazar, Antonio de Oliveia. 1963. *Declaration on Overseas Policy*. Lisbon, Portugal: Secretariado Nacional da Informacito.

Seeman, Berthold. *Reports of Missionaries*. Paper presented at the Anthropological Society of London, June 22, 1863.

Sheffield, J. R. 1973. *Education in Kenya: A Historical Study*. New York: Columbia University, Teachers' College Press.

Sik, Endre. 1970. *The History of Black Africa*. Vol. 1. Budapest, Hungary: Akademiai Kiado.

Smyth, H. H., and Mabel M. Smyth. 1960. *The New Nigerian Elite*. Stanford, CA: Stanford University Press.

Sobel, I. 1982. "The Human Capital Revolution in Economic Development." In *Comparative Education.* Edited by P. G. Altbach et al. New York: Macmillan.

Sogge, David. "Angola: The Client Who Came in from the Cold." *Southern Africa Report* 15, no. 4 (2000): 4–6.

Sommering, S. T. 1785. *Concerning the Physical Differences Between Negroes and Europeans.* Frankfurt am Main.

Sroufe, G. "The Assumptive World of Three State Policy." *Researcher: Peabody Journal of Education* 62, no. 4 (1985).

Stinchcombe, A. L. 1968. *Construction Social Theories.* New York: Harcourt Brace.

Taba, H. 1962. *Curriculum Development: Theory and Practice.* New York: Harcourt.

Tabita, I. B. 1964. *Education for Barbarism in South Africa.* New York: Praeger.

Tanoh, M.A. "Rapport de M. A. Tanoh. Minisg del'Education National devant le congres du P.D.C.E." *Education et Techniques* no. 31 (1965): 8–9.

Tchombe, T. M. 1997. "Teacher Education and Deployment in Cameroon." In *Issues in Teacher-Education, Policy and Practice.* Edited by J. Bruce. Cameroon: Felicitas Academic Press.

Thakur, Ramesh. 1999. "U.N. and Human Security." *Canadian Foreign Policy* 7, no. 1 (1999): 51–59.

Todd, L. 1983. "Language Options for Education in a Multilingual Society: Cameroon." In *Language Planning and Language Education.* Edited by C. Kennedy. London: Allen & Unwin.

Trowell, M., and K. Wachsmann. 1953. *Tribal Crafts of Uganda.* London: Oxford University Press.

Turner, T. E, and Young, M. C. 1981. *The Rise and Decline of Zairian State.*

UNESCO. 1962. *Conference Report on the Adaptation.* Paris: Author.

UNESCO. 1967. "House of Assembly Debates." *Hansard* 52. 30–31.

UNESCO. 1995. *Report on the State of Education in Africa. Education Strategies for the 1990s: Orientations and Achievements.* Paris.

United Nations. 1966. *E.C.A., African Agricultural Development.* New York.

United Nations. 2000. *Report of the Panel on U.N. Peace Operations* (A/55/305 s/ 2000/809): New York.

United Nations Development Programme. *Development and Human Report 1998.*

United States Department of Commerce, National Trade Data Bank. 2007. Washington, D.C.

Uganda Government. 1992. "Education for National Integration and Development." Government white paper on Implementation of the Recommendation of the Report of the Education Policy Review Commission. Kampala, Uganda.

Verhagen, Benoit. 1978. "Les Crisis de la Reserche Zairoise au Zaire, 1967–1977." no. 10 (July 1978): 38–62.

Ward, W. E. F. 1967. *Educating Young Nations.* London: Allen & Unwin.

White, Charles. 1977. *An Account of Regular Gradation in Man.* London.

Whyllie, R. "The New Ghanaian Teacher and His Profession." *West African Journal of Education* 8, no. 3 (1964): 175.

Wilson, J. Zoe. 2005. "Certainty, Subjectivity, and Truth: Reflections on the Ethics of War Time Research in Angola." In *Research Conflict in Africa: Insights and Experiences.* Edited by E. Porter, G. Robinson, M. Smyth, A. Schnabel, and E. Osagie. New York: U.N. University Press.

Winterbottom, Thomas. 1803. *An Account of the Native Africans in the Neighbor-hood of Sierra Leone, with an Account of the Present State of Medicine Among Them.* 2 vols. London: John Hatchard, Booksellers.

Wolpe, Hazold. "The Debate on University Transformation in South Africa: The Case for the University of West Cape Town." *Comparative Education* 31, no. 2 (1993): 276.

Wolpe, H. 1992. "Towards A Short Term Negotiating Policy on Education and Training." National Education Policy Investigation: Working Paper.

Women's Commission for Refugee Women and Children. 2004. *No Safe Place to Call Home: Children and Adolescent Night Commuters in Northern Uganda.* New York.

Women's Commission for Refugee Women and Children. 2005. *Learning in a War Zone: Education in Northern Uganda.* New York.

World Bank Comparative Education Indicator. (Oct. 15, 1975).

World Bank. 1990. *Policy Paper on Primary Education in Nigeria.* Washington, D.C.

World Bank. 1995. *Priorities and Strategies for Education.* Washington, D.C.

World Economic Financial Surveys. Sept. 2006. *World Economic Outlook.* http://www.imf.org/external/pubs/ft/weo2006/02/data/index.aspx.

Young, M. C. 1978. "La Faculte des Sciences Sociales a l'UNAZ: Reflexions autour d'un mandate." *Etudes Zairoises* 1 (1978): 154–180.

Young, M. C. "The African University: Universalism, Development, and Ethnicity." *Comparative Education Review* 25, no. 2 (1981): 145–162.

INDEX

ABOUT THE AUTHORS

JIM NESIN OMATSEYE is the Dean, Faculty of Education and Professor of Educational Philosophy and Policy Studies at the University of Benin in Nigeria.

BRIDGET OLIREJERE OMATSEYE is a Senior Lecturer, Institute of Education Doctorate in Educational Philosophy and Policy Studies, at the University of Benin in Nigeria.